WAS ALICE CRIMMINS CON-VICTED OF THE BRUTAL SLAYING OF HER TWO CHILDREN BECAUSE OF WHAT SHE DID—OR BECAUSE OF WHAT SHE WAS?

"Kenneth Gross has laid bare every insidious detail of the case . . . a penetrating study . . . Every character from beat cop to D.A. is vividly portrayed, their ambitions and motives bared, their backgrounds and genealogies thoroughly delineated . . . an overwhelming indictment of the American system of justice."

—*Playboy*

"A story as compelling as any work of fiction . . . should send shivers through the New York court system."

—*Chicago Tribune Book World*

THE
Alice Crimmins
Case

Kenneth Gross

BALLANTINE BOOKS · NEW YORK

Library of Congress Catalog Card Number: 74-21306

ISBN 0-345-25072-9

This edition published by arrangement with
Alfred A. Knopf, Inc.

Manufactured in the United States of America

First Ballantine Books Edition: October 1977

For Risa and Leslie

"What sort of things do *you* remember best?" Alice ventured to ask.

"Oh, things that happened the week after next," the Queen replied in a careless tone. "For instance, now," she went on . . . "there's the King's Messenger. He's in prison now, being punished: and the trial doesn't even begin till next Wednesday: and of course the crime comes last of all."

"Suppose he never commits the crime?" said Alice.

"That would be all the better, wouldn't it?" the Queen said.

—LEWIS CARROLL,
Through the Looking-Glass

INTRODUCTION

One steamy night in the summer of 1965, when I was a young reporter for the New York *Post,* I was assigned to "cover" a station house in Fresh Meadows, Queens, where the police were investigating the murder of two children. It was a routine assignment—I was to sit outside the station house during the night, waiting to see if the case would be broken. The regular reporters had filed their overnight stories and gone home. It was understood that nothing was expected of me unless the murders were solved. I was to dull my imagination because it would be inconvenient to interrupt the story that had already been filed and set for the next day. For twelve hours a newspaper's editors hoped that the version they were committed to would hold. Until the edition was on the street, one brief radio bulletin could make it obsolete and seem foolish. Reporting, I was beginning to discover, was largely a matter of waiting and self defense.

The gray veteran police reporters slouched possessively against the squad cars in the street. They were a special breed, balancing loyalty to a newspaper against an affinity for cops. There was a particular pallor to these men, who dressed like detectives and radiated a kind of insider's insolence. They were proud of their techniques—they had already found the nearest telephones, impressed the local merchants and residents with their importance, and now waited patiently for some detective to feed them a fresh scrap of information. The hoods of the police cruisers were cluttered with cold coffee containers. In time, a detective broke away from a pack of his colleagues and waited until one of the trusted veterans sidled over for a brief exchange. In the established ritual, the veteran passed along bits of what he had been told to the newer men, then headed for the telephone with his richer version. It struck me, as we stood helplessly on the sidewalk, that we were at the mercy of the detectives. And the word that was filtering out from this precinct was that Alice Crimmins was guilty and it was simply a matter of time until she cracked.

What was particularly treacherous about the process was its elusive effect. The newspapermen would salt the accusation into conversations with editors at their home offices. Editors are always dredging reporters for spicier gossip, even when it cannot be printed. Editors are expected to know more than they print. They obtain the material from reporters, who are then credited with a kind of mystical expertise. The reporters get the word from detectives, who may be trying to manipulate public opinion, impress superiors, or apply pressure to a suspect. Whether or not the specific accusation sees daylight, it poisons the coverage. And the process all hangs on the thread of a subtle code— the editor does not challenge the reporter too closely because the reporter has privileged sources. The editor finds it comfortable to believe that the reporter is in intimate contact with policemen who must be protected. The reporter does not question the detective too closely for fear of drying up his source.

The editor would like to believe that the reporter knows—really knows—something special. The reporter is convinced that the detective has complete access to the facts of the case. The detective is suspicious of the reporter; he worries that the reporter knows too much to be manipulated and is only looking for information critical of the police. What takes place are shadowy conversations in which each party tries to find out how much the other one knows, while suggesting his own familiarity with the facts. This makes for exaggeration and error. There grows a fund of "common knowledge" which never has to be proven and is accepted by those who want to demonstrate their connection with the case.

In 1965, the "common knowledge" that Alice Crimmins had killed her children was burnished with rumors of scandal. This mother had slept around indiscriminately. There were not many women police reporters that season, and it would have taken extraordinary courage for one to go against the boys' explanation. Like some black policemen, women had to be tougher on their own to prove themselves.

So, that sticky summer night I was told to leave the station house and get over to the woman's apartment with a photographer. She was expected home to feed her dog, and my assignment was to watch. There were a dozen newsmen and photographers standing on the mall outside her apartment when she appeared on the arm of her estranged husband. The flashbulbs flickered in her face like a swarm of fireflies. She sobbed and her husband begged the photographers to stop. They persisted, following her to the door and waiting until she came out, when their lights pecked at her again.

"Why?" I asked one photographer.

"The bitch killed her kids!" he replied.

It was exactly what a detective had told us an hour earlier. The same detective had said she was a "cold" woman who never cried. The photographer merely repeated what he had been told.

As her car pulled out of the parking lot, a photographer maliciously popped his light in the windshield, blinding the driver. He made no attempt to aim or focus.

And the only thing we knew for certain was that Alice Crimmins had just lost her two children.

In time the case receded in my mind. I had other assignments, and I harbored the sloppy assumption that the police couldn't always be wrong. I was vaguely aware of a trial, but the details were a blur. Through the years, what I knew about the case was punctuated by the persistent whisper of guilt. Lawyers, secretaries, housewives, public officials would repeat rumors they had picked up somewhere and pollinated somewhere else.

In 1971, working for *Newsday,* I was assigned to write a magazine article about Alice Crimmins. One detective called and told me she was guilty, that there were incriminating statements which could never be introduced at a trial. But when I tried to pin down that assertion, I found there were no corroborative tapes.

Finally, Alice Crimmins decided to grant me an interview. She had been isolated from the press from the beginning, at first under the advice of her attorney and later because of the momentum of bad publicity. She had never allowed an interview of any depth or duration, and it was her attorney's opinion that she should now counter the negative image. The attorney had heard that I was open-minded and decided to trust me. I spent one afternoon talking with her and there were later interviews.

What impressed me was the difference between the person and the public image. Alice Crimmins was shy, not stridently aggressive. She explained her estrangement from the press: she wanted her vindication in a courtroom, not in a newspaper. The courts and prosecuting attorney are charged with maintaining the sanctity of the courtroom, but in this situation they were using extralegal methods, while Alice Crimmins insisted on the law.

As I began examining the details of the case, I was not able to satisfy myself about her guilt. The purported evidence was always buttressed by prejudice and fear. Whether Alice Crimmins was a nice person or someone morally beyond redemption, the law was supposed to be administered without fear or favor. There are times, however, when threats to society are masked behind evasions or couched in acceptable excess. The Alice Crimmins case, I came to believe, was perceived as frightening because the women's movement was just coming into existence when the case broke, and the implications—a housewife grown rebellious and out of control—terrified those who felt a stake in maintaining the status quo. Through the late 1960s and early 1970s the most advanced feminists failed to grasp the significance of Alice Crimmins. Many shrank from one of the questions raised—whether motherhood is an authentic role for some women.

The sexist bias in the case was impossible to escape. Her social habits were permanently grafted onto the central question of her guilt or innocence. Whenever I raised the possibility of her innocence, my friends had a neat explanation: I was in love with Alice Crimmins.

When I began to work actively on this book, I was constantly asked: "Is she guilty?" as if I possessed some special insight. The question struck me hardest when it was raised by lawyers and prosecutors and judges with connections to the case. After all the investigation over the years, there remained that single haunting question: "Do you think she did it?"

It was troublesome but, from the standpoint of the law, beside the point. The technical questions of guilt and innocence are intended to be resolved in a courtroom, a place where passions are supposed to be replaced by logic. The formality of the courtroom is meant to satisfy the cheaper doubts and the needs for revenge and vindication. The law demands suspension of simple curiosity. The rules and rituals are designed to protect against unsupported gossip and prejudice. It is, perhaps, human to want an answer. But there are mysteries incapable of solution. The easiest answer may be wrong. The truth may lie outside the known possibilities.

There were problems in researching this book. Officials who had never been shy to pronounce Alice Crimmins guilty were reluctant to explore their own roles. They retreated behind technical codes of silence, codes that had been conveniently ignored when that served their interests. And some people were ashamed of what had happened.

There was one man whose sense of outrage had never dimmed: Harold Harrison, Alice's first attorney. He was brutally honest, even about himself. He introduced me to people who had refused earlier to be interviewed. I am grateful. I should also thank John Cummings and Henry Shankman, who know what they did.

Some policemen, notably Phil Brady, came forward and revealed themselves candidly. Others required protection, and their names and circumstances have been altered to avoid injury. Some active policemen, prosecutors, and judges have been disguised to protect careers. There are men and women whose lives collided with Alice Crimmins' and whose marriages would be affected if they were identified. The names have been changed, but the fabric of the story is intact. There are enough broken lives in Queens.

1

She slapped off the alarm clock and heard the sound of the air-conditioner. And the silence. It was morning and the woman of the house woke up with an abrupt feeling of dislocation . . . listening to the mechanical sound of an air-conditioner instead of breathing. When she had separated from her husband months earlier, she had replaced him in the bedroom with an air-conditioner. When she awoke, she still felt a mixture of strangeness and relief.

She moved quickly in the morning, without a sluggish aftermath of sleep, as if keeping an urgent rendezvous. She washed, hardly staring at her face in the mirror. It was an interesting face, with powerful internal animation. Some of her friends were more beautiful in a classic, brittle way. Their bones might photograph better, their skin would show smoother texture. But cameras couldn't capture what flashed behind this woman's amber eyes. She radiated something elusive, as if she harbored and was privately amused by some vast secret. At the lounges and bars where women tested themselves insatiably, this woman had a life force more compelling than most of her peers.

Hers was not a simple appeal. There was a suggestion of vulnerability, a quality that made men fumble to light her cigarette or fetch her drink. For some women, desirability was a gift. They accepted their own good looks with a kind of regal carelessness—living off the interest as the very wealthy do who never touch capital and never dream that it could be squandered away or used up. Not this woman.

She worked quickly on her makeup. It was an important part of her, the makeup. It would be misunderstood later, dismissed as cold vanity. But when she was a young girl in the pale convent schools of the Bronx her face had always been scrubbed raw. Makeup was not for good Catholic girls. The deep-pitted scars of adolescent acne had burrowed into her a feeling of permanent inferiority. Later, after her marriage collapsed and she left that rigid system of values, she would cloak her face in pancake, as if all modesty rested on that mask. She would apply the eyeshadows and liners with the devotion of an acolyte. It would take her the better part of an hour each day to perform this new devotion. But the great affliction would be disguised with expert care, and no one would take her for less than a flawless beauty. The scars would remain on her psyche and she would never appear in public without first going through the makeup ritual. Only when she had finished each section would she look at the complete face instead of the working fragments. Only then would she look at Alice Crimmins.

It was Wednesday, July 14, 1965. Lyndon Johnson had just announced that the United States was taking a decisive step into Vietnam, but another shadow had captured the headlines: Adlai Stevenson had fallen dead of a heart attack on a London street corner, and his photograph—taken moments before he was stricken —gave a final weak smile from the front pages of New York's newspapers. To some, Stevenson's passing seemed to signal an end to public grace. Change and resistance to change were in the air. On a street corner in Queens—one of New York City's two boroughs east of the East River—Jimmy Jemail, the *Daily News* Inquiring Fotographer, was stopping people to pose the day's typically loaded question. This particular day Jemail asked how people felt about the use of children in street demonstrations. In Queens, to which parents had fled to escape urban streets, such a question touched raw nerves. "I feel strongly that children should not be involved in violence of any kind," Ella Klein, a florist with an uncomplicated smile, told Jemail. "Parents may be led to believe there will be no violence in a demonstration, but how do you know? If there is violence, it will make an unfavorable impression on the children that will last all their lives."

Such an explanation was easier to handle than the complicated questions raised by the demonstrations themselves—civil rights, peace. It lifted the issue beyond the reach of critics. Who could challenge a parent's impulse to protect a child?

In the summer of 1965 the questions of change, protest, and violence were compressed into the contest for the Mayoralty of New York City—a post mythically held to be the second most important job in the nation. Only the Presidency was said to be more potent. The truth was more elusive. The Mayor of New York commanded great access to the media. The city was located in the ganglia of magazine, newspaper, and network headquarters. Yet the job had a strange draining effect on political power. New York City Mayors would retire in disgrace or impotence, somehow never able to use their high visibility to launch themselves into national office.

For more than a decade the Mayoralty had been held by Robert Ferdinand Wagner, son of one of the state's most illustrious Senators. Wagner had never quite measured up to his father, who was the author of farsighted labor legislation and a man of infectious charm. Wagner the son was a short man with puffy eyes and droning syntax. By the sheer force of his ancestry he could lull New Yorkers into a sense that slippery values could be held and that loss of control could be checked. But Bob Wagner had undergone a shattering ordeal and was exhausted. His wife, Susan, had died in 1964 after a withdrawn, lingering contest with cancer. He would recoup his ambition in private.

Traditionally, the campaign for the Mayoralty would begin in earnest after Labor Day, but the Democrats were already trying to elbow each other out of the way. Abraham Beame, a feisty little accountant, was plunging head first into the lineup like a half-crazed halfback. Frank Hogan, the remote Manhattan District Attorney, was testing the wind from his lofty perch

3

with sanitized straws that never seemed to touch his own hands.

The apparent front runner was the dignified City Council President, Paul Screvane, a clubhouse politician who had graduated into sudden importance. There was a strange paradox to Paul Screvane. Blessed with a halo of gray hair and an imperial carriage, he had the look of breeding. And yet his background was a scramble with tough-talking New York City union leaders and building contractors. Somehow, even when he was Sanitation Commissioner and in the crossfire from both sides, he had managed to keep their friendship. Now he had the support of Robert Wagner. Screvane and Wagner were more than political cronies. During Susan's illness Screvane had befriended Wagner and, with his natural heartiness, drawn the Mayor into social distractions.

Alice Crimmins made one final appraisal in the bathroom mirror. Her fresh slacks and blouse were tight enough to suggest restrained sensuality—a mood Alice always tried to evoke. On this particular day it might have occurred to some women to appear subdued. She was to meet her attorney to plot strategy in a looming custody fight over her children. Her estranged husband, Eddie, had brought the suit. Not that Alice had any doubt that she would retain custody of the two children —Eddie, Jr., a chubby five-year-old, and his sparkling sister, Alice, one year younger, whom everyone called Missy.

If the unusual quiet from the children's room registered with Alice, it was stacked under the other considerations of the day. As she paused to stare at her carefully arranged face under the sprayed frame of strawberry-blond hair, there was one important aspect to her face that could not be disguised by powders and rouge: defiance. In the last few years Alice Crimmins had broken the social taboos of her class, of her religion, and of her sex. But apology was not in her makeup. To do what she had done required an important source of energy. The raw force of her mutiny carried her through.

4

When she had completed her face, Alice turned her attention to the creatures who shared her life. Circling her feet impatiently was Brandy, the half-Spitz bitch with weak bowels. "OK," cooed Alice, clasping on the dog's leash. A week later Brandy would surprise everyone by giving birth to a single pup. The dog had delivered a litter during the previous winter and had never regained her configuration; her stomach remained low-slung enough to conceal the new pregnancy. Alice, not realizing that Brandy's recent whimpering was the result of pregnancy, had been dickering with a neighbor to buy another dog—she wanted one for each child.

This particular day Alice wore her defiance lightly and there was a certain spring to her step as she tugged Brandy around the ragged footpaths of Regal Gardens. She would smile quickly for the men, but wait until the women smiled at her before she replied. Experience had taught her that the women in the neighborhood resented a young, attractive mother who could be seen going in and out of her home with a string of different men. So Alice would hoard her smiles, giving one only in return, like a Christmas card.

By 8:30 a.m. she could usually hear the clatter from the children's room. Little Eddie and Missy were exuberant, noisy children. Like many children of preoccupied parents, they had grown self-sufficient. Their mother was absorbed in work and a complicated sex life and so the children were left to explore the world through the window of their room.

Neighbors heading for work in the mornings would see Eddie and Missy sitting in the window—chubby, smiling, waving happily to anyone. A few times they had climbed down from their perch. Once they had been found on the lawn of the apartment complex, wearing only their pajamas in the snow. Alice had spoken sharply to the children then, but she was not really alarmed. After all, they were far from the traffic, protected by the girdle of lawns and mall. And who would harm two such adorable children?

On the morning of July 14, 1965, Alice Crimmins heard nothing from the children's room. On most days she could measure the excitement in the rising laughter as the children anticipated their liberation, for Alice kept their door locked by a hook-and-eye on the outside. For Eddie and Missy, the day officially began when their mother unlatched the lock she had installed to keep them out of the refrigerator. But today Alice didn't hear the familiar laughter as she flicked open the latch.

The jarring telephone left him trembling. In the furnished room that he had rented less than a mile from his estranged family, Eddie Crimmins was still groggy from his fitful night. Eddie was an airline mechanic at Kennedy Airport, accustomed to working odd shifts. But since the separation, sleep had become elusive.

"Eddie? Have you got the kids?"

Even in anger, that voice could tug the limits of Eddie's grief. Even when all the tenderness had been bled out of their contacts, even when they only exchanged bitter accusations, even then it didn't matter—he cherished even these.

"No." He tried to sound indignant, still not quite grasping the question. He rubbed the sleep out of his face.

"Eddie, don't play games with me!"

They were testing each other, reading voice prints over the telephone. In the breakup stage of their relationship, things did not always mean what appeared on the surface. There were tactics and reprisals involved and each had to be able to read beyond the conversation. This complexity was compounded for Eddie by the emotion he still felt for Alice. In the strange bed, in the unfamiliar room, he was closer and more poignantly involved with the barking voice on the telephone.

"I don't have them," he replied.

"Eddie! Don't fool around! Do you have them?"

In retrospect, Eddie Crimmins remembers that his wife's voice had taken on a rasp of hysteria. She had begun the conversation in anger and it had risen to fear. "Don't do this to me, Eddie." She was starting to believe him.

"They're not here, Alice," he said.

6

"Eddie, please don't do this to me!" She was pleading.

"They're not here, Alice!"

"Eddie, they're missing!"

Alice Crimmins would tell people that one of the reasons her marriage failed was that Eddie fell apart when she needed him. They had been married for seven years, and, at twenty-six, she was looking for someone strong, someone she could lean on in a crisis. But in the first stages of this crisis she let Eddie take charge.

"They're not in their room? Did you look outside?"

She had taken a quick look outdoors, she told him.

"Go look again," he said. "Check with the neighbors. I'll be right over."

Eddie Crimmins jumped out of bed and headed for the shower. His concern was not overwhelming. The kids had probably climbed out of the window, as they had done before. They were doubtless cadging a free breakfast from a sympathetic neighbor right now. He washed quickly, certain, when he emerged from the shower and heard the telephone, that it would be Alice to tell him gratefully that he had been right, that the kids climbed out in their underwear and were fine. They would have to be stern with the kids. . . .

"Please, Eddie, if you have the kids, tell me. Please, Eddie, please."

"Did you look outside? Did you check the Eybergs'?"

She had. Her frantic voice told him that the children were truly gone.

2

The Queens Criminal Courthouse lies on a hillside overlooking the spokes of the Grand Central Parkway, the Van Wyck Expressway, the Long Island Expressway, and Queens Boulevard. There the breezes are always stale with automobile fumes.

Morty's Luncheonette, across Queens Boulevard from the courthouse, catches the crosscurrents radiating from that hub. In the mornings policemen sip steaming coffee at the counter beside rubbery junkies; stewardesses who live in the nearby apartment highrise grab takeout containers to nurse on the ride to the airport, hiding their suffering eyes behind sunglasses; attorneys who handle cases like fast-food chefs chatter carelessly at worried clients.

Harold Harrison preferred the table in the window. The people who sat there usually had business across the street. They would examine the traffic and the people going in and out of the courthouse like soothsayers studying entrails, trying to read their own future in the flow. On the morning of July 14, Harrison sat with two other men. They spoke to each other, but their eyes were on the action in the street. It was a cozy group— Harold Harrison, an attorney, and two detectives. They seldom found their interests in collision. Indeed, they shared a view of life that was shaped by their mutual experiences. It was a philosophy that was vaguely cynical. They also shared clients. When the detectives arrested someone, they would make a separate evaluation: if the suspect looked as if he/she could afford a fee, the detectives would mention their friend Harold Harrison. When the detectives needed legal help—to draft a will, close a mortgage, settle a suit—Harold Harrison would handle it and there would never be any talk about a fee. It was not an uncommon unspoken arrangement between policemen and lawyers in Queens.

Detective George Martin was looking forward to an easy day in court. Martin had been a New York City detective for almost a dozen years and had developed an occupational laziness that was a prelude to retirement. The assignment in Queens suited him. In Queens he never heard a shot fired in anger. Queens was a place where policemen lived. Manhattan, the Bronx, and Brooklyn were occupation zones where junkies and gamblers operated boldly. But Queens was home turf.

Today George Martin had a routine court-calendar case: a burglary committed by a young drug addict, the son of a hard-working laborer. The kid had left behind a complete set of fingerprints. Very sloppy. It was a familiar tragedy for George Martin. The boy was an ungrateful child of the suburbs who had turned to drugs and crime out of sheer boredom. There was little satisfaction for Martin in such work. He regarded junkies as hopeless; and the father of this one was doomed to live out his later years making bewildered apologies in the wake of his son. The courtroom would become the old man's church where he would perform penance for his mystifying failure. The inevitability of it all left Martin feeling helpless. His single passion was to spend time in his private plane. Flying gave him a sense of control that he could never duplicate on the ground. A terrible tragedy had almost blighted his hobby. One of his daughter's friends had taken a ride with Martin in his plane. When they landed, she had leaped out and got tangled in the propeller. The girl had been killed. Harold Harrison had taken charge of the legal details, relieving Martin and cementing the relationship between the two men.

George Martin was an easygoing man. He was not driven—not like his eager partner, Gerard Piering, who was new to the detective division and anxious to

9

prove himself. Jerry Piering was in his thirties, but his moral code, like the bristling crew cut over his sagging boyish face, was somewhat out of sync with the times. Piering was an ardent Catholic, the father of six children. Within the shelter of the church and his family Jerry Piering felt safe. But outside, his values were under siege from forces he found difficult to grapple with.

It was not always possible to define duty. He could, for example, shrug off a brother officer's infidelities, but insist that a woman had to remain faithful. Even in repose Piering's face seemed in a permanent scowl. And he was capable of strange explosions that appeared to come out of nowhere. "I'll tell you something," he once told George Martin, "I've got six kids at home. If anything happens to them, it's my wife's fault. She's in charge while I'm not there. Anything happens, I blame her." It was the sort of remark that masked layers of unspoken rage. Martin recalled that Piering often left him feeling uncomfortable. Jerry Piering, he would come to understand, was always looking for someone to blame—and he did not forgive easily. In his next case Piering would get his chance to test himself. All the ingredients of his threatened world would tumble together in a single stew, and he would try to sort it all out.

"I think I'll check in," said Piering before the coffee arrived. Martin, the senior partner of the team, did not object. He had worked with Piering for a year and had surrendered the initiative to this eager beaver long ago.

"Eager beaver," said Harrison after Piering left for the telephone, and Martin chuckled at his friend's ability to read his mind.

Piering did not sit down when he returned from the telephone. "Couple of kids missing in Kew Gardens," he said, standing over the table.

"Well," replied Martin, "there's safety in numbers."

Piering just stood there. "They got a search going."

"It's bullshit," said Martin. "Forget it."

"I'm gonna go," said Piering.

It's been my experience that the kids are over in somebody's basement or in somebody's attic," recalled Martin

10

much later. "Or somebody's house having an ice-cream soda. Or some other bullshit. Particularly if there are two. There is no doubt, the proper hindsight is twenty-twenty, he did the right thing and I didn't. But this is, you know, it's not the norm, if you will. It's not the norm."

George Martin fished out the keys to the unmarked police car and handed them to Jerry Piering. "I'll go over to the courthouse and cancel our cases," he said. "I'll meet you over there."

Jerry Piering was already out the door.

Eddie Crimmins had placed the call to the police at 9:44 a.m. The time was registered precisely by the instruments at the Central Switchboard in the Queens Communications Bureau in Jamaica. The men operating the telephones there were trained to drain emotion out of their voices. Accustomed to dealing with hysterical civilians, they would reply with calm authority to instill confidence and allay alarm. Often the people calling in were frantic, reporting robberies in progress, and they would sometimes hang up without giving any address, name, or any other detail. No matter how controlled the voices sounded, the level of excitement was always high.

"My name is Crimmins, Eddie Crimmins. My children are missing. . . ."

Eddie had been reluctant to bring in the police. He had hurried over from his rooming house. When he pulled in, he saw Alice coming back from another circuit of the area. She was carrying a bundle—a jacket and shirt she kept in the car. Eddie took her free hand in his. They were both trembling.

Theresa Costello watched Alice and Eddie go inside. Standing on the mall, she stared at the window without looking at it; it was almost a reflex to see if the children were there in their spectator seats on the mall. She remembered passing it last night. On her way to a baby-sitting assignment she had passed underneath the window about 8:30 p.m. She had heard Alice's voice, full of adult reproach: "Now, Missy, say your prayers!" And then she had heard Missy's tinkling little voice, unable to sound solemn: "God bless Mommy and Daddy. . . ."

11

Theresa Costello shivered, experiencing an uncanny fear. It was the last time she had heard Missy's voice. She hadn't paid much attention then; she had been rushing to her baby-sitting job and she was very conscientious about her work. At fourteen, Theresa was considered a prize on the mall. Mature beyond her years, she was one of those natural parent substitutes, imbued with good common sense and unflappable. Children sensed an ally in her. Theresa had become particularly fond of the Crimmins children. They were comfortable with each other, and Alice felt safe leaving the children with Theresa.

On the morning of the disappearance Alice had come to Theresa's door looking for the children. Theresa had left her breakfast on the table to help look for Eddie and Missy. As Alice and Eddie went through the apartment again before calling the police, Theresa stood on the mall with a few other neighbors, staring at the window as if she had never seen it before. It was wrong. She stared harder and harder, the way some people can repeat a familiar word again and again until it acquires new and strange intonations.

The casement window was cranked open to about seventy-five degrees—almost the ninety-degree maximum. It had been closed last night when she passed. She remembered that she had heard the voices slightly muffled. It had been closed because there was a hole in the screen and the window had to be kept shut to keep the bugs out. Another thing struck Theresa: The screen was no longer in the window. It was outside leaning against the wall. Next to it was what is known as a porter's stroller—a converted baby carriage with a box mounted on it. It was directly under the window. She remembered that last night the stroller had been farther down the mall, under another window. All this suggested that, wherever the children were, they had got out through the window. Or, more precisely, been taken out. They couldn't have moved the stroller over to their window. There had been persistent rumors of prowlers in the neighborhood. A few blocks away, someone had even tried to lure a young boy outside. Theresa was suddenly very frightened for Eddie and Missy.

12

There were twenty-five identical three-story build-ings in the apartment complex where Alice Crimmins lived. The hedges and occasional splashes of white railing did little to relieve the impact of repetitious, institutional red brick. People often became confused searching for the right address.

Six minutes after Eddie Crimmins called the police, Patrolmen Michael Joseph Clifford and MacKay Flint double-parked on the street outside 150–22 72nd Drive. It was not difficult for Clifford to pick out the address from a platoon of identical buildings—Clifford lived on 73rd Avenue, three blocks away, and had mastered the coded mysteries of Kew Gardens addresses.

Eddie was waiting outside for the police. Clifford paused. "Ed," he said. "Hello!"

Clifford, who was twenty-three years old, six years younger than Eddie Crimmins, recognized the man from the neighborhood bars. He had never known his last name, but he remembered long evenings of sitting together and drinking beer in the local pubs. In the dark, anonymous bars the snatches of conversation had been abstract and impersonal. He'd known that Ed was having trouble at home, but he'd been only a sympathetic listener in a bar. Now, as a policeman, it took on professional significance. The first question Clifford asked was if there was a separation and a custody fight.

When they had moved inside the house Clifford had another jolt: he also recognized Alice. He had worked as a checker in a local A&P before joining the police force, and had seen Alice and the children shopping. She was someone to be noticed. Clifford, a bachelor, had paid particular attention to the striking redhead. But he had never connected her with his drinking part-ner of the bars.

Clifford put authority into his voice, pushing away the diverting intimacies of dealing with neighbors. If this is a custody-fight tactic, he warned them, it was a very bad idea.

"If this is a game, you better stop before it goes too far," said Clifford.

13

It was no game, Eddie and Alice assured him. The children were missing.

Two or three times they went through the routine. If this is a trick, stop it now before it goes too far. The patrolmen took Eddie and Alice into separate rooms, but both parents insisted they had no idea where the children were. Clifford went to the phone and started to dial the precinct. His finger paused halfway through, giving them one last chance to call it off. Neither moved. Clifford, the son of a detective inspector—ironically, the detective inspector who would be in charge of the case—reached the precinct commander on the phone and said that it appeared to be an authentic disappearance; they would require a lot of manpower for a massive search.

When Jerry Piering arrived at 11:00 a.m., he found precinct cars parked at random angles all around the mall, as if to punctuate the seriousness of the situation. Small knots of confused residents—men without socks; women in curlers and pinched faces, arms folded protectively across their chests in poses familiar to fearful tragedy—crisscrossed the malls without apparent pattern. No one wanted to stand still. Uniformed policemen moved briskly in and out of buildings, making basement-to-roof searches. Jerry Piering, the first detective to arrive on the scene, was struck by a curious uncertainty about all the activity. The search was halting because Eddie and Alice Crimmins were still trying to convince the police that their children were indeed missing—that they hadn't hidden them from each other. It was a story never accepted by everyone.

3

"Eddie! Missy! Can you hear us?"

The police sound trucks, starting from 72nd Drive, made wider and wider circles, like ripples in a pond.

"Eddie! Missy! If you can hear this, come out onto the street!"

The search was spreading. It had started in the 107th Precinct in Fresh Meadows and traveled like rumor toward Flushing. Now the commanders were arriving—men with stars on their shoulders, flanked by captain and lieutenants, chauffeured by plainclothes detectives. As their braided caps bobbed through the collecting crowds, a stiffening of attention made itself felt among the lower grades of police. The senior police officials were accompanied by men with brief-cases—inside the briefcases were contingency plans for drawing reserve manpower from spare units around the city.

In the newsrooms around the city, the police re-porters recognized that this was an event rich in danger and universal appeal. Without much discussion or reflection, the reporters headed for Queens.

A green flag had been planted outside the entrance of 150–22 72nd Drive, where Apartment 1-D had been isolated by uniformed policemen. Alice Crimmins' apartment had become a police command post. Next door, Mrs. Robert Yoquinto was conscripted to brew vats of coffee to fuel the police. It was a welcome diversion for her. She didn't want to be helpless and hand-wringing. Making coffee and sandwiches, she could feel that she was being useful. Mrs. Yoquinto hoped to bring coffee and sandwiches to Alice Crimmins, but her neighbor was blockaded behind a wall of frantic activity.

The press photographers were always ahead of the reporters. Their quick arrival was no trick. Tommy Gallagher was a staff photographer for the *Daily News,* which kept a dozen radio cars scattered around the city for just such emergencies. Often Gallagher would arrive before reinforcements and find himself pinned down under murderous crossfire. A veteran of fifteen years with the *Daily News,* Gallagher was pulled off of his regular assignment—which was the tedious stake-out at the World's Fair, waiting for some pseudo-event such as a press agent causing a young starlet to fall into a fountain.

Gallagher lugged his heavy camera case out of his gray radio cruiser and began looking around to see how to best "cover" the disappearance of two small children. It was a delicate operation. The police had very tight limits in such situations. If the children were recovered quickly, the police would be grateful for a front-page picture of the rescuing officers and the two children wearing the cops' hats. But if the situation was truly serious, then Gallagher would have to contend with a layer of hostility. The higher brass might spot a stray photographer and tell the nearest man in uniform to "get that guy out of here." Journalists were always considered a nuisance by police during a crisis. It was almost as if the reporters' and photographers' presence was a kind of challenge.

Gallagher's first thought was to shoot some establishing pictures—a distraught neighbor or an anxious father or, ideally, a tearful mother. Instinctively, he knew that the best picture, under the circumstances, would be that of the mother of the two missing children. People could identify with her and he was in the business of vibrating nerves. If the tearful mother was a cliché, the *Daily News* was not in the business of "new journalism." Its readers operated lathes and rode the subway and looked for predictable reactions. They had a predictable vision of how a mother who lost her two children was supposed to react, and it

16

would tear at something fundamental if they couldn't find it. Newspaper photographers are supposed to sense and capture in a single frame the essence of any story—a politician loses an election and he looks sad; the temperature climbs past 100 and people walk around without coats and with their neckties undone; Miss America is crowned, overcome with joy. . . .

And Alice Crimmins should be sobbing for her missing children. But she was not available for Tommy Gallagher. She was inside Apartment 1-D, telling a story she would repeat a thousand times.

Gallagher was not dismayed. A photographer learns early that if he is blocked from the ideal shot, he takes what he can. It's called "getting it in the bag."

Click! A picture of the hectic arrival and departure of grim detectives, shields hanging from their breast pockets, making cellar-to-roof searches.

Click! A picture of neighbors, caught in half-surprised concern; even in the worst circumstances, one can't help smiling at the camera as if some voice in the ear has whispered "Cheese."

Click! A picture of two uniformed patrolmen sitting in their cruiser, studying photographs of the missing children—the faces of the policemen are tense.

Click! A wide, long-distance shot of the area, revealing its nature—the low garden-apartment buildings with chipped, naked brick. Later, police photographers would take similar pictures to show the density of the hedges, the conditions of lighting, the positions of doors and parking area. Gallagher's pictures would be printed in gray in the newspaper, but even the police color photographs could not add much hue to the dreary landscape.

Click! A picture of the empty window in the children's room. This was perhaps the most evocative photograph Gallagher would take—the unspoken absence of the two children crying out at the viewer. (That photograph would provide an important record, since it would show the condition of the window—without the screen, open to a seventy-five-degree angle, and with a porter's stroller underneath. Inexplicably, police photographers neglected to shoot the pictures Gallagher took.)

Jerry Piering wanted this case. He wanted it from the first with a kind of high-school yearning. When he had telephoned the precinct, he had spoken to Detective Sergeant Kurt Gruenthal, who was in temporary command of the 107th Squad Detectives while Lieutenant Ray Jones was on vacation. Gruenthal's reaction to the bulletin was phlegmatic:

"It's a grounder."

"Listen," said Piering with superior instinct, "I've got kids and what worries me is the age."

"OK," said Gruenthal with a shrug, "if you want it, take it."

Piering's instinct told him immediately that this was a detective case. When he first arrived on the scene, he was overshadowed by the uniformed forces, for whom it seemed an appropriate job. The case did not require elaborate detection—merely careful sweeps of the neighborhood. The uniformed men were blocking out the standard search techniques, avoiding duplication. They saturated the neighborhood with teams who went from door to door, house to house. They were bound to find Eddie and Missy with shoe leather, not brilliant detective work.

But Jerry Piering never believed it. Of course he wanted to make second-grade detective, and he knew that promotions within the detective command were propelled by important cases, good instincts, and lucky hunches. This time Piering's instinct told him that the uniformed men were looking in the wrong place. Piering had staked out the one place where the uniformed men were not allowed—inside the head of Alice Crimmins. He would never look anywhere else.

Piering was new to the job, but he was intent on being thorough. He went through Apartment 1-D, treating it as evidence. In the crowded, frantic confusion of the morning Jerry Piering would note the condition and contents of each room. And he began to form hard opinions. There were a dozen empty liquor bottles in the garbage. Alice would explain that she had been in the middle of cleaning the apartment. She had been told by an attorney to expect an inspection visit from a court agency in connection with the custody suit. And so she had been painting the foyer and cleaning up. Getting rid of the liquor bottles was part of cleaning up. She had wanted nothing to suggest she was an unfit mother. Piering noted the bottles and the explanation, but he did not like this woman in the tight toreador slacks and thick makeup.

Patrolman Mike Clifford had already taken Piering aside and explained the complication—husband and wife were separated and in the middle of a custody fight. Clifford showed Piering the hook-and-eye latch on the door to the children's room.

"What's that doing there?" Piering asked Alice Crimmins.

"I had to put that up because Eddie would sneak out of bed and raid the refrigerator," she explained. "He'd make himself sick."

In his hand Piering held a black address book that Alice had dropped outside; it had been part of a key-holder attachment. The names of men outnumbered names of women by four to one. He didn't like Alice's explanation about the lock on the children's door. He saw it as something sinister, rather than as a mother's attempt to prevent a son from overeating.

From the first confrontation there was an instant chemical reaction between Jerry Piering and Alice Crimmins, and it was not affection. Piering had the reputation among his brother officers of being something of a martinet. He was only just over the height requirement to become a policeman, and some detectives who worked with him said his size caused a kind of gruff assertiveness, an inability to admit mistakes. There was, they said, a harshness that would have been tempered by someone more confident of himself.

Other detectives found it difficult to warm up to Piering. He would not drink on duty, although he would not turn in his brother officers who did. Perhaps because of his height complex, his first reaction was always to overpower a suspect. So the tactic he employed with Alice Crimmins was to be tough. And Alice Crimmins flinched.

"From the first minute, I never had the feeling that they"—the police, or, more precisely, Detective Jerry Piering—"were interested in finding my children," she would recall later. "I got angry."

19

Detective George Martin flashed his gold shield and rode the bus across Jewel Avenue to Kew Gardens, still annoyed by his partner's overeagerness. He had been left without the radio car, which, as senior partner, he was entitled to. His brooding was interrupted by the sudden whoosh of a helicopter. Through the bus window he could see that it was a police helicopter and was executing an intricate grid search—hovering, plunging down, then sucking itself up again for height, like a gull working to spot a fish. And George Martin, with a sinking feeling, could hear the police sound trucks crying for the two missing children.

One helicopter was running at rooftop level when Martin left the bus at 150th and Union Turnpike near Main Street. He had been going to meet Piering primarily to retrieve the car and gloat in his senior wisdom. But now he felt like a truant. Hundreds of cops were running communications trucks through the streets; they were looking on rooftops and watertowers for the children.

"Holy Christ!" thought Martin with a jolt. "This is for real."

Alice and Eddie Crimmins were sitting frozen on the couch in the living room of the apartment when Martin arrived. Jerry Piering was on an easy chair.

"You know, if you know something, if either of you are hiding something, you should tell me now. Don't let this thing go too far!"

Eddie would look at Alice . . . Alice would look at Eddie . . . Piering would study them both, but nothing broke. "Is there someone who has a grudge against you?"

"We divide them up," whispered Piering to Martin after filling him in. "You take Eddie. I'll take the bitch."

There was a brief interruption as Eddie was rushed to the 110th Precinct; a young girl had been found and there was a flurry of hope that it was Missy. The girl was ten years old, however, and bore no resemblance to Missy. Still, Eddie walked over to her and touched her before he said it wasn't his daughter.

Jerry Piering took Alice into her bedroom. George Martin was slipping into a depression. Alice's room

20

was air-conditioned. Martin and Eddie Crimmins stood in the superheated children's room.

The case had eluded Martin, but he was an old professional. In the summer of 1965 he was forty-seven years old and had more than two years to go before retirement. Like many of the other detectives who would be involved in the case, Martin was a product of the parochial schools of New York City. His father had been a pharmacist, broken during the Great Depression. Martin vividly remembers standing in the street with his father when the family store went bankrupt. His father pointed to the man directing traffic and said: "He's got more job security than I'll ever have . . . with all my education." That was when George Martin decided to become a cop.

He and Eddie Crimmins stood awkwardly in the center of the children's bedroom. Neither man seemed to want to touch anything. It was as if the room itself were stricken.

"What do you think, Eddie?"

Eddie shrugged. Then he looked at the open window without the screen. "That must be how they got in," he said.

Over the years Martin had developed a flexible rapport for dealing with people. He had spent World War II as a cook in the Coast Guard, and in questioning people he would divert their guard with his rambling anecdotes—earthy and rich in inelegant detail ("It was so hot on that ship that the sweat ran down between the cheeks of your ass and you could mop the floor with it"). If Martin had a strength, it was an ability to connect with a guy like Eddie Crimmins, an airplane mechanic who worked with his hands and spent time in neighborhood bars, showing the first signs of a beer paunch. They spoke to each other in short jabs.

"Whaddya think, Eddie?"

"I dunno."

"You think she hid 'em on you?"

"Maybe, but I don't think so."

Both men looked around the room. The beds had been slept in. The window was open. The screen was off, lying outside on the ground. But there were no

21

signs of a struggle. As they looked, each man was aware, although neither of them spoke of it, that the thing they were really looking for was blood.

Jerry Piering stood while Alice Crimmins sat on her bed. Piering wanted to emphasize the formality of the relationship and so he braced in a kind of attention. The distance between them was more than space. It never crossed his mind to put her at ease, to comfort her.

Alice was conscious of the buzz of the air-conditioner. Her legs were like rubber. The man standing over her couldn't keep the cutting edge out of his voice. It was strange. Usually she would dismiss such a man with the flick of an eyebrow, but now she was obliged to submit to him.

"Yesterday," he was saying. He wanted to know what she had done yesterday. It was hard for her to answer. She had to pull herself away from the dreadful possibilities of today.

"We went to the park yesterday," she said. "We had a picnic."

Detective Jerry Piering wrote on Form UF-16, his field memo book. He was all business, functioning, creating a record.

"We went on a picnic to Kissena Park yesterday afternoon," said Alice Crimmins.

"What time?" asked Piering.

"Oh, I guess it was about two-thirty."

July 13 had been a perfect day for a picnic, even if Alice Crimmins' days did start a little late. She was a night person who spent long tracts of time in the bars and restaurants of Long Island. If she awoke before noon, there usually had to be a reason. The children learned patience, or were taken care of by one of Alice's helpers.

On that Tuesday she had piled the children into the front seat of her four-year-old Mercury convertible and driven six blocks to the park. They had taken along meatball sandwiches and soda, and the children were too impatient to wait to eat. Little Eddie had gone down the slide again and again. Alice had pushed

Missy on the swings until she got tired. Then she had sat with other mothers, listening halfheartedly to this one's grief with a mother-in-law; to someone else's dinner coup. It was comfortable and lazy, sitting in the shade, watching the children run out of energy.

Jerry Piering jotted it down, omitting the parts that had no business in a police narrative. He was only interested in the parts he could check.

Alice remembered leaving the park at about 4:30. She could pinpoint the time because she had to stop at a corner telephone booth to call her attorney. She knew he might not be there after 5, so she made certain to leave by 4:30. The telephone call was to Michael LaPenna, the attorney representing her in the custody suit. LaPenna was busy. He told Alice to call back later, he would be working late.

"Whatdja do then?"

"We came home. Oh, I picked up some things for dinner first."

Alice said she'd stopped in a neighborhood delicatessen and bought a package of frozen food, a can of string beans, and a bottle of soda. Her purchases in the delicatessen were always modest and spur-of-the-moment. She enjoyed cooking, but often she was carried away by the whim of a summer afternoon and would be forced to conjure meals on the run. She said she had bought frozen veal. At the time it would seem a trifle, perhaps not worth noting. Later a dispute would rage over whether it was in fact frozen veal or frozen manicotti.

When Alice and the children reached home, a few neighbors saw them walking from the car to the apartment. Later, people would remember Alice walking with the brown grocery bag while the children skipped carefree ahead.

Alice left the children outside to play while she went in to call LaPenna. Piering wanted every detail, precise times. Why was all this necessary? Alice wanted to know. What has this to do with the disappearance? Why wasn't he outside looking?

"It's just routine," said Piering.

Alice punched out cigarettes one after the other. OK. OK. She understood. Her nerves were on the

23

ragged edge of hysteria, but she understood. She went on with the narrative. She talked to LaPenna about the custody case, which was scheduled to come up for a hearing in a week. Alice had learned that a former maid was going to testify against her and she was worried. The maid, Evelyn Linder Atkins, claimed that Alice owed her six hundred dollars, but Alice said that was nonsense. The maid had hinted that if she got her money she wouldn't be available to testify, said Alice. Alice Crimmins was not the sort of person who would tolerate a shakedown. It was just another messy detail, said Alice, shaking her head.

"Yeah?" said Piering.

Then Alice had made another call. A friend. But he was busy. In conference. He had told her to call back.

"Who?" asked Piering.

Alice looked at Piering for a moment. This man was violating her privacy. She was trying to decide whether to hold anything back.

"His name is Tony Grace."

The flashing diamond pinky ring adorned a hand that had spent a lifetime performing hard labor. Anthony Grace was fifty-two years old—precisely twice the age of Alice Crimmins. He was a small, thick man with a pencil mustache and the raspy voice of someone who had once been strangled. Grace's name was stenciled on hundreds of trucks and pieces of heavy machinery throughout the state. His contracting firm built highways and parks all over New York State. He might have developed more polish on his rude climb to become a millionaire, but his social mobility did not suffer. He could sit in his favorite bar in the Bronx and point out famous politicians and mobsters he knew.

Among his friends was City Council President Paul Screvane. Because of their interlacing business interests, Grace had come to know almost every important New York City official. When Alice Crimmins became Grace's girlfriend, she came to know them, too.

On the day that Mayor Robert F. Wagner's engage-

24

ment to Barbara Cavanagh—sister of Deputy Mayor Edward Cavanagh, Jr.—was being publicly announced, Tony Grace was fending off telephone calls from Alice Crimmins.

4

It was an accident that Jerry Piering was assigned as the detective in charge of the Crimmins case. Since Lieutenant Ray Jones was on vacation, his chores fell to Sergeant Kurt Gruenthal. A cautious man who was on the police promotion list waiting for appointment to lieutenant, Gruenthal was eager to court the friendship of members of the force. By surrendering the case to Piering, he was not so much avoiding risks as accumulating debts.

George Martin stepped out of Piering's way without recriminations or protest. It would have been difficult for Martin to challenge Piering's right to the case, even if he had wanted to. Perhaps Ray Jones might have insisted on assigning the case to the senior detective, George Martin. But Martin was already a first-grade detective and so he retreated in order that Piering might get some credit and a shot at second-grade detective. Martin also suspected that by passing up the Crimmins case he might be saving himself a lot of hard work . . . and grief.

While Piering was poking around the kitchen and going through the garbage, Martin was making a routine search of Alice's bedroom, the room with the air-conditioner. He was not looking for anything in particular, but he would know a find when he came upon it. The vanity was cluttered with an assortment of sweet-smelling cosmetics that perfumed the entire

25

room. The closet was jammed with an assortment of bright summer clothing. Martin noted that the clothing was inexpensive—labels from Macy's and Gertz—and kept in neat condition.

And then he saw something sticking out from under the bed. It was a pastel overnight bag. He reached over to pick it up, grateful that he was not outdoors in the unbearable heat, marching up and down the neighborhood.

"Do you have to do that?"

Alice Crimmins was standing in the doorway, her hands on her hips, trying to suppress her anger. The police were pawing through her private things. Strange men stomped in and out of her bedroom, handling her intimate papers, her clothing, her underwear. Their clumsy, careless manner left her feeling violated.

"I know what I'm doing," replied Detective Martin. "You've got two kids missing." He unzipped the case and immediately regretted it. The case was filled with cards—birthday greetings, comic valentines, holiday cards—some of them signed. The detective lifted a batch and began to read them. "Holy shit!" he said. He had stumbled upon a greeting card from Paul Screvane, President of the City Council, likely to be the next Mayor. There was a telegram from the present Mayor, Robert Wagner, inviting Alice to attend the opening of the Verrazano Narrows Bridge. There were dinner programs autographed by Mayor Wagner and Senator Robert Kennedy. There was a card from Tony Grace, the contractor who had constructed a small park underneath the Verrazano Bridge. They all had the same opening: "To Rusty." To the important city officials she was known only as "Rusty," a kinetic redhead who appeared and disappeared in their lives at convenient moments—she was one of the pretty smiling faces at their social assemblies; a party light who would glow until the men of power grew tired or bored and shut her out. Martin knew instantly that Alice Crimmins traveled in important circles and sensed that a hopeless complication had entered the case. He didn't want any part of it. But at the moment all he could say was "Holy shit!"

Ruth Mandelbaum watched the two policemen going from store to store along Main Street, a few blocks west of the Crimmins apartment, in one of the shopping districts. Her desk was in the window of a small insurance firm where she worked as a receptionist, secretary, and soft counterpoint to the asset-eyed men. Ruth Mandelbaum was a swollen middle-aged woman who gave herself special credit for gifts of insight and prescience. The latter, which she charged to some dim ancestor who had passed along genes of witchcraft, kept Mrs. Mandelbaum alert. She could always spot trouble coming up the block. She was in the middle of her morning coffee break, chatting with her daughter on the telephone, when she saw it coming.

"I'll have to call you back, Sheila, something's going on."

Mrs. Mandelbaum seldom noticed the faces of policemen. Usually the uniform alone was enough to create an identity. But today she noticed the policemen's faces. They were very young and seemed very anxious. She was already out of her chair and at the door when they reached the office. Her boss, a chubby man smelling of cologne, was standing next to her.

"We're looking for these two children," said one of the young policemen, holding out pictures of Eddie and Missy. Mrs. Mandelbaum's boss, a short man, had to peer over her shoulder. Guided by some interior logic, the policemen went to the woman instead of the man.

Mrs. Mandelbaum looked gravely and carefully at the two photographs—not because she would have recognized the children, but because she felt some obligation to form. Ruth Mandelbaum saw hundreds of children every day from her window on Main Street. It was one of the more pleasant aspects of her job, the ability to divert herself to the street and a passing pack of children. After 3:00 p.m., when school broke, she derived satisfaction from watching the youngsters bursting with happy energy.

The small, preschool children passed all day, by the hundreds. This was a crowded section of Queens, busily breeding large families. But the children were always attached to an adult—even if the strings were loose and invisible. Whenever she saw a young child, she would instinctively look behind for the attending parent. It was something she never thought about, but realized instantly when the police showed her the photographs. She would have noticed an unattached child.

"They might be wearing pajamas or underwear," said one of the policemen.

All along Main Street, like some tide that the policemen had drawn after them, storekeepers stood in the doorways looking up and down the street.

Mrs. Mandelbaum's coffee was tasteless and cold by the time she got back to her daughter. "What kind of mother lets her children run loose like that?" said Mrs. Mandelbaum, and then, without thinking, "By the way, where are Mark and Lisa?"

By midmorning there were hundreds of detectives and uniformed policemen walking in pairs looking for the two missing children. More than a mile away, teams walked slowly through Cunningham Park, dreading every bush. Using their nightsticks, the policemen explored the undergrowth in Kissena Park.

One detachment spread out on both sides of the access road to the Van Wyck Expressway. There were wild, weedy patches where neighborhood children built secret warrens or tree houses, where teenagers left traces of midnight trysts—beer cans and contraceptives. Lately, new tenants had moved into the stretches of greensward. Rats, driven away from the World's Fair grounds in Flushing Meadow Park, had temporarily nested on the uninhabited islands, like swimmers pausing in the mid-ocean of highways.

It was in no way an ordinary assignment for the policemen in the area. Most of them were parents. Most had children near Eddie's and Missy's ages, and they could easily imagine this nightmare happening to them.

Abe Silverman had always warned his children to stay out of the open lot a few doors from their home on 162nd Street. Besides being an eyesore, the lot was a dangerous dumping ground. There were wild flowers

28

which attracted children into the area, but Silverman knew that there were outcroppings of broken glass and rusty cans. "I never want you to go in there without an adult," Silverman told his son, Jay, nine years old, and his daughter, Leslie, who was three years older.

On July 14, Jay Silverman was furious. He had just fought with his sister and stalked out of their attached home in search of mediation. He walked quickly up 162nd Street. The dirt path that led past the empty lot turned into Jewel Avenue, a major east-west artery. Jay found himself heading toward the library, less than half a mile away, where he expected to find his mother. His indignation was high as he made the trip that he had made so often, the pale youth with glasses who always seemed buried in a book.

Jay's mother wasn't at the library and, with his anger unspent, he headed home. He kicked up dirt as he passed the empty lot near his home—the forbidden place which held so much allure. Automatically Jay glanced at some movement. A small cloud of flies hovered over something just off the footpath. Jay looked down.

Perhaps it was because his father was a designer for a toy company, or maybe it was an inability to accept cruel possibilities, but the first thing that Jay Silverman thought when he looked down was that he had come upon a broken doll. Of course, some part of him realized that it was not a toy. He was looking at the broken body of Missy Crimmins.

5

At 1:45 p.m. on July 14, 1965, there was an abrupt change of tone in the Crimmins case.

"Hey, Jerry, you wanna take this call?"

Detective Piering listened for a moment, then told Alice Crimmins that she had to go with him. There was no appeal in his voice. He did not tell her where she was going, or why. But she could tell that something had changed dramatically. Alice did not argue. She attached a leash to Brandy and went with Piering and Martin, wedged between them like the filling in a sandwich.

The unmarked police cruiser raced the eight blocks to the scene, a little pocket of urgency punctuated by a flashing red light and a mournful siren. No one spoke; everyone was absorbed by the details of the transit, by the frightened faces lining the streets. At the end of Jewel Avenue the street was blocked off. Uniformed patrolmen paced back and forth, delineating the limits of crowd penetration. They left the police cruiser in the middle of the street. Jerry Piering grabbed Mrs. Crimmins under the armpit and walked her across the street. The crowd pulled away.

Alice Crimmins looked down and saw her daughter and swooned.

Jerry Piering purposefully had not told her where they were going or what they expected to find. He had wanted to test her reactions, convinced that he would be able to read guilt or innocence in her expression of pain. He was ready when she crumpled and grabbed her. George Martin was unprepared. Stunned, he just stood watching.

"Do you recognize her?" asked Jerry Piering.

Mrs. Crimmins, sagging in his arms, replied, "It's Missy."

The two detectives walked the stricken mother back to the unmarked car. Another car had just arrived. Eddie Crimmins, flanked by two policemen, was about to go through the same ordeal. He was walking with Sergeant Gruenthal and another detective. Alice mumbled something, but Eddie didn't seem to believe her. He just kept heading toward the shroud of flies where his daughter lay.

Alice Marie Crimmins—known by everyone who loved her as Missy—was dead. She was lying on her side with her back to the street. She had been dead for several hours. Exactly how many hours would be very difficult to pinpoint.

The police technicians circled her as if she were something contaminated, as if the job was too unbearable to begin. They had to follow the compelling professional routine to fight off a stab of emotion. The textbook ritual was explicit—keep the crime scene intact; keep the bystanders back; keep contact with command.

Still, it was very difficult. Missy's legs, overstuffed like sausages, were stiff now with rigor mortis. The knees, smudged with little scabs from exuberant tumbles and careless play, were lifeless. The worst part was her head. She looked as if she might be sleeping. And the pretty blond hair and once bright blue eyes were covered with fly-egg larvae.

Jay Silverman had been pushed back with the rest of the crowd. After his discovery he had run home, the fight with his sister forgotten. Neighbors had rushed out with Jay, skeptical of his alarms. The radios in Queens had been broadcasting news reports of two missing children, but radio bulletins had only abstract claims on their attention. The dead child in the lot was overwhelmingly ghastly.

Jay Silverman stood with his mother, almost lost in

31

the pack waiting for the police. In the years ahead he would have many bad nights, and his sister would not be able to sleep alone without lights. Jay would achieve his growth going in and out of courtrooms, telling of that moment when he found Missy's body. He would be forced, by the requirements of law, to relive it again and again.

One of the first to answer the alarm was *News* photographer Tommy Gallagher. It took the police forty-five minutes to arrive, because many sector cars were involved in the search. A few minutes after 2:00 p.m. Detective Frank Frezza showed up. To the people on the street, it looked like the appearance of just another photographer. Frezza, however, was a police photographer who had learned his craft during World War II in combat. His pictures would be different from Gallagher's. His job was to record the crime scene for possible courtroom use. He took eight pictures—five in black and white, three in color.

It was 2:45 p.m. by the time Dr. Richard Grimes arrived at the vacant lot at 71–31 162nd Street. In thirty-eight years as an Assistant Medical Examiner, Grimes had been exposed to almost every variety of violent death. He had performed thousands of autopsies and had a professional detachment from death. And yet he was moved by the sight of Missy Crimmins.

He touched her tiny leg. It was still warm; but that was from lying in the sun. He tried to flex the limb to test the degree of rigor mortis. The right side of Missy was pale. Her blood had settled to the left side —because of gravity. Technically, the condition is called lividity.

There was something tied around the child's neck. It proved to be a pajama top. The arm of the pajama top had been knotted into two ligatures; but it wasn't tight. Dr. Grimes could fit his fingers between the balls of the ligatures and the child's neck.

He noted that there were bruises on the neck. Some spittle had dribbled out of Missy's mouth—a froth that had run down her lips and onto her neck and was caked dry. The fly eggs were so thick that they obscured the eyelids and the forehead. Dr. Grimes had to keep brushing flies away from Missy's face. He

32

made a few notes and then released her to the detectives.

"Pretty little girl," said someone in the crowd.

Dr. Grimes walked away quickly; he was not prepared to listen to that kind of talk.

6

Jerry Piering didn't need Dr. Grimes or anyone else to tell him he was dealing with a homicide. He had seen it coming all day.

The police car headed back to the apartment. Alice Crimmins was in an apparent state of shock and Piering was plotting his next moves, beginning to realize that his correct guess would place him in a powerful position with his colleagues. No one would try to take the case away from him now. When they reached the home mall, hundreds of people were jammed on the patchy lawns. These strangers and neighbors had sensed tragedy, without having to be told. They cleared a path as Piering led Alice past the newspaper photographers. Piering noted that it was the cameras which started Alice's tears. He recorded that, along with the memory of the liquor bottles, the tight slacks, the heavy makeup, and a theory began to congeal in his mind. Alice Crimmins had failed his final litmus test when he showed her Missy's body. She had wept for the cameras, not for her child. The swoon he dismissed as theatrical.

Piering brought Alice back into her bedroom, sat her on her bed, and paced for a moment before launching on the tactics that he was certain would crack the case.

"Do you have any enemies?"

33

She shook her head.

"Think, Alice. Do you know someone who would want to do this?"

She paused and then shook her head again.

The apartment throbbed with even more activity as the criminal division of the Police Department moved in. In the children's room, technicians were dusting for fingerprints. They had to take a set of elimination prints—fingerprints of all the people known to have handled things in the apartment so that they could be compared with any strange, unaccountable prints. They fingerprinted the parents, neighbors, baby-sitters. They took the children's prints from their toys—Missy's from a plastic tea set and a doll carriage; Eddie's from a truck and the toy chest. The technicians also dusted the windows and the windowsills. They found one strange fingerprint on the third window pane from the bottom. It was an adult fingerprint and it would remain a mystery. In all the years that the case would be investigated, among all the thousands of fingerprints tested, that particular print would never be matched.

The fingerprint dust spilled on the crib where Missy had presumably been taken from her sleep; it fell on Eddie's cot, where he had kicked the sheets around in a nightmare. The window screen, inside now, was dusted, as was the bureau in front of the window.

In the early stages of an investigation it is impossible to know what will become important. In the first hectic moments the job of the investigator is to capture a kind of still-life; to freeze all the details before things are changed and touched. Police photographers went through the apartment, but, curiously, did not take many photographs. The standard procedure was for the photographers to operate under the orders of the investigating detectives. Jerry Piering was busy with Alice Crimmins, and when the subject came up, he was uncertain. He assumed that the photographers knew their job and would overshoot—take more photographs than were needed. Later it would be recalled that this was Jerry Piering's first major case and senior commanders would excuse this lapse. But when veteran detectives moved into the investigation, they felt hampered and frustrated by the lack of physical evidence.

One of the important items that was overlooked, the seemingly insignificant top of a bureau in the children's room, would later become a ferocious battleground. Piering would claim that when he first came into the room he detected a thin film of dust on the bureau top—thus eliminating the possibility that the children had left the room through the window since they would have needed to go over the bureau. (Curiously, a murder case had been solved a few months earlier by just such a piece of evidence—a film of dust on a window pane had proved that the murderer had been admitted through the front door. Piering had worked on that case.)

But the technicians dusted the top of the bureau for fingerprints before it could be photographed. Piering would develop a theory that the children must have left through the front door because he was certain he had seen a film of dust on the bureau top. There was a lamp on the bureau and it had a round base. When he'd moved the lamp, it had left a circle in the dust. Eddie and Alice Crimmins would dispute Piering's story, as would Alice's brother, John Burke. The lamp on the bureau had tripod legs, they all said. In addition, many people had come into the room before Piering arrived; Eddie Crimmins had leaned out to look for the children when he first showed up. Patrolman Clifford had reached out of the window to flick an ash from his cigarette. If they had all leaned out that way—between the plastic barrel bank and the bowling trophy on the sill—it would have been virtually impossible not to brush the bureau.

The film of dust and the lamp were not noted in Piering's first reports, but much was overlooked in the first flood of discovery. Other items—to become tricky points of disputed testimony—went unrecorded except in the files of self-serving memories. As the years passed, some of the details would become cemented with importance. A mote of dust would grow in significance and be glazed with certainty.

While Piering was absorbed with the details of Alice's day with the children, other detectives were

35

questioning everyone in sight, nailing down stories before people started talking to each other, comparing testimony and subtly shifting themselves into favorable or important roles. Later the stories would be strung together like a chain in the detective squad room. Calmly, with reflection, investigators would be able to read the reports and fit the bits and pieces together, sifting out error or mutations of imagination.

In the bedroom Alice and Jerry Piering were squaring off, measuring each other.

"OK, Alice, no more bullshit! Let's go over this whole thing again. ... ."

Before, when the case involved two missing children, some care had had to be taken with the parents. The children did, after all, belong to Eddie and Alice.

"I don't want to hear any more of your bullshit. What the fuck happened yesterday?"

In death, Missy Crimmins belonged to Jerry Piering.

There was no startling confession; no shattering drama to explain something monstrous. There was only the repetition of the mundane story—full of the petty details that go into the makeup of life within a broken home, in a boring suburb, with tacky subplots. If Detective Piering was listening to pick out some unusual telltale chord to vibrate his deductive ear, it was in vain.

July 13—just another summer day. As Alice told her story again, Piering was trying to penetrate the fortress behind which Alice Crimmins hid herself. A sometime secretary, Alice had found that working as a cocktail waitress was more lucrative and suited her changing tastes. One side benefit was that it gave her more time with the children. If it threw her into a life of high excitement, where relationships were ultimately more bruising, that was not such a high price to pay for escape from the banal drudgery of being just another housewife. Still, she considered herself a fine and loving mother.

On the Tuesday morning before the disappearance the children had been particularly voluble. They had been out with their father the day before for the first time in two weeks. He had been too busy, moving to another furnished room. Alice had been especially tolerant of their chatter, partly to woo their affections back from their father and partly out of curiosity. While she cooked breakfast, she questioned them obliquely. Where did Daddy take you? What did you eat? Did you have a nice time?

Missy sat dreamily over her egg, and Eddie's hands were greasy with bacon fat. He was very much like his father, thought Alice—too impatient to wait for a fork, and clumsy. He spilled part of his milk.

In nine days there would be a custody hearing. Eddie had hired an attorney and was making a serious effort to take the children away from Alice.

Alice Crimmins had been brought up to connect her feelings for her children and her marriage. Gradually she had been able to separate the emotions. It had become clear to her one night in the spring of 1965 as she sat with a friend in an all-night diner on Northern Boulevard—one of a breed somewhere between a restaurant and greasy spoon where the waitresses wore thick eyeshadow. Late on this Friday night the room vibrated with unspent gaiety. At one table a group of high-school seniors were celebrating graduation, their prom faces still flushed with excitement. At another table a drunk sat weaving over a plate of ham and eggs, unable to decide whether to try eating or stagger back to the men's room. Two Nassau County policemen attempted to concentrate on heaping plates of free stew while a counter man chattered incessantly at them about an unfair speeding ticket.

Ruth Cranston and Alice Crimmins sat in the booth at a window. They always made a point of being nice to waitresses. Although they regarded the profession of cocktail waitress as grander, they knew what it was to be pestered or kept waiting or forced to listen to rude, ragged jokes.

For a while Alice and Ruth ate in silence. They had been talking—parrying the stream of glib entendres that passed for conversation in the Heritage House, the bar in Huntington where Alice worked as a cocktail waitress.

Ruth was tired, feeling her face sagging from the strain of smiling all night. It struck her that Alice had

37

extra sources of energy; that she paced herself better and *enjoyed* what Ruth Cranston regarded as a hectic rat race.

Yes, Alice explained smiling, her life was fun now —compared to her past. She felt an exhilarating sense of freedom. Ruth didn't understand—Alice had two kids, a husband who gave her $40 a week, and worked long and hard to support herself.

I don't mind, said Alice. Compared to the prison she had lived in, this life was free. Before, she had felt trapped. Now, anything was possible.

Ruth's feet tingled with fatigue. She would have preferred a steady husband and no obligations. No, she thought watching Alice's enigmatic smile, she didn't understand at all.

The first year of the marriage had not been bad. Alice was working and stretching with her first stirrings of independence. She and Eddie had their own apartment, but it was lonely when Eddie was working nights, and gourmet dinners seemed pointless for one.

Alice was happy when she got pregnant. It was an early birth, and the next year she was pregnant again. But by 1960 Eddie was working more and coming home less. It was not that he didn't love Alice; but he had been brought up to believe that a woman remained home, uncomplaining, while a man went out drinking with the boys. The arguments became bitter. Alice went through the entire range of fury and retaliation. And then she smoldered silently.

For days, then weeks, she wouldn't speak to Eddie. They would visit friends, never talking to each other. It was a strange and frustrating contest. One Sunday morning they woke up sullen. They had not been speaking for two days. Alice prepared the children for a visit to Johnny and Marilyn Bohan, while Eddie sat around angry. When the children were ready, she simply started to leave. Eddie ran to catch up and got into the car to drive. For two hours they drove in utter silence, broken only by the occasional noises of the children.

When they arrived at the Bohans', Eddie spoke to Johnny and Alice spoke to Marilyn. The Bohans and Crimminses had been childhood friends. Alice and Eddie had also been childhood sweethearts. He had been working at an A&P in the Bronx in 1953, Alice had been going out with a Puerto Rican boy, but her father, Michael, had attacked the boy with a knife. So Alice picked someone who would be acceptable to Michael Burke. Her father never approved of any of her boyfriends except Eddie. And Eddie courted her family. Michael Burke worked as a repairman for the Con Edison Hell Gate plant and Eddie's father also worked for Con Edison. "He's a good Catholic boy," said Michael Burke, giving his blessing to the union.

As much as Alice Crimmins resisted her mother, she always hoped to please her father. He was rough and crude, but he exerted a powerful influence over his daughter. They shared the same stubborn pride and their clashes of will became famous. When he died in May 1965—a few months before the disappearance of the children—his daughter went through a period of profound mourning. In some ways she never fully recovered.

After Missy was born, Alice Crimmins decided not to have any more children. So she was fitted for a diaphragm and tried to keep it a secret from Eddie.

"What's this?" he cried when he came across the device and foam in her purse.

She tried to explain, but a diaphragm so violated his Catholic conscience that he would never forgive her. Eddie, whose brother Tom was a priest, attended church regularly. Alice's religion was more erratic, and after the events of that summer she stopped going to church. The relationship between Alice and Eddie deteriorated until, on June 22, 1965, Eddie Crimmins went to Family Court on Sutphin Boulevard with his attorney, George Marfeo, seeking custody of his two children. The affidavit he filed before Judge Paul Balsam is filled with repressed bitterness and frustration.

The petition of Edmund Crimmins respectfully alleges and shows:

1. That petitioner is a resident of the State of New York, over the age of 21 years and resides at 173–31 Grand Central Parkway, Jamaica, New York.

2. That petitioner is married to Alice Mary Crim-

mins, who resides at 150–22 72nd Drive, Flushing, New York. That an infant boy was born of the marriage on October 17, 1959, and an infant girl was born of the marriage on October 24, 1960, presently residing with the respondent.

3. That petitioner and respondent are living apart in a state of separation but are not divorced.

4. That the said infant children reside with the respondent at address stated above.

5. That petitioner and respondent separated on or about the 5th day of February, 1964.

6. Immediately after the separation, my wife began to indulge herself openly and brazenly in sex as she had done furtively before the separation. 6a. That no previous application has been made for the relief sought herein.

7. My wife entertains, one at a time, a stream of men sharing herself and her bedroom, until she and her paramour of the evening are completely spent. The following morning, the children awake to see a strange man in the house.

8. My son, who will be six years of age, is aware that something is going on that is not right. His statements to various people that his mother has a lot of men cousins that come to the house and stay overnight and his obvious embarrassment when he tells about it is indicative of his awareness.

9. Petitioner will present ample credible evidence to the Court that my children are in serious danger of being irreparably damaged by the unwholesome environment in which they are living.

10. Petitioner will also present to the court evidence that a clean wholesome environment is available for my children, one in which they will have a fair chance in life.

Wherefore petitioner prays that a Writ of Habeas Corpus issue directed to said Alice Mary Crimmins returnable before this Court for the purpose of delivery of said infants Edmond [sic] Crimmins and Alice Marie Crimmons [sic] from the custody of said Alice Mary Crimmins and that petitioner may be awarded the custody of said infants.

(signed) EDMUND CRIMMINS

Although the spelling of some of the names had been botched by Marfeo, Edmund Crimmins further swore that the contents of the petition were "true."

Yes, thought Alice Crimmins as she shared a meal with Ruth Cranston in a diner sometime before dawn, this life was better than tossing alone in her apartment. She didn't have Eddie anyway when he was out working or drinking. She was too much alive to stay home watching television. She would not settle for an occasional night out with friends.

If she was not happy, she was more at peace than when she'd lived with Eddie.

Through Tony Grace and Assistant Sanitation Commissioner Sal LoCurto (once Grace's business counsel), Alice had retained Michael LaPenna, a Bronx attorney with a good reputation in such matters. He had assured Alice that the courts would be very reluctant to take children away from their natural mother, but this case had some complications and she should not take any chances. An agency would probably inspect the apartment and he wanted it to be reported as a proper environment for children. So Alice was in the midst of a major cleaning job—painting the foyer, throwing away liquor bottles, replacing the screen in the children's bedroom. There was a hole in the old screen; sometimes the children would drop their toys out through the hole onto the mall, playfully, almost like throwing a stick for a dog to fetch. After she had installed an air-conditioner in her bedroom, Alice had a spare screen, and she decided to replace the broken one in the children's room with it.

On Tuesday morning she spoke to LaPenna. He told her to call back in the afternoon—they had to straighten out the business with the maid, Evelyn Linder Atkins. Alice told Piering she was angry about Evelyn's claim that she was owed six hundred dollars. Alice admitted that she owed Evelyn some money, perhaps a hundred and fifty dollars, but nowhere near the higher amount. Her entire relationship with Evelyn had turned into spite. They had never really been close; she didn't like the idea that Evelyn had once had a

41

white boyfriend. "If I ever catch her screwing in the house with the kids here I'll kill her," Alice had told one of her own boyfriends, a detective, who had seen Evelyn and her escort groping together in a car in the parking lot and reported it to Alice.

It didn't matter what the source of the conflict was; what mattered was that Eddie had enlisted Evelyn in the custody battle. In fact, the custody battle itself could be traced back to Evelyn. It was the maid who had called Eddie one Friday afternoon in February and told him that Alice had not returned from work and she was left with the children, without food and without money. Eddie had rushed over and taken the children to his mother-in-law's house in the Bronx. Evelyn had never returned to the apartment in Kew Gardens Hills.

Her explanation to Piering struck him as lame. It was perfectly understandable, she said. She had gone to a *bon voyage* party aboard a boat with Tony Grace and Sal LoCurto and Charlie Fellini (a developer of Freedomland). Alice went with a friend, Margie Fischer, who had an apartment above Alice's. They had too much to drink and the men playfully locked them in a washroom. By the time they were out, the boat had sailed.

There was no way to get off the boat, so Alice went to the Bahamas. Grace bought her an airline ticket and she flew back to New York on Sunday night, but by then Eddie had decided to fight her for the children. The incident had driven one more ally into Eddie's corner—Alice's own mother. Alice Burke was a pinched woman who lived in the Bronx and had given up trying to understand her daughter's behavior. In May, when Michael Burke, her father, died, Alice and her mother stood across the bier from each other at St. Raymond's Church in the Bronx. They had undergone a long estrangement. When Alice had broken from her husband, both parents had been stricken by the failure of the marriage. From under her black mourning veil Alice Burke began to scream at her daughter: "You killed him! You killed him! You killed him!"

Alice Crimmins took her father's death hard, but suffered in her own fashion. She had been particularly close to her father at one time, but the years and family demands had driven them apart. Alice no longer accepted the church dogma that was the touchstone of her father's life. It was hopeless for Alice to try to explain it to her father—the slow drifting away from formal religion. She still believed in many of the things taught by the church—she believed in good and evil and the existence of heaven and hell. She believed that Jesus Christ understood and delivered personal absolutions. What she couldn't accept was the hypocrisy of the church—priests claiming to deny flesh while privately indulging; hollow sermons that didn't seem to have any relation to her life and needs.

On the night her father was buried, Alice Crimmins went to the Broadcaster's Inn on Long Island and met three men and two women and had too much to drink.

When she came home from her unplanned cruise, she called Joe Rorech, a building contractor, to meet her at the airport. But he got tied up in a snowstorm. So Alice called Eddie and he came out to the airport to bring her home. On the ride back to the Queens apartment, they had another of their cutting exchanges:

You left Evelyn without any money.
There was a hundred dollars in the house and she knew it.
There was no food in the house.
She knows she can always buy food.

The words were like little nicks, drawing emotional blood, leaving tiny scars.

What kind of mother are you?
There's nothing wrong with my kids.
Where were you?
None of your business.

Less than two months later Eddie began the custody suit. The idea was not so much to take the children away from Alice as to bring Alice back into the fold.

She had strayed, but everyone was ready to forgive and forget. Everyone except Alice.

While the children played in Kissena Park that Tuesday, her determination to hold on to them hardened.

Her fury about the suit had been no secret. "I'll take them out of the country if I have to," she had told Joe Rorech. "I'll never let Eddie have them."

She did not want her children to grow up under the canopy of the church. She taught them prayers, but had resisted enrolling them in parochial school. Eddie had been badgering her about that just before the disappearance. Alice had seen and sampled the weight of money and power. She knew what beauty and wit could accomplish. She was dazzled by the men who moved cities and built roads.

"I'd rather see them dead than with Eddie."

Alice Crimmins was careless with words. She knew she could use them to wound her husband; she could drive men to the edge of expectation with hints and double entendres. She had learned to employ verbal brinkmanship to keep interest alive, or decisive putdowns to ward off vulgar approaches.

"I'd rather see them dead than with Eddie."

She would learn that words could cut both ways.

7

The thing that Detective Piering picked up from the cold progression of Alice Crimmins' day was a pungent suspicion. She had notebooks full of men's names. A woman like that, Piering deduced, would automatically deal in evasion and lies. She dangled too many men to be truthful. As his ballpoint pen moved across the

the page of his own notebook, he did not trust a single word she said.

"OK, you called the lawyer. Whatdja do then?"

"I had to call him back when I got home; he was busy. So I picked up some things for dinner. . . ."

He wrote down the name of Sever's Delicatessen. Soda. String beans. Etc. From her home she called LaPenna again and he told her that he wanted to see her the next day—that would have been today—to talk about the case. He warned her again that there could be an inspection visit any time and that she had better be careful. He didn't sound as sanguine about her chances as he normally did and she felt uncomfortable.

Missy and Eddie were outside tossing a ball around. And laughing. She put the package of frozen food in the oven and looked at her watch. She couldn't remember the exact time, only that she checked it to time the dinner. Then she opened the can of string beans and set the table for dinner. She telephoned Tony Grace at his office in Whitestone. He sounded brusque.

"I'm busy; lemme call you back."

Outside, Theresa Costello was sitting on the cement porch, tossing the ball to Missy and Eddie, giggling delightedly. They were the sort of children who always enticed adults into their games. Theresa pretended that she had been fooled into playing. She could hear Mrs. Crimmins in the kitchen, rattling pots and pans.

"Missy! Eddie! Let's go! Supper."

"Ahhh," protested Eddie.

"I gotta go eat, too," said Theresa, settling it.

No one intended to live forever in Regal Gardens—not at first, not when the moving vans arrived and the spectators on the lawn stared with a mixture of prison pity and just-wait smirks. For some, Regal Gardens was a white, lower-middle-class staging area halfway between the escape from the city and the house on Long Island. There, before the commitment to mortgages and lawn care, the bad marriages were sorted out and life styles were settled. But nothing seemed permanent and this affected even the relationships between

45

neighbors. There was an element of reluctance on the part of some residents to commit themselves to deep friendship, since they might be moving again soon. The relationships grew gradually, grudgingly, the way that people accepted living in Regal Gardens.

In many ways Theresa Costello shared Alice Crimmins' dissatisfactions. She understood the arid existence that could spawn such restlessness and envied Mrs. Crimmins' strength in establishing her own standards. She was not put off by the obdurate gossip that set Alice Crimmins apart. She saw through much of it as plain envy.

"I liked her very much," she would say later. "She was a good person."

It was a judgment not **made** lightly. The week that Alice moved into the larger apartment with two bedrooms—in March 1962—Theresa saw her on the mall with the two infants.

"Hi," Theresa said to Missy.

Theresa became more than Alice Crimmins' babysitter. Two or three times a week she would stay with Eddie and Missy until Alice came home at 1:00 a.m. Later Alice would hire a live-in maid at thirty-five dollars a week, losing the steady services of Theresa as a baby-sitter, but Theresa was always her friend. And even if their ages made it unlikely, it was important to Alice to have the approval of the fourteen-year-old Theresa Costello.

Piering again pressed Alice for details about the children's last day.

"Let's go for a ride," Alice suggested after the children had finished dinner. The children piled into the back seat of her Mercury convertible and they started riding toward Main Street. It was not a random choice. Alice had a plan in mind; she wanted to find out where Eddie had moved.

Eddie Crimmins had left his furnished apartment on 164th Street at the end of June. He was now in another flat a few blocks away, overlooking the Grand Central Parkway.

"I figured it was close because his phone number stayed the same," Alice told Piering.

In the escalating custody battle Eddie and Alice had been tracking each other's lives with amateurish zeal. She knew he had planted a crude bug on her telephone and was assembling evidence to use against her. She half suspected he had a girlfriend and wanted to find him living with someone. It was her only hope of countering his assault on her character in court. "Look for Daddy's car," she told the children, as she cruised the streets off Main Street.

Alice drove around for more than an hour, until it was almost dark, and then she headed home. Nina Schwartz, who lived across the mall from her, saw Alice and the children coming home. Mrs. Schwartz watched for a moment, then closed her window because, she said, it was "cool and breezy."

No one has disputed that Alice Crimmins was a fastidious parent. The children were always clean, and with little Eddie's propensity for getting messy, unusual attention was required. Some neighbors thought Alice was a little too fastidious. No sooner would one of the kids smear his or her face than Alice was ready with a washcloth. There were things about her that defied understanding. She didn't mind putting on the scantiest costume as a cocktail waitress—in fact, she preferred a costume—but she refused to wear anything that would show her cleavage. From the waist down, she had no rules. There was another thing: with all the men she had been with, she never undressed in the light. This shyness was mystifying, in view of the fact that she shed her inhibitions in the dark. It was an irreconcilable paradox that clouded everything she said.

She told Detective Piering that after coming back from the drive she had undressed the children, washed off their ice-cream stains and the accumulated debris of the day's playing, put fresh T-shirts and underwear on them and put them to bed.

It was at this moment that Theresa Costello passed under the bedroom window on her way to a baby-sitting job across the mall. "God bless Mommy and Daddy," she heard Eddie say.

47

It had surprised Theresa that Alice insisted upon the children's evening prayers. The first time she baby-sat for Eddie and Missy, the boy told her they had to do something first before going to bed. Theresa watched as Missy and Eddie got on their knees in front of their beds and, half stumbling, said the prayers.

"Do you always do that?" Theresa asked little Eddie. "Yup," he replied.

Alice's unusual religious faith was an incongruity that Theresa came to accept.

On the evening of the disappearance she heard Missy giggling. "C'mon, Missy, no more fooling around," she heard Alice say.

"God bless Mommy and Daddy . . . and Brandy," she heard Missy say. Then she crossed the mall to keep her appointment.

Alice, meanwhile, had a busy night. She brought the screen from her room into the children's room. But then she noticed some dried turd on the screen and realized she couldn't put it up. After Brandy gave birth months earlier, they had used the screen to fence in the pups and it had never been properly cleaned. Alice reset the children's screen in the window, without bothering to bolt it into place. It was only leaning against the window because she intended to clean hers and affix it at the next opportunity.

She had always kept a clean apartment, but now Alice had to look at it through the eyes of a city agency. She collected empty wine and liquor bottles to throw away. She made a pile of old clothing—mostly Edmund's. By 10:30 she was exhausted and slumped on the living-room couch, watching *The Defenders* on Channel 2.

Tony Grace hadn't called back, and she telephoned a Bronx bar where she knew he would be—the Capri —and asked for him. It was Tuesday night, and on Tuesday nights Tony Grace drank whiskey at the Capri bar on Williamsbridge Road, within sight of her mother's window. Grace was a big man in the Capri, a place that seemed to belong to another time— a time of Italian crooners singing "Isle of Capri"; of ambitious secretaries with rhinestone rings ordering Crème de menthe; of double-parked Lincoln Continentals. Inside the Capri the lighting was mostly shadows, the seats were made of leather, and there was a suggestion of violence in some of the men who drank there.

"You didn't call me back," she said coolly when Grace came to the telephone; her legs were tucked under her and she was tapping ashes into an overflowing tray.

"Ah, I got busy," said Grace impatiently. She sounded like a wife.

"I could come over for a drink."

"Where are you?"

"Home."

"I'm only gonna have a drink and go home," said Tony.

"Are the bowling girls there?" she asked, referring to a group of women who used the excuse that they were going bowling to get away from their husbands.

"No. No, I'm alone."

"I'm having a lot of trouble with the custody thing."

"What's the lawyer say?" asked Grace. He had directed her to LaPenna as he would a friend to a favorite barber.

Alice was itchy. She knew he was with the bowling girls and had no intention of going home early. She didn't like the sound of her own voice. They hung up, each feeling some dissatisfaction.

She didn't brood for long. Sometime after ten, the telephone rang and the roles were reversed. Joe Rorech was calling from a bar in Huntington, Long Island, where Alice had once worked, and he wanted her to join him.

"Hey, guess who's here," he said, trying to kindle some interest. Alice listened politely, but he sounded drunk. He had in fact been drinking all day. He was with his cousin, Bob Rorech, and a business partner, Dick Nevins. There was an exotic singer performing and Rorech tried to make it sound inviting. But Alice was merely polite.

Once Joe Rorech's calls had excited Alice Crimmins. That had been when he seemed like a huge success; when he was considered the biggest home-improvement contractor on Long Island and there seemed to be no limit to his potential. She'd been impressed by the way he piled people onto airplanes for weekends in Las Vegas; the way he traveled first class and seemed a bottomless spender; the way he could drink from lunch until all the bars closed and never seem drunk.

But the glitter had gone out of their romance. Joe Rorech was no longer the fastest contractor with the newest Cadillac. He was the sad father of seven children whose business was beginning to fail and who sounded like a lush.

"Why don't you come on out?" he asked.

"I don't have a sitter," said Alice.

They both knew there had been a time when he had only to suggest a rendezvous and she would make some arrangements. But that time was gone. She was tired now. He was a jealous man and he knew about Tony Grace and the other men in Alice Crimmins' life.

"I can't get a baby-sitter," she said, and Joe Rorech returned to his Scotch mists.

Alice went back to watching television. At midnight, she told Detective Piering, she took little Eddie's hand and walked him from his cot to the bathroom, where he emptied his bladder. She tried to shake Missy awake, but the little girl just moaned and rolled over in her crib. Alice let her sleep.

She thought she relatched the door, but the memory was hazy. The hook-and-eye lock had been put up when she still lived with her husband. One morning little Eddie had left his room and made himself sick by gobbling everything in the refrigerator. The parents had agreed to install the lock.

After she checked the children, Alice took Brandy for a walk. She passed a neighbor, Bob Yoquinto, who was walking his boxer. They waved to each other and she smiled. She sat on the stoop for a moment; the night was clear, and it felt good to inhale fresh air. There were distant sounds, perhaps coming from late celebrants at the World's Fair. Traffic was light in this section of Queens, which was like a bypass road that had been made obsolete by a superhighway.

Alice didn't bother to bolt her front door since she was sitting out front. But habits and memories are deceptive. Times and events sometimes blur and are hard to separate into components. Perhaps it was another time that she sat outside without locking the door. Alice was almost certain, she told Piering, that she shot the dead bolt to the front door when she returned. But she was not positive.

She went into her room, turned on the air-conditioner, and fell asleep in her clothing. She heard a sound in the rear, perhaps a child crying, but she wasn't certain. Something woke her at a quarter to three. It might have been a scream, or just a random noise, or a nightmare. She went to the bathroom and washed and prepared for bed. Nothing seemed unusual or disturbed.

As she was stepping out of the bathroom, the telephone rang. It was Eddie, who sometimes called at this hour.

"Evelyn says you owe her money," said Eddie.

"Oh, yeah. Well, she's such a good friend of yours, go ask her yourself."

She did not sound upset, Eddie would recall later. She didn't sound nervous as if something drastic had happened. He said that she acted normal—that is, nasty.

The telephone call from Eddie made Alice angry. She had gone to see Evelyn about the debt, but the former maid wouldn't even let her come in. Alice took Brandy out again, cooling off. She sat on the stoop for about ten minutes, then went back inside. She took a bath and went to sleep sometime between 3:30 and 4:00 a.m.

"That's it?" asked Piering.

8

"The situation is mushrooming."

*—Detective Piering to Edmund and Alice
Crimmins before Missy's body was found*

Edmund Crimmins sat in a squad room of the Fresh
Meadows Precinct, flanked by two detectives. He was
trembling. The room was thick with the suggestion of
violence. There was a desk and two chairs, but no
window. There was the artificial light of a naked bulb
and the unblinking presence of the detectives. The
starkness was meant to be intimidating.

"How did you kill her?" asked Sergeant Kurt Gruenthal.

Eddie Crimmins didn't say anything—he was still
absorbing his daughter's death.

"You better tell us how you did it," said Gruenthal
with more than a little menace.

"I'll tell you anything you want to know, but I didn't
kill my daughter," Eddie replied. Gruenthal and Detective George Martin just stared at Eddie.

In the aftermath of the discovery of Missy's body,
it had been decided to keep the parents separated. If
there was a chance that they were in it together, the
police didn't want to give them an opportunity to lean
on each other for support. There was another, more
subtle reason. In the summer of 1965 there were no
women detectives in the New York City Police Department. Eddie Crimmins could be handled according

52

to standard procedures. If they were rough with him, he would simply have to stand it. There was no mystery in his role. If he had killed his child, the motive would have been a simple one—jealousy, rage, revenge—or it might have been an accident. Such explanations were familiar ground and the police were confident they would get the truth out of Eddie by using standard investigative tactics. With Eddie they could be as tough as the situation demanded. Alice posed a complication. She was a woman, and to the men of the detective command she had the mystique of a woman—that is, she was unfathomable. Furthermore, she was an unusual woman. She didn't crumple and fall apart, as they expected a grieving parent would. They would have to come up with a different kind of roughness to deal with her.

As the questioning of Eddie went on, the police became aware that his attention strayed. One level of his consciousness coped with the questioning. But other levels were going through the torment of the sudden tragedy.

The feelings of both parents about their children were complicated and inextricably bound to parcels of love and guilt. Children inevitably feel some guilt at the breakup of the marriage of their parents—and in this case the parents inevitably would feel guilt about the death of a child.

Eddie Crimmins loved his daughter, but every time he looked at Missy he saw his wife. Missy was a golden child, one of those precious offspring who turns out to be everyone's favorite. Her features, like Alice's, were thin and finely drawn. And, like her mother, she was gifted with unbounded charm that would make perfect strangers want to hug her.

The father was drawn to his son—little Eddie with his thick, fumbling hands that matched his awkward, erratic personality. Little Eddie's features might be coarse, but there was the unmistakable potential of strength about him. Like his father, Eddie had developed a kind of dogged loyalty; he would not let anyone near his sister. He hovered over her like an umbrella. Nina Schwartz, the neighbor across the mall, would remember that when her own son pulled some hair from one of Missy's dolls, little Eddie came thundering to her rescue. Unafraid, he told the larger child: "Don't you ever touch my Missy; don't you ever touch my Missy." Always it was "my Missy."

The father had tried to introduce his son to a manly world, once taking him on a camping trip, leaving Missy behind because she was too young. But the separation was unbearable for little Eddie and they had cut short the trip to come home.

Alice understood her husband's crude attempts to overcompensate for Missy's dominance, but the problem was impossible. She favored Missy and would feel guilty about neglecting her son. She was determined that young Eddie would grow up different from his father—she told that to many people.

As the detectives were questioning the father about the death of his daughter, he was coming to a terrible realization. He told them how protective Eddie was about Missy. If anyone had tried to harm Missy, Eddie would not have quietly allowed it to happen. If someone had killed Missy, that someone would have found it necessary to kill little Eddie, too.

But there was no time for grief at the Fresh Meadows Precinct. Eddie's story had to be tested again and again. There is simply no way to reconstruct stories except by picking them apart, bit by bit.

"Let's hear again what you did yesterday, Eddie," said Detective George Martin.

Eddie was off from work on Mondays and Tuesdays. He worked as a mechanic for TWA from 4:00 p.m. until midnight on other days. This Monday, after the two-week absence, he had taken his children to a park. They had got along well, he told detectives.

Tuesday, Eddie had played golf. He was not a particularly good golfer, but he found some solace in the long stretches of green and the occasional concentration. He had made a 7:00 a.m. appointment to play on a public course at Bethpage in Nassau County and had got up at 6:00 a.m. to keep it. Later in the day the links would be crowded and hot, and if he timed it right, he could catch the All-Star Game on the clubhouse television.

On July 13 he did not shoot even up to his usually mediocre game. Having seen the children again, he was brooding about the custody battle. Not even the long drives and hard slices could divert him.

After playing eighteen holes with a friend, Eddie drank three beers in the clubhouse and watched the baseball game on television. He was an ardent fan of the Mets and they were in the cellar of the ten-team National League, twenty games out of first place. But in his distraction he left before the game ended, probably around 2:00 p.m. (There was one curious coincidence: sitting at the bar after a strenuous eighteen holes of golf was John Kelly, a Brooklyn detective who specialized in murder cases. Neither man noticed the other, but they were destined to meet.)

When Eddie Crimmins left the golf course, he had a destination in mind. He had driven out to Nassau County that morning with another purpose in mind. He headed now for Huntington.

The house on Sandra Drive had a thick green lawn, a swimming pool shielded in the back, and was protected by two Doberman pinschers. The shrubs had been trimmed professionally. Like the man who lived there, the house was pampered and barbered to reflect a certain degree of achievement in life. But, like the man who lived there, it was overreaching. The house rested on the quicksand of impossible mortgages. The man who lived there was Joe Rorech, Alice's sometime lover.

Eddie Crimmins drove by slowly. On a Tuesday afternoon in July the driveways along Sandra Drive all seemed to have built-in station wagons. The women of the houses drove the cars with vinyl wood paneling while their men were away in their summer suits and dark sedans. Eddie Crimmins was looking for a beat-up four-year-old Mercury convertible with a ripped top. He was not certain what he would do if he found it. Maybe just chalk it up as another point to bring out in court. Maybe just accept again that he had lost his wife.

But Alice's car wasn't there—she was taking it to

Kissena Park with the children for a picnic. Reluctantly, Eddie Crimmins pulled out of Sandra Drive and headed back to the expressway.

He arrived home at 5:00 p.m.—the time that Alice was calling her attorney. In his room overlooking the Grand Central Parkway he could hear cars inching along during the rush hour. He said that he stayed there until eleven, watching television. Then he drove along Union Turnpike to a small stand near St. John's University, bought a plain pizza and a large-sized bottle of Pepsi-Cola, and hurried home before his dinner cooled. Eddie Crimmins is a big man—an inch over six feet tall and weighing more than two hundred pounds—and has a large capacity. He finished most of the pizza.

But he was still restless. He drove back to Union Turnpike, a rutted east-west road running from Kew Gardens to the lip of Nassau County. He picked out one of the desultory bars sprinkled like lampposts along the way and sat drinking gin-and-tonics. That was unusual, for Eddie was a beer drinker. He did something else unusual. He made conversation with a bartender named Lou, who would remember the hulking customer who drank gin-and-tonics. There were one or two other patrons in the bar, but there was nothing else to distinguish the people or the place from a hundred other saloons and a thousand other nights.

The other patrons started home by 2:00 a.m. Eddie Crimmins, perhaps thinking of his empty furnished room, ordered another drink. He had his last round at 2:45. Then he did a very strange thing: he made the familiar twists and turns and found himself in the parking lot behind his wife's bedroom window. He said that he saw light in her window and in the living room. And he sat there for a moment.

In his solitude, Eddie Crimmins had come there often. Sometimes he would park a few blocks away, in a place where Alice would be unlikely to spot his car; then he would sneak into the basement under her bedroom. He would sometimes sit there for hours, listening. He had installed a crude bugging device and could hear whatever went on in the bedroom.

Why did you do that? asked George Martin.

It was the custody thing, said Eddie. But it went beyond the custody battle. Putting the bug on her phone, the microphone in her bedroom, setting up the basement listening post—they were acts that Eddie Crimmins couldn't fully understand himself. It was like poking a sore tooth. He couldn't leave it alone.

Once, hearing Alice and a man in the middle of sex, Eddie ran out of the basement and burst into the bedroom. The man, Carl Andrade, fled naked out of the window to his car. Eddie, in the full throttle of anger, could be a frightening sight. Alice had to go out and give the man his clothing, after dressing herself. She was furious with Eddie. How dare he! They had a separation agreement. They would soon be divorced. He had no more rights.

But to Eddie, Alice was always his wife. He was a literal-minded Catholic who refused to recognize divorce. Alice was his wife, and he would sit in the basement listening to his wife's infidelities, tormenting himself.

Eddie told the detectives that he stayed outside the window on the morning of July 14 for a few moments, saw her car and the lights, and left. He said he went home and called up Alice and talked about the maid. Then, he said, he watched a movie on television, read, and fell asleep by 4:00 a.m.

A detective who checked out Eddie's story was bothered by one point. Eddie said he had watched a particular movie after coming home from his wife's apartment. But the CBS programming department said the movie had been on much earlier.

9

Dr. Richard Grimes waited for Missy Crimmins at Queens General Hospital. She was placed on a cold slab in the basement morgue—still wearing the faded white undershirt, yellow panties, and the pajama noose around her neck. Even in death she was a lovely child. Grimes dictated his notes to an assistant—a mixture of his initial findings at the lot and later details from the hospital.

> Examination disclosed . . . no gross evidence of trauma to the ano-genital area. However, the rectal sphincter gapes rather widely; no definite tear of the anal mucosa is apparent. There is no blood or other secretion on the panties. Several superficial abrasions noted over the right popliteal space and over the posterior aspect of the right calf. The fingers . . . show no evidence of injury. . . . The deposits of insect eggs are not only over the eyes but are also over the left side of the forehead and in the folds of the tie. . . . There were a couple of hairs found on the inner aspect of each thigh. On the medial aspect of both upper thighs were found several fibers and several hairs; fibers were reddish; hairs appear brown; one blond hair was found. . . .

So Missy Crimmins died without much of a struggle; otherwise the fingernails would have shown something. She had been strangled or smothered—helpless or impotent. There were no signs of bruises or resistance, only the normal bumps of childhood play. Had Missy been sexually molested? The evidence pointed against it, but not conclusively—things never are conclusive along that line. "Rectal sphincter gapes rather widely. . . . There were a couple of hairs found on the inner aspect of each thigh. . . ."

In death, especially violent death, the body convulses in protest. The muscles make one last great strain—like a final sigh. The brown hairs matched those of the family dog, Brandy. The fibers were identical to the thread of a dress Missy wore. There were no answers, no conclusions, no compelling leads in the preliminary autopsy.

Grimes' immediate task was to put brackets around the time and circumstances of Missy's death for the police. He telephoned Sergeant Gruenthal at the Fresh Meadows station and said that Missy appeared to have been strangled and had been dead from six to eighteen hours when she was found.

There were techniques for fixing the time of death with greater precision—examination of internal organs, chemical tests. The body would be shipped to New York City, where the Chief Medical Examiner, Dr. Milton Helpern, a man with a worldwide reputation in forensic pathology, would supervise the autopsy. And then there would emerge a dispute about crucial details. At first Dr. Helpern would take the position that there was no way of telling for certain whether Missy died before midnight. Later, after it became apparent that there was no other evidence against Alice Crimmins, after a long and arduous campaign by the District Attorney to attack Alice's contention that she had seen the children alive at midnight, Helpern would change his story.

10

The discovery of Missy's body did not interrupt the world's business. It was not a historic milestone, like the concurrent death of Adlai Stevenson. And yet it was a cosmic event, evoking a terrible vulnerability—a reminder of some subsurface horror lurking beneath mannered surfaces.

Minnie Feldman ran up and down Jewel Avenue, frantically calling her three children. They had been spectators at Jewel Avenue and Main Street, watching the unfolding drama. Saul, the oldest, was nine; Jeremy was seven, and he held the hand of his sister, Amy, five.

Mrs. Feldman was half mad with worry. The sirens, the helicopters, the armies of police had driven her near to hysteria. When she finally found the children, she slapped Saul, the oldest, whom she held responsible. "Where were you?" she said angrily.

"We were just watching," he replied petulantly.

Minnie Feldman was sorry. She realized that she had been wrong to slap her son. It was because of the awful fear, and the vision of his body lying in a field covered with flies.

After the news had raced around the city, people tried to reassure themselves about their own families. This impulse was evident during the great blackout, after assassinations; citizens reached for telephones and the lines became swamped. The lines to Queens on that Wednesday were overburdened.

"Did you hear about it?" asked Raymond Bonelli,

60

an import clerk in Manhattan. He was talking to his wife, Kate, in Kew Gardens. It had taken him forty-five minutes to get through. Kate had already spoken to her mother and two girlfriends and she had three other friends to call and begin by saying, "Did you hear?"

"It's terrible," said Kate Bonelli. "I'm not letting the kids out of the house."

From her window she watched police detachments sweeping through the bulrushes down by the subway-train yards near Flushing Meadow Park—a frightening place where she imagined that all sorts of vice took place after dark. Twice, uniformed policemen had knocked on her door and showed her pictures of the missing children. The first time the officers had had pictures of Eddie and Missy. The second time they handed her only a picture of Eddie.

Nick Farina felt as if he had just been reactivated into the Army. In a sense, he had. Farina had just become a detective, but on July 14 the city was short of man-power and so he was called back into uniform. He was permanently assigned as a plainclothes detective in the 107th Squad, the Fresh Meadows Precinct. Early on July 14 he squirmed back into uniform and drove to an unfamiliar precinct in Richmond Hill. It was the first time he had worn the uniform since being appointed a plainclothesman two years earlier, and he itched in discomfort.

As he drove from his Nassau County home, Farina flicked on the car radio. The music was interrupted every half-hour by an annoying roundup of news. Farina, still piqued about being put back into uniform, was only half listening as the radio announcer came on. The words flickered at his attention like a feather.

"A four-year-old Queens girl was found dead to-day . . ."

The words tickled his professional interest. Homicide? What precinct?

". . . massive police hunt continues in the Kew Gardens section of the borough for her five-year-old brother, Eddie Crimmins . . ."

The bulletin launched Farina's eyebrows.

". . . *the body of little Alice Crimmins, known as Missy, was found in a vacant lot* . . ."

Farina continued to drive to the assigned precinct in Richmond Hill in a daze. He had more than a professional interest in the case. He was one of Alice Crimmins' boyfriends. As he drove, he kept thinking of the delightful children——Missy clutching a doll and sitting on his lap and teasing her brother, Eddie, while Nick Farina waited on the couch for their mother.

When he reached the Richmond Hill station, Farina called his home precinct in Fresh Meadows, certain he would become an important part of the case. He was excited when he got the clerical man on the phone, but the man said everyone was busy——Jones was on vacation, Gruenthal was handling things, and everything seemed to be under control.

"Look, Nick, Piering caught the case," said the clerical man. "You know, he stands to make second on this."

"Yeah, I know. I'm not trying to be a hero, I just thought that I could help, you know, since I know the broad and all. She might talk to me. I could help. I know the broad, you know? I *really* know her."

"I'll tell him, Nick. But, you know, Jerry stands to make second on this and how's it going to look?"

Farina couldn't believe it. He was angry. He gave the clerical man the telephone number of the booth he was calling from. He said he'd wait around for a call. Otherwise they would be able to reach him through the Richmond Hill Precinct.

But no one called Farina back. In his ill-fitting uniform he patrolled the unfamiliar streets of Richmond Hill while Jerry Piering——and a score of other detectives——tried to pry information out of Alice Crimmins, by now a reluctant witness.

11

The lines in her face had been driven deep into an expression of permanent anguish. Alice Burke had spent a lifetime in a hopeless Jansenist reach toward grace. The tracks of her disappointments etched a frown.

Unflinching, she stood outside Apartment 1-D. Her fingers dug into the arm of her son, John. He told the uniformed policeman at the door that he was Alice Crimmins' brother and the woman shivering in the summer heat beside him was her mother.

"Wait a minute," said the policeman, closing the door behind him.

Alice Burke had come to comfort her daughter in their mutual agony. It was no small gesture.

They had never got along, mother and daughter. There were too many unkept promises between them.

The mother, born in County Limerick in 1909, was taught unquestioning obedience as a child. She was drilled to believe that a woman suffered almost anything from the men in her life—her father and later her husband—and kept her feelings locked inside. As a child in Ireland she had obeyed her father. As a wife in America she had obeyed her husband. It was the natural order of things in her world. When she had a daughter, there were unspoken expectations. Alice Burke named her Alice. But she was bewildered by the untamed child who obeyed nothing but her emotions.

The daughter suffered her own disappointments. She could never explain them to her mother. Somehow young Alice kept sliding away from her mother's values and her mother's church. She could never talk about her exploding dreams to a mother whose soul was weighed down by the constant dread of damnation. Alice would call her mother "cold" and bitterly fold her impacted ambitions inward. She would suffer in silence. She would marry Eddie Crimmins to shake off her mother's name—and all the strangling family demands.

The family abyss was immediately forgotten in the face of the disappearance of the children. Now mother and daughter had something to share, something they could both understand. Alice Burke understood the loss of a child.

"You can't see her now," said Detective William Corbett.

"Where's Eddie?" asked John Burke.

"He's at the station house," replied Corbett.

"Where's that?"

The Fresh Meadows Precinct headquarters looked more like a heating plant to service the Metropolitan Life Insurance Company's garden-apartment complex than a New York City police precinct. The flat brick building was covered with ivy and surrounded by shrubs, blending softly into the background.

Shortly after 7:00 p.m. John Burke and his mother stood before the high magistrate's desk asking if they could see Eddie Crimmins. The man behind the desk was sympathetic, but said they would have to wait. It was awkward. Outside, reporters and photographers were clustering to pounce on anyone connected with the case. Like empty shell casings marking a battle, used coffee containers and cigarette stubs accumulated outside the station house. The detectives, meanwhile, never stopped. The uniformed men turned out for a change in shifts. And Alice and John Burke felt naked as they sensed the eyes of the policemen and saw the whispering just out of earshot.

The afternoon was a blur. There were stark moments, however, that would stand out. Alice Crimmins re-

64

members clearly the demarcation between the time she was treated with some tenderness and the moment she became a murder suspect. She was in her bedroom with Detectives Jerry Piering and Bill Corbett. They had been circling, suggesting but never actually saying that she was a suspect. Piering had been clumsy. Corbett fancied himself subtle.

"Alice, would you like a priest?" asked Corbett.

She shook her head no.

"You know," began Corbett, "sometimes a mother can hurt her own child accidentally."

Corbett spoke softly. He told Alice that he understood things. He had taken a few psychology courses in college. He used the word "hurt" to take the sting out of what he was suggesting.

"Sometimes an accident can happen. It can happen to anyone."

"I didn't kill Missy." Her voice was a razor blade.

"Look, Alice," said Piering, "this thing, you know, you can't shock us. We've seen it all. Why don't you let us get you a priest?"

She didn't want a priest.

Every so often the door to the bedroom would open. A high-ranking officer would whisper to Piering or Corbett and leave. And then Alice Crimmins was jolted into the full reality of her situation. At one point in the afternoon, when she looked through the open door, she saw a policewoman.

Eddie Crimmins, meanwhile, was undergoing a relentless interrogation.

"One of you two did it," said George Martin in the room inside the detective squad complex of the Fresh Meadows Precinct. "If you didn't do it, she did. Or maybe you did it together?"

"I swear on my children . . . ," he said, then choked on the words.

The telephone in Alice's apartment never stopped. The calls were brief. The policewoman who answered explained that the telephone had to be kept free in case someone wanted to ransom the child who was still missing. Friends of Alice and Eddie called with offers of help.

Michael LaPenna called after Alice failed to keep her appointment to discuss the custody suit. John Burke phoned LaPenna back and told him he might be needed. LaPenna arrived at the apartment in the afternoon, and the police led him into Alice's bedroom. Her eyes were red and sore.

"Could you leave us alone?"

Corbett and Piering stepped outside.

"What happened, Alice?"

She looked at him hard. He had been briefed by the detectives and now he, too, was suggesting she had had something to do with Missy's death.

"Do you know what happened?" LaPenna asked.

"All I know is when I woke up the kids were gone," she said.

"Did you have anything to do with this?"

"No!" she cried.

She went to the Fresh Meadows Precinct with LaPenna. It was still light out and Alice remembered watching from the station window as night fell. They led her into the detective lieutenant's office and sat her behind the desk. They left her alone for a few moments—to think about all the dreadful possibilities, to feel the great weight of authority, to worry about her dead daughter and missing son. It was at the precinct house that Alice began to think that she needed additional legal advice. Michael LaPenna might be competent to handle a simple custody case, but Alice thought that he was over his head in this situation. She didn't like the way he kept deferring to the detectives. Everyone seemed preoccupied, including LaPenna, and Alice began to feel frantic.

"I want to make a telephone call," she told Deputy Inspector Thomas McGuire, detective commander of Queens.

She wanted to reach City Council President Paul Screvane. If the police had taken the trouble, they might have discovered at this stage of the case that Alice Crimmins knew Screvane. The threads were right in front of them. Michael LaPenna had been hired through Tony Grace, the Bronx contractor. Grace had important city contracts, and he counted Paul Screvane—once the city's Sanitation Commissioner—as a friend. Screvane had been with Alice Crimmins socially. As had the Mayor, Robert Wagner. She didn't expect that Wagner would remember her name; their encounters had been brief and almost anonymous. She dialed one of Screvane's aides, who said he would pass along the message. But Paul Screvane was the leading Democratic candidate for Mayor of New York and if he were linked to this particular woman—no matter how harmlessly—it would be political disaster. The telephone call was never returned.

As it grew dark, the lights went on at the World's Fair. Cars hurried down Main Street. People were coming home from work or heading for an evening of dancing and Belgian waffles at the Fair.

Two-man police teams, meanwhile, were going from door to door, hoping to catch a clue from someone who had been at work or out shopping earlier. Across the mall and one block east from Alice's apartment, two uniformed men were canvassing 72–21 153rd Street. The business became ponderously routine. They would show the pictures of the children, wait while the tenants stared and clucked at how tragic the situation was. And then the residents would hand back the pictures and say that they knew nothing, had seen nothing.

In Apartment 3-A a nervous woman with fluttering hands and an inappropriate smile shook her head even before she looked at the pictures. She said she hadn't seen or heard anything. In fact Sophie Earomirski was convinced she had seen and heard something very significant, but she couldn't bring herself to tell the policemen. Sophie had a reputation among her neighbors for exaggeration. There was, for example, the time she had sworn that a yellow mouse ran up her arm at the World's Fair. And the times she had had to be hospitalized for her "nervousness." She didn't want to appear a fool again. So Sophie Earomirski shook her head and said she had seen nothing and heard nothing.

12

"I see something very specific when you mention welfare. I see a picture. I see half-naked kids on a tenement stoop. The mother is drunk and there's no father around. It's a very frightening picture to me."

—One of the Detectives on the Crimmins Case

The 102nd Precinct headquarters is in Richmond Hill in central Queens. It is an old building and the staircase leading up to the divisional detective command post creaks under the weight of almost a century of crime. The old-timers said you could read it all in the field reports of crime filed on the second floor of the 102nd—that the change from rural tranquility to urban terror was recorded there as on a Rosetta stone.

The old-timers suffered lingering regret at the differences. The burglaries were inexplicably crueler. Instead of clean professional break-ins, homes were sometimes damaged pointlessly. Instead of the occasional teenage drinking excess, kids were shooting dope. Family fights were more savage and often irreparable.

Instead of neighborhoods stitched together by one-family homes, cheap apartment houses were sprouting like blisters. People who lived in the apartments were transients—strangers who were careless about the tissue of community.

The reports would come into the 102nd from the various precincts of Queens and the men sifting through them became like Regular Army soldiers trying to grapple with an elusive guerrilla enemy. They could confront the surface crime—the rapes or murders or burglaries—but, like Jerry Piering, most detectives had come to believe that the crime was only a surface symptom. Somehow, in the mid-1960s, Queens had lost its adhesion. The shared values and beliefs and standards had become unstuck. The old-timers would tell you what was wrong. They would spit out the "problems" like a bad taste: "Welfare." "Abortion." "Divorce."

Bernie Jacobs climbed the old staircase inside the 102nd shortly before 5:00 p.m. on July 14. Technically, he was about to take charge of the Alice Crimmins case. In the procedural charts of the New York City Police Department, the lines of authority are as precisely drawn as a pyramid. A detective is responsible to his squad commander, who is responsible to the division commander, who is responsible to the borough commander, who is responsible to the Chief of Detectives, who is responsible to the Police Commissioner, who is responsible to the Mayor. It is all very neat on paper. Reality is a little sloppier. Politics and ambition blur the lines of the chain of command. The skin of a line police officer is as fragile as an eggshell. The Mayor can rage against high police commanders, who serve at his pleasure. But a detective is cushioned by fraternal and professional organizations. If a Mayor reached down to a common detective, the shriek of politics would explode. In reality, the pyramid is tender.

Jacobs understood situational protocol. A New York City policeman for twenty-two years, he had not become a detective lieutenant by mashing toes. The Police Department was an agency dominated by Irish Catholics. By tradition and inertia, Irish Catholics floated into the choice assignments—such as the detective division. This case, in which Irish Catholic morality was to play a crucial role, Bernie Jacobs tactfully left in the hands of Jerry Piering. After he had checked in at his home precinct and driven over to Kew Gardens Hills, Jacobs was assured by Piering that he had things "under control." Jacobs was not a blundering presence, but something was bothering him. He didn't like this thing being conducted in Alice Crimmins' apartment.

Jacobs talked to some of the other commanders. They, too, wanted to take Alice to what they euphemistically called "our environment," meaning the precinct house. They felt more comfortable surrounded by communications and stark green walls. Jacobs did not feel compelled to press the issue. For one thing, his boss was on the scene. By the sheer whim of the rotational chart, Jacobs had become detective commander of Queens at 5:00 p.m. But Deputy Inspector Thomas McGuire, the detective commander of Queens, had not gone home at 5:00 p.m. McGuire, a short, balding man with thick glasses, was prowling the Crimmins apartment, his inspector's shield flopping out of his breast pocket. He, too, wanted Alice to be taken to "our environment," but Piering was reluctant to break the mood. Every so often Piering would brief McGuire and Jacobs.

If Jacobs was popular among his brother officers, McGuire was somewhat aloof. An attorney, he did not talk in police jargon. The cops under him said he spoke with a Boston accent, but it was simply his education washing his speech.

By mid-afternoon Jacobs and McGuire had managed to convince everyone that Alice would be easier to handle at the 107th. Just before they left, there was a telephone call which the police answered. One of them handed the phone to Alice. It was Joe Rorech. "I can't talk to you now," she said. "The children are missing and the police are here. I have to keep the telephone open."

As she sat in the lieutenant's office of the 107th Precinct, Alice Crimmins had time to reflect on the frantic hours. She had been questioned again and again. Each time the tone of the questions had got tougher.

70

"Piering was very rough with me from the beginning," she would recall later. *"He was very rough. They brought me back into the children's room and kept asking me what was missing. The only thing I could find was the blanket off my son's bed. It was blue plaid. All the slippers and the shoes that the children owned were in the apartment."*

From time to time they had left Alice and Eddie alone in the children's bedroom. The associations and emptiness were extraordinarily painful.

"Then Piering came back into the house after having gone out to my car; he came back with a blue blanket and threw the blanket into my face and said, 'What were you doing with this in your car?'"

It was the blanket she had used for the picnic in Kissena Park. She had spread it on the grass when she and the children ate meatball heroes and drank soft drinks.

The "nastiness" did not soften at the precinct. There McGuire seemed obsessed with her sex life, she recalled. While the detectives were questioning her, Alice was thinking of the dead body of her daughter.

"I don't remember if they uncovered the body or if it just wasn't covered when I approached. I was approximately ten feet away from her when I recognized her as being my daughter. I don't remember if I saw her face. I don't remember if I passed out or not. I think I recognized the body as being that of my daughter. I don't remember if she was dressed or undressed. . . . I don't remember anybody saying anything to me."

McGuire and another man were in the lieutenant's office with Alice. Jerry Piering stepped out. McGuire had asked him to leave them alone.

"McGuire asked me about my personal life . . . the men I had known. I answered truthfully all the questions because I was trying to help the police find the murderer of my child."

Both Eddie Crimmins and Detective George Martin were hungry. During a lull in the questioning the two men went to a diner on Union Turnpike for bacon and eggs. The long questioning paused while they ate and drank cup after cup of steaming coffee.

Outside, a few reporters and photographers waited in ambush. Martin spotted them as they were coming out of the diner.

"Do you have anything to say, Mr. Crimmins?"

"Nothing," muttered Eddie, his head ducked as he hurried toward the unmarked sedan. "Nothing."

George Martin grabbed Crimmins under the arm. "Look," he tried to explain to the father. "Your child is missing. Why don't you ask these guys to help? Make an appeal to the public?"

Crimmins did not quite understand. Martin explained that a concerned father should make some sort of public appeal for his child's return. Awkwardly, Eddie Crimmins came back to the group of reporters and said he wanted to appeal to the public—if anyone knew where his child was, or if someone had taken the child, please return him home.

Martin stood off to the side watching, and decided that he was dealing with someone who was "very dumb." "I mean," Martin would say later, "I had to practically drag him up to make a normal appeal. He just didn't understand. Not too swift."

On the basis of such judgments, it was decided that Eddie Crimmins did not have the requisite imagination, intelligence, or cunning to plan and execute murder. Furthermore, the police would conclude, a man of his limited wit would not have been able to sustain a cover story in the face of interrogation. They simply never took Eddie Crimmins very seriously.

13

The technicians had finished with Apartment 1-D. The surfaces had all been dusted for fingerprints. The items had been inventoried.

"One child's baby carriage—blue."

Alice Burke sat crumpled in a chair in the living room. John Burke tried to comfort his mother and to find someone in charge. He was concerned about his sister.

"My sister has a heart murmur," he told one detective after another. "She should have a doctor look at her." But no one seemed to pay attention.

One detective dismissed the request with a flash of anger. "She doesn't need a doctor," said the detective. "She needs a priest. She's our major suspect."

Alice Crimmins was dazed and utterly drained when she returned to the apartment on LaPenna's arm. It was 11:00 p.m. Mother and daughter fell into each other's arms, weeping. John Burke folded his arms around his mother and sister and cried.

The policewoman was camped in the apartment for the night. Alice Burke took off her coat and began to make tea. While she waited for the water to boil, she started scrubbing the sink. Her daughter went to work on the cabinets. They took out a pail and a mop and washed the floor.

John Burke did not find it strange that his mother and sister were scrubbing the apartment. He had seen that reaction to stress before. When his mother was having problems with his father, she would be seized with a burst of housecleaning. As he watched the two women ferociously attacking every stain, he thought it probably helped to wash away the bitter reality.

Neither woman slept that night. At daybreak, their hands raw and red, they were still sloshing around in the cleaning bucket. By daybreak one or the other had turned countless times to stare at the silent telephone—trying to make it ring. All night long, policemen had been in and out of the apartment.

The second day broke hot again.

Alice and Eddie Crimmins were compelled to consider arrangements for their daughter's funeral. "I really don't want to think about it," Alice told her mother.

"You have to," said Alice Burke.

George Martin and Jerry Piering went home for a change of clothing and a shower, but the adrenalin of the case kept them going around the clock. By daybreak they were back at the 107th plotting moves designed to crack Alice Crimmins. When they came to take her away, they were brusque. In ordinary circumstances, what they were about to put her through might be cruelly unnecessary. But Jerry Piering considered it vital.

The Manhattan Medical Examiner's office is located at 30th Street and First Avenue—part of a hospital complex. Alice was hurried through the corridors and down a flight of stairs. Some men in white wheeled a stretcher to the door. They lifted the blanket and Alice Crimmins swooned. Again, when she saw the lifeless body of her daughter, she fell into the arms of Jerry Piering.

It was not necessary for the mother to identify the child before the final autopsy, although Piering would defend it as "routine." John Burke could have done it, but Piering wanted to keep the pressure on Alice Crimmins. She had angered him again. On this second day she was again immaculately groomed, and just seeing her did violence to Piering's concept of grieving motherhood.

In the car back to Queens, Piering again hammered at her story. Is there anything you forgot to tell us?

74

Are you certain you fell asleep at four? Did you accidentally kill Missy?

Alice Crimmins was tired. She had not slept. Piering was badgering her about things she thought were irrelevant. What about the search for Eddie? she wanted to know.

On the second day this search was more systematic and more organized. The police teams were equipped with neighborhood maps. A local officer accompanied each team to ensure that all areas were covered. Block by block, buildings were canvassed. A list was kept to check off which tenants had been questioned; they would return to find the ones on vacation or away.

When Alice returned to the apartment, there was a long string of callers. Johnny and Marilyn Bohan drove in from their home on Long Island. Emily Vernon, a friend of Alice's mother, arrived exploding with energy. Why hadn't a doctor been called? she asked Piering. This poor girl is exhausted on her feet.

Emily got in touch with a doctor, who telephoned a nearby drugstore to prescribe Valium for Alice. Emily picked up the prescription and supervised the reluctant Alice as she swallowed two.

"But what if someone calls about Eddie?" Alice protested.

"There are plenty of people here to answer the phone," said Emily, cutting off the argument. "Just take the pills."

While John Burke made arrangements for Missy's funeral at St. Raymond's in the Bronx, teams of detectives were rounding up anyone in the vicinity with a history of sex crimes.

Milton Helpern had been a doctor since 1926, and New York City's Chief Medical Examiner since 1954. His list of honors and credentials ran several typewritten pages. Dr. Helpern was regarded as the nation's foremost forensic pathologist. He would estimate that he had performed, supervised, or been present at twenty thousand autopsies.

The attending pathologist at Missy Crimmins' autopsy, William Benenson, was sixty years old. Assisting Benenson was Michael Baden, a young physician in his first week on the staff of the Medical Examiner. Missy Crimmins lay on the sunken table latticed with drains to carry away the fluids from the probing autopsy. Dr. Benenson dictated into an overhanging microphone. The findings would be transcribed into the official autopsy report.

Alice Marie (Missy) Crimmins: Case No. Q65–2955.

Dr. Benenson ran through the routine. He made a visual observation of Missy and noted her normal development. He took sample swabs from her vagina and rectum to see if she had been sexually molested. The acid phosphatase tests would show bacteria, but no spermatazoa. There were tests of the major organs —brain, liver, kidney, heart, and stomach.

Samples were taken for chemical analysis—routinely. There was no evidence of drugs or brain damage. The contents of the stomach were sent to Alfred P. Stoholski, whose title was "microscopist-criminalist."

SPECIMENS: Stomach contents of Alice Crimmins.
ANALYSES AND TESTS REQUESTED: Identification of all undigested food particles.
RESULT: Vegetables: Carrots, potatoes, green-leaved (such as spinach or parsley), lima or string beans.
        Fruit: Having color and texture of peach.
        Other: Macaroni, chewing gum. Also, many small dark-brown fruit seeds. . . .

Copies were sent to Dr. Helpern, Dr. Benenson, and Inspector Wolfgang Zanglein, who was chief of Queens Homicide.

It was not a particularly long or difficult autopsy. Dr. Helpern was not present for much of it. The tricky part would come later when the District Attorney and police were constructing the case against Alice Crimmins. There would be a time when Helpern recognized the rumblings of a staff revolt by his subordinates. He would take the case away from Dr. Benenson and testify in open court.

Excerpts from an interview with one of the doctors assisting in the autopsy of Missy Crimmins: "*The question came up as to whether or not one could circumstantially implicate Mrs. Crimmins as far as the District Attorney's office was concerned. Now, as an aside, our concern to run a Medical Examiner's office properly and effectively and impartially can't be, you know, whether or not a specific individual is the culprit. You see, our concerns aren't to indict a given person. That's up to the District Attorney's office.*"

The squabble never broke into open warfare. Benenson would retire quietly after Dr. Helpern exercised the privilege of his office and assumed the case. Other doctors in the Medical Examiner's office became convinced that Dr. Helpern had lost his scientific detachment and became a part of the prosecution team.

"He feels very strongly that Crimmins was, you know, a nasty woman who was guilty," said one of the doctors who assisted in the autopsy of Missy Crimmins. In time, the doctor said, as the prosecution groped for anything substantial for a courtroom test, the contents of the stomach became more and more important. If the stomach contained a lot of food, the authorities could fix the time of death:

If Alice Crimmins fed the children at about 7:00 p.m.;

If she claimed that she saw Missy alive at midnight;

If the stomach contained a great amount of food— say, for example, it was completely full—then Missy either could not have been alive at midnight or must have been fed again before being killed, since the digestive process would have been under way in five hours.

When it seemed clear how crucial the time factor was, others associated with the case said that Dr. Helpern became more certain about his recollection of the size of Missy's stomach during the autopsy. None of the other participating doctors, not even Dr. Benenson, would have such a clear recollection. Dr.

Helpern vividly recalled it being like "a full purse." "It's gotten bigger and bigger," said one of the doctors who did not agree with Dr. Helpern.

But on July 15 Dr. Benenson concentrated on finding the immediate cause of death. The pinpoint hemorrhages in the mucous membranes in the throat and vocal cords indicated that pressure had been applied to the neck. In the absence of other injury, the result was almost self-evident: Missy Crimmins had been asphyxiated.

14

Nick Farina reported to the 107th Precinct early on July 15. He was not scheduled to come in until evening, but he showed up before noon.

The day he had spent in uniform patrolling the 102nd Precinct had been torture. He was convinced he wasn't cut out for pounding a beat.

Farina couldn't understand why no one had called him back after he revealed that he knew Alice Crimmins. The case was splashed all over the newspapers, radio, and television. He understood that jealousy and ambition could shut out detectives from a hot case, but he couldn't believe that they would ignore him completely. Maybe they hadn't understood him when he said he knew Alice Crimmins. Maybe they didn't understand how well he knew her. On July 15 he was determined to make them understand.

Even the tin shield of a plainclothesman was a key to a golden life to Nick Farina. In the spring of 1964 he was in his late twenties, well over six feet tall and ruggedly handsome. He was two other things—single and a plainclothes detective in the 107th Squad. He had made a few good arrests and now there seemed to be no limit on his good fortune. He ate in the finest restaurants and couldn't pick up the check. The choice of women for a handsome single detective was endless.

"One night we're sitting around the squad and we get a squeal," he recalled. "Right out at the desk. This guy is there. His car was in the lot near the precinct and someone broke in and took a briefcase. Not a big deal. But this guy is a buff, you know?"

There are always police buffs, who hover around policemen like moths. Some are attracted by the uniform, some by the mystique.

"So this guy, Pete Malone, has this big Caddy, and me' and my partner go through the motions—filling out a report and all. I can see this guy is money. Juice. He has a dozen corporations, it turns out."

Pete Malone spent a lot of time at the 107th Squad, and not necessarily to check on the burglary in his car. He just liked hanging around policemen. Malone never let a cop pay for a drink—and he and his detective friends spent many nights bent over the bars far up on Union Turnpike. Sometimes a girl would come over, sent by Malone like a complimentary drink. And there was an apartment in Whitestone, tastefully furnished, well equipped with liquor and the sort of casual food for quick entertainment. In the cabinets were crackers and cans of exotic spreads. No one lived in the apartment, which Malone kept for assignations. He also loaned it to special friends—like Nick Farina, who had his own key.

One night in the winter of 1964 Nick Farina was in the 107th Squad Room and there was a call from Pete Malone.

"Nick, you gotta come down here," he said excitedly, mentioning a bar on 81st Street in Manhattan. "There's a babe here you are not gonna believe. She's got a body that's out of this world."

It was after midnight when Nick Farina squinted into the darkness of the 81st Street bar, looking for his friend.

"Nick, hey, Nick!" Pete Malone was half out of his chair, introducing Nick Farina around the table. "I want you to meet Tiger."

79

"Hi," said Farina, reaching across to shake hands with the woman. But he was watching the redhead half smiling at him from the side of the table.

"And this is Rusty."

"That's how I knew Alice Crimmins," said Farina later. "I always knew her as Rusty. Her hair was flaming red. But it wasn't her hair that drew you to her. She was striking. She was twenty-five years old then and lovely. I can't tell you how lovely she was. Small, you know, but dynamite. She had a great laugh; a great personality."

It was as if the homecoming queen and the football hero were being introduced at a fraternity smoker when Alice Crimmins met Nick Farina. Each was a recognized star in his or her own peculiar galaxy. Alice was the celebrity swinger who dangled paunchy executives in the string of week-night Long Island cheater bars. She would make guest appearances in Manhattan, but she preferred the suburban steak-house bars, where the competition was less spectacular. Manhattan was crowded with pretty women with uncomplicated lives. On Long Island most of the women were working on their second family cycle. In that setting Alice Crimmins bubbled like fresh champagne.

And Nick Farina was the macho king.

"So, we danced," recalled Nick Farina.

They danced and there were promises in the music and the way that they moved together. "She said that she might have some legal problems sometime and maybe she should take my telephone number. And I took hers."

In less than a week there was a message slip on Nick Farina's desk that said "Rusty called." Pleased, he phoned her back. "I think they had a prowler in the neighborhood or something," said Farina much later. "Also she wanted to talk about her legal problems with her husband. So, naturally, I went over."

The dates were erratic and surprisingly cold-blooded. Farina would show up and play with the kids for a while while Alice got ready. "She took a lot of time getting ready," he recalled. Nick Farina liked Missy and Eddie. They were, he remembers, friendly and well-cared-for kids.

There would be elaborate instructions to the baby-sitter and then they would have a quiet dinner at one of the better restaurants in Queens. Alice would sip Scotch mists. She'd acquired the taste for Scotch mists with a wealthy contractor who had also taught her how to handle herself and order expensive dishes.

"It was never sneaky," recalled Farina. "She was never afraid of being seen. She was never ashamed."

After dinner Farina would take her to a motel or his friend's apartment, where, in private, Alice was even more uninhibited.

"She had a pretty rigid sex life with her husband," said Farina. "She had a really healthy sense of her body and herself. She wasn't ashamed of any of it."

But something did bother Farina. There was sex, but never any intimacy. She would make certain that she and her partner were both satisfied. But there were certain parts of Alice Crimmins that no one could ever touch.

During the later stages of the affair Nick Farina was dating a girl he would eventually marry. He continued to see Alice through the fall of 1964 and into the winter. But the relationship withered.

"Occasionally she'd call and we'd talk about her problems with her husband," recalled Farina. "She was thinking about running away. She loved those kids."

Farina found Sergeant Kurt Gruenthal in the furor of the 107th Squad Room. "Could I see you a second, Sarge?"

Gruenthal took Farina into the bathroom.

"Listen, Sarge, I tried to call you yesterday."

"Yeah, I know, we were a little busy."

Farina started to tell Gruenthal about his relationship with Alice Crimmins. "See, I thought that since I knew her so well, I could—"

Gruenthal held up his hand. "Wait here," he told Farina.

Gruenthal came back with Jerry Piering, who held Alice Crimmins' address book. On the facing-cover page were Farina's name and the telephone number of the 107th Detective Squad. Gruenthal tore out the page and ripped it into little pieces, says Farina; then he flushed the pieces down the toilet in the adjoining bathroom.

"Now you have nothing to worry about," Farina says Gruenthal told him.

But Farina continued to worry. "Look," he said, "I'd like to tell McGuire about this. I mean, I don't want him coming to me to tell me about it. I want to tell *him*. There's no way I can keep this secret."

The relationship would haunt Farina's career. Despite his efforts to inform his superiors, he was thwarted. Later he would be flopped back to uniform for failure to report his connection with Alice. He would also come under suspicion by his friend and neighbor Jerry Piering. One day months later he would see Piering photographing him with a telescopic lens as he walked out of his house. The pictures would be used to show to potential witnesses.

"That bastard," recalled Farina. "I would have posed if he asked me."

15

"There is no need to tell anybody how we feel about this thing. We want anybody who has any idea whatever to help us. We will appreciate it. You know, we lost a daughter. We have a lot of hope we will find our son."

—*Public appeal by Edmund Crimmins*

City Housing Authority police swept Pomonok Apartments, a thirty-five-building complex directly opposite Queens College on Kissena Boulevard. It was an incinerator-to-roof search and it, too, was futile. Assisted by Sanitation Department workers, police went to the city dump and sifted through 300,000 tons of garbage taken from that area of Queens. They found nothing of any value.

There were things they could have been looking for. Jerry Piering claims that in the garbage on the morning of July 14 he saw a package which had held frozen manicotti. Piering says he also saw a plate of leftover manicotti in the refrigerator. Alice Crimmins swore she had fed her children frozen veal.

There are techniques for determining who is telling the truth. If Piering had saved the manicotti package he claims he saw, it would have been admissible evidence. If he had made a notation in his notebook, the record would be admissible as evidence. But on July 14 perhaps the relevance of the manicotti did not strike Piering. After the autopsy report came in, listing "macaroni" in the contents of Missy's stomach, the significance of the dispute became clear. If Piering had seen manicotti, that would be consistent with the autopsy report and one might conclude that Missy died before midnight. If Alice had fed her veal—and there was no mention of meat in the autopsy—then Missy might have been fed again before she died. Or else she might already have digested the meat, thus throwing off the time factor in the autopsy report. Later Piering would have to rely on his memory to prove that Alice had fed the children manicotti. Neither side could muster support for the last meal.

John Reiersen was twenty-nine years old, and the co-owner of a German delicatessen at 72–40 Main Street. Alice Crimmins was one of his prized customers. The death of little Missy was a blow to Reiersen and his wife, who worked in the store. "Those kids were marvelous," he would recall. "They had a proper upbringing. They were real good kids. You didn't have to coax them or bribe them with a slice of salami. They behaved because they were taught the right way. You find very few kids around like that."

The police, in retracing Alice's steps, went to Reiersen, who told them that he remembered Mrs. Crimmins coming in. "I have a very distinct recollection," he said. The detectives were skeptical and tried to break down Reiersen. At first it was the standard testing of a story that the police perform on every witness. Later it took on greater zeal. They suggested that they had better information than Reiersen's. They dropped hints that they had absolutely incriminating evidence against Alice Crimmins—that his prized customer had made statements on tapes that would explode her version. The police told the story about the incriminating tapes to almost anyone who would listen. After it became clear that there were no incriminating tapes, they simply winked and said that there had been.

But it wasn't the tapes story that made John Reiersen hesitate. It was an idea subtly planted by one detective.

"You know," said the detective, "death could have been from poison."

The power of that suggestion was impressive. If Missy had been poisoned, and if the last meal she had eaten had come from Reiersen's food, then it could be concluded that Reiersen sold poisoned food. So Reiersen entertained some doubts. He would still "distinctly recall" that Alice had been in the store on July 13, but he could not remember what she had bought. He could never swear whether it was veal or manicotti. Enough doubt had been planted in Reiersen's mind so that his testimony would be useless for a defense.

At the 107th Precinct, detective teams were being assembled to begin a deep investigation on the background of Eddie and Alice Crimmins. From parents, teachers, and friends they would reconstruct the two lives.

In the case of Eddie, it seemed more or less straightforward. At Kennedy Airport the detectives talked with airline employees. It was hard to believe that the big, clumsy man could work with surgical precision on complicated jet engines. Yet Eddie was known as a competent dependable mechanic. He was a "regular guy," someone with whom you could sit around the locker room and shoot the breeze about baseball.

"Not very bright, though," said one of his supervisors.

Jerry Piering and George Martin learned one disturbing thing. Eddie had gone to Alice and told her he had exposed himself to little girls in the park.

"I told Alice about the park incident," he would say in an affidavit.

> I don't know why it occurred but I told Alice about it because I was despondent. I was trying to make up excuses why it happened and I was blaming her maybe because of the marriage difficulties we were

having. I never received any medical help for this condition.

The police questioned me about this incident—I don't know for sure who told them about it. It may have been Alice, they never told me. But I denied it. But the police continuously used this as a threat to me and threatened to expose me in Court and embarrass me publicly in connection with the incident.

One of the reasons I told this to Alice about the incident [was] because she started to blame herself about the breakup of the marriage and I wanted to show her perhaps that I was partly at fault and this may have been one of the reasons. The police had continually wanted me to say that I committed the crime on my daughter or that Alice did and threatened to use this incident to expose me. They asked me if a similar incident happened with my kids and I said absolutely no. In fact, it never did.

Alice never believed me when I told her about the incident. She thought I was saying it to get back at her. . . .

In their investigation, the police found that Eddie had sneaked into the apartment more than a score of times when Alice was out, just to be around her things. He also listened with his crude bugs in the basement when she was with other men.

As the police went back over Eddie's background, a single theme emerged—Alice Crimmins. There were no other girlfriends. Even when she was bringing men home, he was faithful to her. Even when she flaunted her affairs, he was ready to forgive and forget. With his children gone, his first concern was still Alice. This devotion was dismissed as pathetic by the detectives. They could not understand this physically powerful man who was rendered helpless and cringing by his faithless wife.

Among the detectives Eddie came to be known as "the Poor Soul." This took on added poignancy later when it was learned that Alice Crimmins, in her inflated social orbit, had known Jackie Gleason.

"Alice and Wonderland," said Jerry Piering. "You start looking at people's lives and the filth that you come up with can make you sick. Sometimes I tell my wife, Helen, that we should get a couple of acres somewhere, get in the middle and put up a fence and a sign—anyone crossing over gets shot."

16

There were extra dimensions to the investigation of a woman who in a few years had ricocheted from the life of a discontented housewife into an unrestrained swinger. The black address book was like a scorecard from a winning season. The men in the book ranged from neighborhood tradesmen to important city officials. There were women in the book, many of them married, who were available for parties—or sympathy. They formed the chorus of Alice Crimmins' ambition. To the police they came to be known as "the bowling girls." They got the name because they told their husbands they were going bowling at night when in fact they were involved in multiple lives.

"Do you know how many marriages could blow up from this?"

The detectives were slumped around a large desk in the squad room of the 107th Precinct. Inspector McGuire was late and the waiting men were inhaling the steam from the coffee containers like firemen using respirators after swallowing smoke. Dozens of detectives had been conscripted from squads all over the city. In the first few days they would be deployed around the city to assemble stray bits and pieces of evidence in the Crimmins case.

Some would slip into the underworld, making contact with reliable informants to see if this subculture knew anything about the killing; they would check into the prison shelters where street gossip about crime often travels faster than radio news bulletins. In an important case, all contacts and sources would be tapped, all favors would be called in.

DD5—Confidential Police Report—Drug dealer named Chico from 116th Street was asked to ask around about the Crimmins case and see if any of his people knew anything.

Inspector McGuire sat on the edge of the desk in the squad room to talk to the men. "Now, you have to be careful," he said to the men about to go into the field to interview people. "You don't have to let husbands and wives know if someone's been screwing around. I mean, use your head."

Marriages were only one volatile ingredient in the Crimmins address book. Reputations and careers were also at stake. The people would have to be handled with tact and skill. Mishandled, the book could be a live grenade.

"So, you talk to people, you use your heads."

Jerry Piering shook hands with Jerry Byrnes, a crack detective in Queens Homicide. He would become one of the insiders, the detectives who would stay with the case after most of the others had gone home. It was an easy partnership.

Like a lot of other cops, Byrnes came out of World War II and into the Police Department. He had grown up in Forest Hills, graduated from Richmond Hill High School, and had one child. At five ten and 270 pounds, he was a barrel of a man. He had a pleasant, round face and dressed in the uniform of a New York detective—toneless suit with a flash of color in the necktie.

Byrnes was about to plunge into a strange and unfamiliar world—a world that shriveled in daylight; a world of first names and bad imitation rock music; a world of quick, guilty sex in strange beds and silicone love. It was part of the world of Alice Crimmins.

"It was amazing. Here I was trying to question this woman about a homicide case, right? So I arrange to meet

*her in this bar. She has to get a baby-sitter; the whole bit.
I meet her there and she's dressed to kill. Everybody's
saying hello to her at the bar—she's no stranger. OK. So
she can't start without a couple of drinks. I'm still trying
to work and she's having this party! She starts getting
personal with me. With me. She asks me if I'm happily
married and all that crap. About Alice Crimmins, I tell
her. Oh yeah, she says. Sure, I know Alice. Everybody
knew Alice. Great kid. A lot of fun. 'Listen,' she says, 'do
you know that my ex-husband is nine weeks behind in his
payments? I mean, if you were divorced, would you leave
your wife stranded, nine weeks behind in payments? How
about another drink?' So I let her go through this bullshit.
For three hours I'm pumping drinks into her like she's got
a wooden leg. Three fuckin' hours! And it's all bullshit.
Finally, I say don't you have to get home to your kids,
and she looks at me like I'm crazy. She got up to walk
to the ladies' room. When she passed under a light, I got
a good look at her face. It's really hard to see in some of
those bars out in Nassau County. She looked like somebody's wife, you know what I mean? She looked like she
was too old and too tired to be out hustling drinks. I
could practically see the stretch marks on her stomach.
It almost made me feel sorry for her."*

It was a colloquial term indicating that he was going
to stay close to her, but it was not without its irony.
Jerry Piering was "married" to Alice Crimmins. On
July 15 the police moved her around. First to the 102nd
Precinct, then to the 103rd. She remembers walking
through tunnels and asking someone to call her mother
to tell her that she was all right. Once George Marfeo,
Eddie's attorney in the custody case, came to take her
home from the 103rd Precinct. But she was soon back
on the same treadmill—going through the same corridors, answering the same questions. She lost track
of the precincts. But always she was aware of Jerry
Piering's frowning presence.

*"Well," said one detective, defending the process, "if
you disorient someone, if they get confused about the
details of where they are and what time it is, then they
won't be able to think of the cover story. It's a good way*

of cracking through the defenses of a phony story and maybe to find out the truth."

Alice Crimmins was exhausted. But she wasn't allowed to lie down and rest. No one ever touched her physically, but she did suffer on that second day. She was kept moving and confused.

"Did anyone call my mother?" she asked Inspector McGuire.

"Don't worry about it," she was told.

No one called her mother.

"Did you tell Eddie that you were never going to let him have the children?" persisted Piering.

"So?"

"Did you?"

"I guess so. What's wrong with that?"

Alice doesn't remember coming home on the night of the 15th. She was disabled by exhaustion and tranquilizers. She passed out on the couch. When she woke up, she was alone and frightened. The telephone rang.

"Who is it?"

There was no answer.

"Who is it?"

She heard heavy breathing at the other end. She dropped the telephone and ran outside. There was a police emergency van nearby, but it was empty. People on the mall stared at Alice.

She hurried back to the house and slammed the receiver back on the telephone. Soon her mother showed up. And then the homicide detectives assigned to stand guard over Alice Crimmins were back. They had gone for coffee, certain that Alice was safely asleep. Later, when it was impossible for her to shake the shadows, Alice would remember almost wistfully the feeling of being alone.

17

On Friday, Eddie and Alice Crimmins were reunited. They hadn't seen each other since they had identified their daughter's body in the lot. Eddie had been kept only a few paces behind on the same dizzying circuit as his wife, but they were carefully separated. Between interrogations Eddie had slept at his mother's house in the Bronx. On Friday he returned to the apartment in Kew Gardens Hills. The reunion wouldn't last, but they did find some temporary comfort together. They had been bled dry of tears and so they sat on the couch, parched and sobbing. Eddie held Alice's unsteady hand and she rested her head on his shoulder.

Friends kept trying to buoy the parents' hopes for their missing son. But the efforts sounded hollow and desperate, and the parents slumped into a doomed quiet.

"Honey," he said, "let's go to church."

There was no resistance left in Alice Crimmins. She put on a high-necked dress and arranged her hair. The detective on duty said it was all right to go to church. But Alice stopped in the hallway. Somehow her own appearance bothered her. She wanted to show her grief. It wasn't her fault that people couldn't read it in her expression. So she draped a black sweater over her shoulders like a cape. It was eighty-one degrees outside.

Eddie and Alice, trailed by an unmarked police car, drove a few blocks to St. Nicholas of Tolentine Church on Parsons Boulevard and went to confession.

The Catholic Church, with its chalices and smoky rituals, had lost its mystery for Alice Crimmins. Neither did it invite confession. The formality merely made her stiff. If she had to expose her soul, she preferred an ear of comparable vulnerability.

Piering, meanwhile, was back at the apartment waiting to resume the questioning. But Alice made one more stop. She had to buy a black dress to wear to Missy's funeral the next day.

18

The wake for Missy Crimmins was held at Cooke's Funeral Home at Parkchester in the Bronx. Monsignor Gustav Schultheiss, who had buried Michael Burke from St. Raymond's Church in May, tried to penetrate the gloom of the parents and relatives. Schultheiss, who was fifty-six years old, had a soothing voice that seemed to have survived a lifetime of suffering.

"You must realize that Missy is now in heaven," he told Mrs. Burke, who clutched rosary beads in her white fist. She nodded that she understood.

Alice Crimmins stitched herself through the ordeal chainsmoking cigarettes. "My children were very religious," she told friend after friend. "Every night Missy said her prayers."

Eddie was in a fog. He had gone home to shave and change. But in some self-protective way he withdrew into confusion. He lost track of time, and events blurred together in his memory.

Saturday was another day begun without sleep. The funeral was held at 10:00 a.m. in the chapel of St. Raymond's Church, where the ceiling was lower than the arch of the main room. The chapel seemed more intimate and appropriate for Missy. Still, the coffin was heartbreakingly small in the sanctuary where Father Michael Gannon recited the Mass of the Angels. Before the age of seven—the age a child reaches reason, according to the church—a soul passes in perfect innocence straight to heaven. It was a white mass and was designed to invest some factor of joy into the brutal death of Missy Crimmins.

The sun on that Saturday morning was relentless. The temperature soared past ninety degrees. Inside the chapel there were other discomforts. Mingling among the mourners were detectives.

Missy's coffin remained closed. The attention, for the most part, focused on Alice Crimmins, who looked like a young Susan Hayward in her black dress and dark veil.

St. Raymond's had been chosen because Eddie and Alice wanted to avoid attention, but the reporters and photographers were almost as hard to shake as the detectives. Eddie and Alice were no longer parishioners at St. Raymond's, but there were attachments.

St. Raymond's was the Mother Church of the Bronx. It had been constructed in 1841 when most of the borough was farmland. Over the years the Byzantine and Romanesque architecture had been improved and rebuilt.

The sun played through the stained-glass windows on July 17. Some detectives insist that Alice Crimmins committed an act of uncommon callousness in the light of the stained-glass windows. During the mass, according to police officials, she passed a note to one of her lovers in the rear. Allegedly, the note set up a date to meet and was relayed by Alice's former roommate Anita Ellis (known to her friends as Tiger).

However, the note has never been produced and Alice denies that the incident took place. Officials, in court and through newspaper contacts, cited the "fact" that Alice could do such a thing during her daughter's funeral as proof that she lacked concern for the child.

After the mass Alice and Eddie, her mother, brother, and sister-in-law paused for a moment in the cool rectory to recover their strength. There they had coffee and cake and girded themselves for the final ordeal.

Then they piled into the caravan limousines and slowly drove the mile to the burial site. They passed underneath the arch of the entrance to the cemetery of St. Raymond-the-Redeemer in the shadow of the Throgs Neck Bridge. And at a spot near a shrine to St. Anne—the patron saint of mothers—they laid Missy Crimmins to rest in an unmarked grave. There was enough room for another grave right beside it.

19

On Sunday, Cunningham Park was less crowded than usual. On a normal summer weekend even the threatening thunderheads in the sky would not have kept away the softball players or the picnickers or the strolling lovers. Even the bocci players surrendered the park to Colonel Mortimer Kashinsky, leader of the detail of auxiliary policemen who turned out to search for Eddie Crimmins. They were strung out in a human chain, sweeping through Cunningham Park until, at 3:15 p.m., they were dispersed by a cloudburst. There had been a false alarm. One of the auxiliaries cried out that he had found something. Standing back, the man pointed to a bush where there appeared to be a blond-headed body. Another policeman approached the bush and the "body" turned out to be a discarded doll.

The cloudburst temporarily drove the helicopters from the sky, but the search was soon on again in full force. By now few people expected that the little boy would be found alive. There had been no sign of a ransom demand. With his sister dead, logic said that Eddie must be dead, too.

"What about the pants burglar?" said Jerry Piering.

The Fresh Meadows–Kew Gardens section of Queens had recently been plagued by a burglar with a strange quirk: he would break into a house or apartment and attack one thing—the trousers of the man of the house. The thief was bold. He/she struck when the people were home and asleep. And only the hard cash of the man of the house was taken. It was uncharacteristic of burglars, who normally try to avoid contact with people. This one depended on someone's being home.

The pants burglar was an outside possibility in the Crimmins case, but one that Piering would have to consider. There had also been a rash of reports of Peeping Toms. Usually voyeurs are harmless. But psychopaths can grow from minor vices, Piering believed.

Piering read the DD5 field reports coming in from the other detectives on the case. A hard-working cop, he wanted to be prepared when he resumed the questioning.

Piering almost hadn't made it into the department. He was twenty-six years old when he was sworn in, and had kicked around in a number of municipal jobs. Jerry and Helen Piering already had two children when he was scheduled to be sworn into the Police Department in the fall of 1956. Helen was ready to give birth as Jerry was putting on his brand-new uniform to attend the swearing-in ceremony.

"It's time, Jerry," said Helen Piering.

"Oh, no," said Piering.

But Piering didn't panic. He called his father and left to attend the ceremony. At a Manhattan armory he kept slipping away to ask whether his wife had given birth yet. "Any minute," he was told. The new policemen were taken downtown, where they had to fill out endless forms. Piering wasn't allowed to leave the room to call about his wife. Finally he got to a question that said he should list his dependents. He raised his hand and the sergeant recognized him.

"Well, I put down two of my kids for dependents," said Piering, "but I'm sure by now I got another. I'd just like to call and see what sex so I can write down the name."

Piering was excused to make the call. "If that sergeant had given me any crap, I'd have told him to shove the job," he said later.

The third child was Kenneth. There would be three more. Piering's attachment to his family was real and deep. He enjoyed hunting and had had a large collection of shotguns. But when the children came along, he had got rid of the guns. "I just didn't want them around the house with the kids young," he would explain.

Piering's hobbies became making furniture, sailing his eighteen-foot runabout, and trying to establish a second income with a trucking business. The boat was often in drydock, the trucking business became a tax writeoff, but the furniture was a satisfying pastime. Piering would spend long hours in his basement, stripping antique tables or building chairs.

Although he was not well liked by his fellow officers, he had earned their respect for his tenacity and imagination. He had spent only a few weeks in uniform. When he was first assigned to the Bergen Street Precinct in Brooklyn, he had decided that his walking post was too long and his path too predictable. "Some bum could see me walking along Flatbush Avenue, wait until I was out of sight, then break into a house," he recalled. So he laid a trap. He began walking his post and when he got out of sight of the street he leaped aboard a returning milk-delivery truck. He told the startled driver to be quiet and keep going.

"I got my burglar," he recalled. "Pretty good collar."

Piering moved into plainclothes seven weeks after going on the job.

20

Sixty-eighth Drive leads nowhere. Between Main Street and the Van Wyck Expressway the narrow road stops. Sometimes motorists looking for a way out perform elaborate U-turns while residents watch with some satisfaction—the outsider has been momentarily trapped in their maze. Between 136th and 138th streets there is a gentle curve in the road. In the cup of the curve is a courtyard where the private garbage collectors leave a trail of spilled debris. The carelessness irritates the residents of the garden apartments, but they are used to helpless indignation. Their protests are trapped on the same dead-end street.

Vernon Warnecke was on the last day of a two-week vacation from his job in the mail room at the Diners Club. It had not been a particularly memorable holiday. Bored and restless, Warnecke prowled the two-bedroom apartment at 137–39—a few doors in from the street. His wife, Ralpha, watched her husband and made a suggestion.

"Ralphie, why don't you take Daddy down and show him the tree house where the boys play?"

Ralph Warnecke shrugged and asked his father if he wanted to take the walk. Little Ralph was almost ten years old and starting to get his growth. Like many children sprouting up quickly, he was awkward and shy, even with his parents. His father was a withdrawn, self-contained man who understood the need for privacy. Both lived under the roof of a woman who spoke like a scattergun. Ralpha Warnecke said the first thing on her mind—and she was always thinking of something. "Go on, take Daddy down and show him the tree house where you play."

"Wanna go?" asked little Ralph.

"OK," said Vernon with the same economy of conversation.

Actually, Ralph had other reasons for wanting to take the walk. The wooded area usually was filled with bottles—beer bottles tossed into the bushes by teenagers who used the spot for a lovers' lane. That was how Ralph Warnecke got his spending money—cashing in the deposit bottles.

Vernon Warnecke was a nervous man who smoked too much. He stuffed an extra pack of cigarettes into his white shirt and resigned himself to the walk that his wife insisted he take.

"It was as if God told me to send them down there," recalls Ralpha. Now she remembers it as a semireligious event. At the time, however, it seemed more like another instance of her tendency to run things: "You two go and get out now."

They were quiet as they walked down 68th Drive. Later the newspapers would report that they were walking their half-breed dog, Lady. But Ralpha took Lady out around the house. "I just got off crutches," said Ralpha later. "I couldn't walk that far." And there were steps she couldn't negotiate.

Ralpha started to put her hair in rollers while her husband and son were out. She was troubled by the fact that her husband didn't have the money to go fishing on his vacation and had to take walks for recreation.

It was 10:30 in the morning and the street was not crowded that Monday, July 19.

Ralph Warnecke always walked with his head down. Sometimes he found spare change or deposit bottles that way. He had retrieved two beer bottles before they reached the mall flanking the Van Wyck Expressway. He was wearing shorts and had to be careful not to cut his legs in the underbrush. They had headed into the embankment overlooking the expressway where, twenty yards away from the street, there was a hidden

98

tree house. The foliage was thick enough to make it seem private.

In their sweeps for Eddie Crimmins, the police had searched this area three and four days ago. Helicopters were still making stories over Kew Gardens Hills as Vernon and Ralph swam through the branches, but Eddie Crimmins was not on the Warneckes' minds. Like everyone else, they had paid attention during the first stages of the disappearance; they had been properly shocked by the death of Missy, but tomorrow Vernon Warnecke had to return to work and he had other thoughts.

And then Ralph's heart sank in disappointment. The tree house had been boarded up. Father and son stared up at it for a few moments without speaking. Then they started out.

Suddenly Vernon stopped as if he had been jolted. He saw a patch of blue cloth. The newspapers had been talking about a blue-and-white blanket in connection with the missing Crimmins children.

Vernon pushed Ralph away and walked cautiously to the blanket. Using his right toe, he slowly lifted the end of the blanket. Something moved underneath and Warnecke and his son lurched away. As he fingered the blanket, a swarm of flies flew out.

The stench was overwhelming. Vernon Warnecke had been in the war, but he had never seen anything like this. He grabbed his son and started to run. Near the street, Vernon put his leg on a milk crate and spilled his breakfast.

"What was that?" asked Vernon of his son.

Whatever it was had been eaten away by rats and insects. It was black and formless.

"Maybe it was a dead dog," said Vernon, trying to protect his son. "Maybe it was an animal."

"Dead dogs don't have pants on them," replied his son sensibly.

"I think we found a body," concluded Vernon Warnecke.

The search for Eddie Crimmins was over.

21

The police had to keep soaking the area with alcohol. The body was so badly decomposed that when the wet blanket was lifted, the odor was like a physical assault. The flies and maggots were a persistent shroud. A special ambulance had to be dispatched from Queens General Hospital with extra gallons of alcohol. They swabbed the area again and again, trying to drive away the vermin and the awful smell. No matter how much they used, it was almost impossible to stay there.

The body was found about a mile from the Crimmins apartment on an embankment overlooking the Van Wyck Expressway. Dr. William Benenson spent almost an hour scribbling notes:

> The body was lying on a blue and white and yellow checked blanket. The blanket was pulled over the feet; the body is on its right side, with the knees high; that is, the knees were drawn up, the left higher. The back of the neck rests against the clump of bushes; the right upper arm has been eaten away by maggots. . . .

In fact, the descriptions were a matter of convenience. There was no neck, as such. Or arms. The body was simply a blackened, formless mass, chewed and decayed beyond recognition. Deputy Inspector Thomas McGuire and a brace of homicide detectives—men hardened against almost any horror—were sickened by what they found. And it was compounded by the knowledge that once this had been someone's child.

100

McGuire had a professional problem: he was not certain that they had found Eddie Crimmins. There was no face left to identify, and even the fingers were almost all gone. The remains were packed into a mortuary bag and taken to the Medical Examiner's office, where pathologists would try to find some latent prints. "We're almost certain that it's Eddie," McGuire told reporters waiting at the 107th Precinct.

The man had put together his life by sheer nerve. He began with a hammer, doing carpentry and repairs on Long Island. It was a modest business. But in the 1950s the people who had started out with simple Cape Cods were growing out of room. And Joe Rorech specialized in making dormers. He became the king of home improvements on Long Island. He drove a new Cadillac every year, picked up tabs, and carried many girls on his arm. At home he had a faithful wife and seven kids, but that didn't interfere with his business and showy front. The office in Huntington seemed an accurate reflection. It was splashed with wood surfaces and artificial plants.

Joe Rorech seemed almost geometrically constructed. Even his hair was cut to match the planes of his face. He was good-looking. But in his mid-thirties something was happening to Rorech. The effort was beginning to say his strength. The dormer business was tapering off and expenses had started to outstrip income.

Rorech had begun to bore friends with tales of his endless conquests. And he drank more and more to keep up his nerve. The straight, good-looking lines of the self-made Joe Rorech suffered under the influence of alcohol. There were cruel outbursts. There were lapses, blackouts. He hung out in a bar with a female impersonator.

It was eleven in the morning and the detectives who had come to talk to Rorech saw he had already been drinking. His hands trembled. The detectives agreed to continue the interview in a bar. Rorech ordered a double Scotch whiskey and the questioning about his relationship with Alice Crimmins began.

"This isn't going to get back to my wife?" he asked.

"I mean, Gloria doesn't have to know about this, does she?"

"No reason to drag you into this," said Detective Charlie Prestia.

"No reason at all," agreed Detective Bill Corbett. "You just tell us what you know. You help us, we'll help you."

Corbett, the amateur psychologist, had already concluded that Joe Rorech was a slave to his weaknesses and would never be able to take sustained pressure.

They met on the night of January 19, 1964, when Alice Crimmins went to work as a cocktail waitress at the Bourbon House in Syosset. A lot of things changed for Alice that night. Joe Rorech had been dating another cocktail waitress at the Bourbon House—Anita Ellis—but such attachments were perishable and were rearranged by vagrant whims. On her first night as a cocktail waitress, Alice saw only the great wads of money and soft, seductive smiles of important men. One place was the same as another, but there was always motion among the fast crowds on Long Island. In sleek white Lincolns or dark new Cadillacs they went from the Bourbon House to the Heritage House to André's to the Lakeside Manor. Joe Rorech always seemed to have some other urgent rendezvous. It was more than impatience. It was as if he were being chased.

Seventeen days after she met Joe Rorech, Eddie moved out of the Crimmins apartment. He was replaced by Anita Ellis—Tiger. Anita and Alice shared the costs of baby-sitters, the maid, and the rent. They also shared Joe Rorech. This strained, though it didn't crack, their relationship. After all, they had shared a brave adventure—a sisterhood unknown to Joe Rorech. Anita too had a broken marriage and a child. They had too much in common to turn on each other.

Tiger and Rusty knew that Joe Rorech was a vain, though not unattractive, man. He was amusing at times. He would talk delightfully with the women on a range of things of no consequence. But Anita and Alice recognized that he was not a serious man. He did not

102

have the internal fortitude to risk everything for the sake of independence. As they had done. He needed liquor, a string of women swearing undying adoration, and attention. He could never bear to walk into a room and be ignored.

He had a beautiful wife and seven children at home. But he treated Gloria badly.

"This happened in 1962," said Jimmy Curran, a man who broke into the home-improvement business with Rorech. "We went to a convention of the Home Improvement Association in Chicago. Naturally, Joe had a broad along. He always had to have a broad along. Couldn't stand to be alone. After the convention he doesn't want to go home. He flies to Las Vegas with the broad. He told me to tell Gloria that he's sick. Now, she's a friend of mine. I mean, I've had dinner at the house. She's there at the airport, waiting for him. I just ducked her. This guy Rorech was a wild man. He could drink like mad. The cunt really killed him, though. He couldn't leave it alone. He'd always have to have them younger and prettier than anyone else. He would never have been seen with someone like Alice when he was riding high. He met her on the way down. By then he was in all kinds of trouble. Bad checks. Federal taxes. But he still lived the same."

At first Alice noticed only Joe the high roller. She was not put off by the seamier side of the life of a suburban cocktail waitress. She saw aging women trying desperately to connect or hang on—giving quick head in a private room; consenting to faceless sex for "a friend," giving themselves casually for a favor. Alice Crimmins was too young and too much in control to feel threatened.

Eddie tried to warn her. He said she would be sorry. She in turn felt sorry for Eddie, sipping beers in his lonely room night after night, never dreaming how much fun life could be.

Anita Ellis understood, even when Joe Rorech switched his affections to Alice. That had been almost predictable. Joe had told Anita that he loved her. But she knew he had told that to Gloria, to a woman named Ginger, to Alice, and to countless others.

Mrs. Warnecke stood on 68th Drive listening to the commotion and wondering what was going on. An unmarked police car stopped, and one of the men told her what had happened, so she hobbled to the embankment.

Another police car took the family to the 107th Precinct, where Mrs. Warnecke insinuated herself into the center of the discovery. "We don't have a telephone," she told the lieutenant, who listened politely. "So I told Vernon to run up on to Main Street and find one of the police callboxes. I didn't even have a dime, for goodness' sake."

The Warneckes were locked in what Mrs. Warnecke remembers as a tiny room in the 107th. Whenever anyone came in, Mrs. Warnecke would remind him that they hadn't eaten. "I kept telling them that I was hungry," she recalled.

Most of the police had lost their appetites after a look and a whiff of the body. But Ralpha Warnecke hadn't got really close. She was a sturdy woman who almost never missed meals. Finally one of the detectives told the family to go to the corner drugstore. But don't talk to anyone, especially the reporters, he warned. And come right back.

Vernon Warnecke—whose elbow was shattered during the Battle of the Bulge in World War II—led his wife and son through the clamoring line of reporters. Mrs. Warnecke felt a tingle from the attention.

That afternoon would become a high point in her life. The details would be etched in her memory more clearly than her wedding day. She remembers every step of the walk to the drugstore. They ordered sandwiches and coffee, but she was almost too excited to eat. She telephoned her daughter, telling her to come over and feed the dog. She remembers seeing famous journalists waiting to interview her like a celebrity. Jimmy Breslin was there. Polite. Deferential.

And while she was on the telephone the waitress took away her sandwich. She hadn't finished. She decided not to make a fuss and demand a new sandwich. Vernon was grateful.

22

"Detectives working on the case took a very emotional view. When you saw Missy on that slab, with her beautiful blond hair, naked and with the ligature around her neck, she appeared to be a little angel, and they, all of us, have children and we just wanted to work on it, to catch whoever did it. The boy, when they found him, he looked like a bundle of garbage. His whole body was eaten away by maggots —like a bundle of nothing, not even a skeleton."

—Detective Charles Prestia

Alice and Eddie Crimmins were at her mother's home in the Bronx when Jerry Piering came to deliver the news that their son had been found. Alice had taken a powerful sedative, but when she heard the news confirmed, she fluttered into a faint.

Piering himself was under important pressure. He had never handled a murder case before and his first one was growing more complicated every minute. There was the primary emotional factor—two brutally murdered children. The principals in the case were obstinate, uncooperative, and unsavory. The field reports coming in concerned men like Joe Rorech and Anthony Grace, who had powerful motives for evasion.

There were, of course, internecine complications within the Police Department. By his own aggressiveness and by chance, Jerry Piering had "caught" a case that should have gone to a more experienced investigator. The men from Queens Homicide were jealous. They let Piering make blunders. When more seasoned detectives later came into the case, they were amazed that Piering had been allowed to make such a mess of the investigation. Evidence was lost—the blanket in which Missy was found disappeared. Routine procedures were forgotten. The police photographers—who normally operate under the supervision of the assigning detective in a homicide case—had taken pictures inside the Crimmins apartment that were random and incomplete. When one veteran homicide detective joined the case two weeks later and asked for the "interior" shots of the apartment, Piering looked at him blankly.

It was not sabotage. Piering simply did not ask for help. Perhaps because of his pride and youth, he insisted on running things himself. And so there was the spectacle of a hundred New York City detectives running in and out of the 107th Precinct on the instructions of a third-grade detective, Gerard Piering, who was not quite certain what was important in a homicide investigation.

There was also a failure of command. The supervisory police officials at first assumed that matters were under control. Piering kept assuring them that a clearcut case was being developed and they took his word for it. All that was needed was the collapse and confession of one or both parents.

The Crimminses were given Monday, July 19, to grieve. But on Tuesday they were back at the 107th being hammered with the same questions.

"This time," recalled Eddie Crimmins, "there were no holds barred. They said that I did it and they wanted to know the details. When I said that I didn't do it, they

106

threatened to take me down to the morgue and force me to look at the remains of my son.

The sessions at the 107th Precinct became longer and more acrimonious. With a paucity of physical evidence, a confession seemed the only hope for breaking the mystery. To prove murder, the police would have to connect a suspect directly to the deed. They would need a witness, or else persuasive circumstantial evidence. But the main shot seemed a confession. Everyone was working himself into exhaustion.

Tuesday slipped into Wednesday—ironically, the day of the scheduled court case dealing with the custody of the two children. Early Wednesday morning Deputy Inspector Michael J. Clifford started to leave the Fresh Meadows Precinct after the grueling interrogations. Clifford was the father of Patrolman Mike Clifford, the first uniformed officer to answer Mrs. Crimmins' alarm. Inspector Clifford was groggy when he paused to chat with a pair of newspapermen camped outside the precinct house. He thought he was talking "off the record." But almost nothing was off the record to reporters who worked for the New York *Journal-American*. They had been raised in an almost outlaw form of journalism—a vestige of another era when seventeen newspapers had competed for attention on the New York City news stands. In 1965 that brand of journalism was almost extinct. Within a year the *Journal-American* itself would be dead. But the ear of reporter George Carpozi, Jr., reacted to Clifford's off-the-record remarks.

"It looks like an inside job to me," said Clifford casually, under the impression that he was delivering a "backgrounder."

Instead, he delivered the next day's eight-column front-page headline for the *Journal-American*. Carpozi, who had been in the newspaper's doghouse before the case, was suddenly a star reporter again. (Carpozi was a former editor who had been demoted to reporter after an argument with another editor. This story was to be his rehabilitation.)

But the headline had a more sinister effect. It branded the parents as killers and created the momentum for

107

what was to follow. There were secondary repercussions. Clifford was transferred out of Queens and given a lesser assignment in Brooklyn. There were other transfers and demotions.

High police officials had noticed that the Crimmins case was being handled very sloppily.

They buried little Eddie beside his sister that Wednesday morning. Father Joseph McGrath read the interment service. No relatives were present. Eddie and Alice were busy at the 107th Precinct. Father McGrath had been a lifelong friend of Eddie's and understood why no one attended the funeral. Both graves were, and remain, unmarked.

23

On July 28, Detective John Kelly officially entered the Crimmins case. He was taken off his regular assignment in Brooklyn North Homicide and ordered to invest some professionalism in the anarchy of the Crimmins investigation. Kelly was a crackerjack professional. He had never had an unsolved homicide, and in Brooklyn North, covering Bedford-Stuyvesant, more than one was often concluded each day.

Chief of Detectives Frederick Lussen, in charge of all of New York City's detectives, was furious at the image of ineptness. He took the top homicide cops from the Bronx, Queens, Brooklyn, and Manhattan and concentrated them at the Fresh Meadows Precinct.

For the first few days Kelly read the field reports and talked to the detectives who had worked on the case. In two weeks the trails had gone cold and attitudes had hardened. Kelly decided to stay away from Eddie and Alice for the time being. He thought he would be able to work his rough charm on them in time. It was more than a hunch. Kelly was astonished when he read one of the DD5's. It was the report of Eddie Crimmins' activities on July 13. On that day, Eddie told police, he had driven out to Bethpage Golf Course and played eighteen holes of golf, then sat in the clubhouse with a beer and watched the All-Star Game.

On July 13, John Kelly had gone to Bethpage and shot a fast eighteen holes, then he drank a beer in the clubhouse and watched the baseball game. Of course, the clubhouse was crowded and he didn't remember seeing Eddie, but the coincidence seemed almost mystical. "I'll be able to talk to him," he told himself.

Kelly was a believer in the methodical school of detection. You cover yourself carefully. If it takes time, that's the price you pay. Solving cases involves hard work, shoe leather, and the painstaking job of going over the same things again and again until they make sense.

It was easy to misjudge John Kelly. He was big and heavy, but it was a mistake to conclude that his mind worked ponderously. Kelly had never completed high school, but he had an analytic mind. He had the gift of patching together bits and pieces of seemingly random information until he had a coherent story.

John Kelly was born on March 13, 1920, the son of a Bronx steelworker. He attended parochial school, but he was more comfortable on the street. After three years he left high school and became a moving man for the Seven Santini Brothers. Then he went to work for the New Haven Railroad. At the outbreak of World War II, Kelly joined the Marines. As a member of the Fourth Division, he took part in the invasion of Iwo Jima. He emerged in 1946 a corporal. In 1950 he joined the Police Department. He remembers that there were dock strikes going on at the time. He spent four years in uniform, patrolling the Bronx. During the war he had married a Polish girl—Hedwig. Kelly had his share of arrests. Once a pair of gunmen who had held up a gin mill were trying to escape. They had fired a few shots into the ceiling, so Kelly was not taking any chances. The stickup men, however, stumbled into a dead end at a pier leading to the Harlem River. It was either the river or a shootout, and the bandits gave up.

On March 1, 1954, Kelly joined the detective division. He was assigned to Brooklyn. He had a natural aptitude.

In 1962 Brooklyn had a strangler who had killed five women. The man would crawl into a woman's window at night and kill her. He would then jump up and down on the dead body. The man made one mistake. One woman, a nurse, talked him out of killing her.

"We staked out the place—I guess he thought that he had a girlfriend," said Kelly.

There were three detectives on the stakeout. A few nights later the man crawled through the woman's window. "Hold it!" shouted Kelly. The man darted out of the bedroom door and slammed it behind him. All three detectives started blazing away through the closed door. They found the suspected strangler with eleven bullets in him.

"I put three in him," said Kelly.

There was no doubt afterward that they had killed the strangler. The man's prints matched those found at the scenes of the five homicides. The strangling case gave a particularly cynical cast to John Kelly's view of the world. There were good guys and bad guys, and policemen were justified in firing eleven bullets into the bad guys.

When Kelly arrived at the 107th Precinct, he was appalled by the undisciplined mess. Scores of detectives crowded into the squad room. Telephones were ringing. Whoever answered the telephone would check out that lead. "Go up to Main Street and talk to everyone," one of the deputy inspectors told one of the arriving teams.

That wasn't the way Kelly worked. He read the reports. He studied the charts. He examined the physical evidence. He drove around the neighborhood. He talked to residents. He became a familiar sight, sitting for hours on the mall with pigeonlike determination. He got to know families. Habits. He played cards with the people of Kew Gardens Hills. He believed in

110

patience and systematic detection. He talked to store-keepers. He talked to witnesses. They had been talked to before, but Kelly had a knack for drawing out more. Alice told police that she had bought gas at about 8:30 or 8:45 p.m. on July 13. Kelly went to the Gulf station and found two attendants who swore that she had bought gas at 5:30.

In itself, the discrepancy might seem inconsequential. But Kelly punched more and more holes in her story. He was not surprised. People get confused during crisis and memories become jumbled. What would surprise him was that Alice would not concede any error. The men at the gas station were lying, she would say.

Why would they lie?

They're lying, she insisted.

Such brittle certainty only made the police suspicious. Why insist on trivial points, they would conclude, unless deep fear was involved? The normal reaction would be to shrug and say what difference does it make if I got the gas at 5:30 or 9:00 p.m.? But Alice clung to her version like a drowning woman.

Police officials, meanwhile, were trying to patch up Inspector Clifford's public-relations blunder. "Everyone is a suspect," said Captain John Thompson, who refused to be pinned down about the status of the Crimmins parents.

Four days before the murders of Missy and Eddie, just four blocks away from the Crimmins apartment, Mr. and Mrs. Robert Levins were asleep in their apartment at 147–27 71st Avenue. At six o'clock in the morning someone crawled through the basement window and took Mr. Levins' wallet.

In another room four-year-old Robert Levins, Jr., was awakened by the intruder. The man asked the little boy to come with him. The boy said he couldn't because he didn't have his mother's permission. Later he was able to give police a description of the pants burglar. The man was between twenty-five and thirty years of age. He was about five feet ten and weighed about 160 pounds. He had light brown hair and wore dark-rimmed glasses and work clothes.

Next door Mrs. Rose Davis said the same man entered her ground-floor apartment through the casement window and stole a wristwatch and a television set.

After the Crimmins murders a delegation of fifty mothers and twenty-five children went to the Fresh Meadows Precinct and spoke to the commander, Captain James Shannon. They wanted more protection for the children. He promised to put extra foot patrols in the area. Detective Captain John Thompson, however, dismissed the incidents, claiming they were unrelated to the Crimmins case.

The switchboards could barely keep up with the reports of prowlers and Peeping Toms.

At 150–16 72nd Road, almost across the mall from the Crimmins' apartment, two teenage girls reported that someone had tried to break into their apartment. Detectives said the incidents were probably unrelated.

On Friday an armed burglar was reported. The sound of police sirens throughout the night was, at the same time, reassuring and a painful reminder.

24

Eddie Crimmins wanted to talk to a priest. All his life he had been an ardent Catholic. He attended Mass and took Communion regularly. He had wanted his children to have a parochial education. He still cherished the values of Catholicism. He needed to talk to a priest, but he also needed a friend. Father Joseph McGrath had known the Crimminses all his life. His brother had been best man at Eddie's wedding. Father McGrath was something more, though. He was also a psychologist.

Eddie wanted to talk, but he felt inhibited by the

ubiquitous detectives. Could we find someplace where we could be alone?

It was like something out of a movie. Eddie and Father McGrath conspired in hushed voices. One started one way, the other in an opposite direction. They ducked into side streets and backtracked until they had lost the tails. They talked in the gymnasium of Cardinal Hayes High School.

"Why didn't you come to me sooner?" said Father McGrath. "Maybe I could have helped."

Eddie poured out the painful details of his marital breakup. He told the priest about catching Alice in bed with Carl Andrade. About listening to the impassioned trysts from his basement listening post. About her wanton disappearance on a yacht. Her unrealistic ambition.

None of it mattered, Eddie told the priest. He still loved her.

"Will she go to a psychiatrist?" asked Father McGrath.

Eddie shook his head miserably. "She doesn't think anything's wrong with her. She doesn't see anything wrong with her life."

They would work on her together. A few days after the funeral for little Eddie, Father McGrath was invited for dinner at Alice's mother's house where Alice was living. Alice Crimmins had gone to extraordinary lengths, even for her. She enjoyed cooking, and now she fussed over every specialty. The wine had to be right. The dinnerware.

Joseph McGrath was suitably impressed. Every hair in place, and yet she produced a feast. He understood that it was a kind of therapy in the face of her tragedy. After dinner they sat around talking. Gently, Father McGrath led the conversation in the direction of psychiatry.

Why not? he asked. He put it as a challenge. Alice always had trouble resisting a dare. He remembered her as a girl. Her brother, John, a year older than she, had run on his high-school track team. Every morning at Van Cortlandt Park, Alice, her flaming hair trailing like a comet, had paced John around the track, convinced she was a better runner. At least, she would

113

never admit defeat. So Father McGrath appealed now to her pride. Why not try psychiatry?

She agreed, reluctantly. It would be a fiasco. The psychiatrist would probe things that Alice Crimmins considered private. Even a psychiatrist was not allowed near parts of Alice Crimmins that she hid under layers of self-protection. She quit after a few sessions.

Father McGrath experienced his share of police interrogation. When detectives learned that Eddie and, perhaps, Alice had confided in him, they questioned the priest.

The thing that impressed McGrath was the emotional turmoil of the police. "You know what this case was about?" he would ask later. "This was a case in which men were more fathers than police. They had dozens of kids between them. They got all caught up in something. Something very emotional."

Gradually, it became clear that there was not going to be a quick breakthrough. And so the detectives settled down to assembling the mass of information. Backtracking.

In his second interview Anthony Grace admitted that he had lied to the police. At first he told them that he'd never left the Bronx on the night of July 13/14. Later he would revise his story. At about midnight, with a group of women—"bowling girls"—he drove over the Whitestone Bridge to a restaurant called "Ripple's on the Water," where they had a snack. They returned to the Capri by 1:30 a.m.

Ripple's was a few miles from Alice's apartment. Piering wondered why he had lied. Grace shrugged. He was a married man. His wife was in and out of mental hospitals. Soon after the Crimmins children were killed, she entered a mental hospital, where she later died. Tony Grace explained that he'd been trying to spare her—he didn't want her to know he was involved in a sensational murder case.

Detective Phil Brady had been brought into the case because of his ability to take shorthand. Later he had developed a valuable rapport with Joe Rorech. Brady was one of the few people that Rorech trusted.

There was one crucial piece of information in Rorech's story. He told Brady he had called Alice twice that night. The first time was after 10:00 p.m., when he had tried to entice her to come to the Bourbon House. He said he had called her again at 2:00 a.m., but there had been no answer.

Where was Alice during the two-o'clock phone call? wondered Piering.

Of course, Rorech admitted he had been drinking all night—possibly as many as twenty drinks—and he could have misdialed the number. A man who has consumed twenty drinks is not the best witness.

Piering believed that he had enough to confront Alice Crimmins. He talked at length with Eddie about his growing suspicions. "We think she did it," said Piering.

Eddie couldn't believe it. He and Alice had been reconciled, and, he told Piering, he would never live with a woman who had killed his children.

"But her answers don't add up," said Piering.

"Talk to her about it," suggested Eddie. "She wants to clear this up as much as you do."

Eddie suggested that the meeting take place on neutral territory. He knew his wife well enough to believe that she would clench up and freeze if they brought her into a police station again. Piering agreed to meet on her turf. There was a bar in the Bronx where they could hash over all the statements and inconsistencies and clarify their positions. The bar was called the Tender Trap.

Alice Crimmins wore her makeup like a bulletproof vest on August 2. She fortified herself with Scotch. Piering carried a small brown paper bag. The cordiality was forced—Alice knew the detective's opinion of her. She regarded him as narrow and constipated. Still, the drinks dulled the edges.

We have just received the complete Medical Examiner's report, said Piering. According to the report, Missy couldn't have died more than two hours after being fed. (This was not precisely true—it would be months before Dr. Milton Helpern would agree to a two-hour span.)

"Maybe you were mistaken about the time you fed the children, Alice."

She did not reply. Her smile grew tighter.

Piering left openings. Would you like to change the story? He offered a possible scenario: Alice was a swinger; she'd stepped out for a quick tryst with one of her lovers. She might have even left the door open. When she came back, the children were gone. He threw out another lure—it was true that Eddie had had a key, wasn't it?

Her poise never broke. Her voice was measured. "Mr. Piering, I told you what I had done that day." She took another swallow of her whiskey and spilled out some anger: "And I tell you this, Mr. Piering, I don't care what scientific proof you have. In fact, you can take what scientific proof you claim you have and shove it any place you want."

Piering was not undone. He took out the brown paper bag and tried to outflank Alice Crimmins' defenses. "Would you be good enough to identify these things for me?" he said.

He had Missy's undershirt and panties and the pajama top that had been used to kill the little girl. It was a cheap trick, but Alice was out of reach. "Those are my daughter's things," she replied icily.

The meeting lasted for hours. It is perhaps a measure of Alice's reputation at the time that Jerry Piering had not felt safe going alone. At another booth, discreetly hidden from the couple, was Detective Jerry Byrnes.

But none of the traps had been sprung.

25

John Kelly was waiting for Eddie Crimmins at the clubhouse of the Bethpage Golf Club. Eddie didn't know Kelly, so the detective showed him the gold shield. Eddie had just played a hard eighteen holes of golf and Kelly waited for him to change. "Let's take a ride," said Kelly.

"How many times do I have to go over the same thing?" asked Eddie. "I've told the story to I don't know how many cops."

"There's a way you can make it stop," suggested Kelly.

"How?"

"Take a lie-detector test."

They were riding along the Northern State Parkway. It was late September and the trees were turning pale before the fall flush. Eddie stared out of the window of the unmarked police cruiser.

"OK," he said.

A private Manhattan firm, Backster Associates, administered the polygraph test. The machine is not infallible. It measures respiration, pulse rate, and blood pressure. Under stress—for example, when telling a lie—most people will exhibit marked changes in breathing and pulse rate and blood pressure.

Detective Corbett had tried to get Alice to take the test. "I can always tell when someone is lying," he told her, taking her hand. "Their hand sweats." She pulled back her hand.

Eddie Crimmins was strapped into a chair facing a mirror. Behind the mirror, he was being watched. It

117

did not help his nerves to know that he was not alone in the room with the technicians. He could see the flicker of cigarettes behind the mirror.

The test on Eddie ran for more than an hour.

"How old are you?"

The answers would measure Eddie's reaction to objective facts and provide a norm.

"Are you married?"

When asked if he had killed his children, he answered no. When asked if Alice had killed the children, he answered no. The indications were that he was telling the truth.

"Why won't Alice take the test?" asked Kelly as they rode back to the Fresh Meadows Precinct.

"She's nervous," said Eddie.

But the most important result of the test was that the weight of police pressure shifted to Alice. Eddie was willing to take it and she wasn't. Therefore it could be assumed that she had a reason for refusing.

"See if you can convince her," said Kelly. "If she doesn't take it, it looks like she's got something to hide and she's afraid."

Alice was adamant. She did not trust the machine, which made her nervous. For every argument that Eddie mustered for taking the test, she raised fears and fantasies.

"It's not legal," she said. "They don't accept it in court. There must be something wrong with it."

"But it will make them leave us alone," said Eddie.

She held out for three days. Her eyes were puffy. Coffee cups trembled in her hand. She was never without a cigarette when she was awake—and she seldom slept. On the fourth day she capitulated. Eddie called Kelly at the 107th and said that Alice had agreed to take the test, but she wanted assurances that she would be alone in the room with the technicians and no one would be watching her.

"Fine," said Kelly.

Eddie held her hand on the ride down to the polygraph firm. By the time she was strapped into the machine, her nerves were ready to pop. All she needed was an excuse. And she found one.

They had just finished the test questions and were

118

starting on the substantive issues of the case when she tore the wires and tubes off of her arm. She had seen flickering cigarettes behind the mirror, and heard the muffled laughter of the men smoking them. Feeling betrayed and boiling with anger and frustration, she refused to continue the test.

It would be whispered in the press—through detectives close to the case—that Alice shut down the test because she was failing. It became habitual for the police to say nothing publicly about the case. That is, when television newsmen were there and the cameras were rolling, police officials were scrupulously silent about an ongoing investigation.

However, once the cameras and recorders were turned off, detectives would vent their frustrations about the case that wouldn't crack. Off the record, detectives would say, she couldn't pass that lie-detector test. The needle was going right up the wall. Confidentially, we know there are lies in her story. You can't quote me, but she was a rotten mother and told more than one person that she'd rather see them dead than with Eddie. She never cried for her children.

From the beginning, some detectives used the press to poison the public against Alice Crimmins. Detectives and prosecutors spent long lunch hours attacking her behavior, her coldness, her immorality.

Although Alice kept accumulating negative points with the police they had no solid evidence with which to bring charges against her. In the case of little Eddie, it would seem impossible to construct a murder charge against anyone. The body had been so decomposed that the cause of death was never determined. Murder could be "inferred" because of the circumstances of Missy's death, but it was an elusive legal point.

In the case of Missy, a charge of murder could be sustained, but against whom? No one had seen the child strangled. No one had witnessed the disposal of the body.

There were inconsistencies in Alice's story. She said she had tanked up her car at about 8:45 p.m. while two garage men said it was 5:30, but no sinister implication could be drawn from that gap.

She said she had fed the children at 7:30 p.m. and last seen them alive at midnight. The medical estimates, in the fall of 1965, did not place this outside the realm of possibility.

She was cold and hostile to the police.

"She was her own worst enemy," Detective John Kelly would say later. "Her attitude didn't help her."

"See, they wanted me to break down. They wanted me to grieve—not for the sake of my children, but for them —the police. I wasn't going to give them the satisfaction. They were my kids. Nobody was out looking to see who killed my kids. They were just interested in making me break."

What the prosecutors needed to mount a case against Alice Crimmins was a witness. What was required was someone who could provide a flesh-and-blood link between Alice and the deed. The best evidence would have been a witness who saw Alice strangle her daughter, but no one came forward.

Police officials knew they did not have enough evidence to support a case. So by October they began disbanding the heavy concentration of detectives.

The week before he returned to Brooklyn, John Kelly spoke to Eddie Crimmins again. Talk to Alice, he told the husband. "See if she won't take the test again."

Eddie said he would try, but his own polygraph test hadn't thrown suspicion off him completely.

"Truth serum," said Kelly. "Maybe some people can fool the machine, but if you take sodium pentothal, nobody'll bother you again."

Kelly argued persuasively. Grudgingly, Eddie agreed to take the sodium pentothal. Kelly returned to Brooklyn confident that Eddie would take the drug. Later he would learn that Eddie refused when Piering again got "nasty."

26

In the garden-apartment courts of Queens, each mall
became a separate village. The three-story buildings
were constructed around a center mall, and the mall
determined which village one belonged to. There were
visits back and forth between villages, but loyalties
and gossip remained within one's court. This wife was
having an affair with that husband. This wife spent the
afternoon putting away a quart of gin behind drawn
blinds. The neighbors would shield the children
tolerantly, regarding the disabled alcoholic as a battle
casualty of the struggle to survive the courts. The
neighbors would mask the steamy affairs, and if there
was envy, it was not something for which they would
betray a straying member. They might snipe among
themselves, but they would protect one another within
the lifeboat of their own little court.

Each court also had its own clown. On 72nd Drive,
Phil Claymore was the court jester. He would come
home at night from his bruising day at the automobile
agency where he sold used cars and pedal around the
mall on his kid's three-wheeler. The women always
laughed in mock outrage at the incongruous sight of a
grown man riding around the footpaths on a three-
wheeler with his legs stuck out like airplane flaps. Of
course, Phil Claymore was known to have a terrible
temper. Through the walls of the garden apartments,
neighbors could hear him shouting at his long-suffering
wife, Bea, and three children. Occasionally there would
be a slap. While their altercations never reached the

point of becoming beatings, sometimes Bea would come running out of the house, her face red on one side. She would sit on one of the benches biting back tears. Phil would come out apologetically, and buy ice cream for all the children in the neighborhood. Bea would soften and go back inside. She would never complain openly. Such things were forgivable on the mall. Understandable. A man had to cope all day in a world of marginal survival. He'd come home with a barely adequate paycheck. And if the dinner wasn't always ready and the house wasn't always clean, it was possible to read failure into that.

The women were sinking into a world of marginal survival as well. They were coming to understand that life would forever be a balance between buying new drapes or re-covering the couch. They sent their children off to take dancing or piano lessons, like tossing out notes in a bottle. And they turned blind eyes to the sour details—the tracks of ice-cream wrappers planted off the footpaths; the wobbly legs of a year-old kitchen set; the sad taste of too many cigarettes and too much coffee out of Melmac cups; the bitterness of idleness, directionlessness, and comparing.

"Not for me," said Connie D'Amato. "After a while you hear the same dreary stories. The same women talking about the same soap operas—their lives."

Connie D'Amato was an exception. She was young; she had no children. Her husband was a writer and she was studying to become a musician. She was a friend of Alice Crimmins, with whom she had much in common. They both regarded the courts as a dead end and were determined to get out.

"She was not only a great mother," said Connie, "she was a great person. She was alive, you know? One of the few live people in that court."

In time Connie would tell the same thing to the police. She would offer to testify in court that Alice Crimmins was a good mother and a good person. But the police found out that Connie was having an affair with a man in her school. In fact, on the day the children were found missing, Connie was driving to Maine with the man while her husband was away on a writing assignment. The police persuaded Connie to withdraw her testimony. Otherwise, they suggested, they would have to tell her husband about the other man.

Many of the women in the courts spent their Friday afternoons at L'Vie, the beauty parlor on Main Street. Fridays and Saturdays were always busiest at L'Vie, and for Mr. Jerry, who ran it, it was sad. The women spent hours wistfully reading fashion and fan magazines. Their heads were primed and washed and rinsed and colored and teased, and, somehow, it was like an assembly line. Mr. Jerry could comb out one head, then move on to the next, never noticing the face underneath, never changing the slightly arched contempt of his eyebrow or chatter. Sometimes a woman would tell Mr. Jerry to take special care, that she was going to an affair. In that part of Queens, "going to an affair" meant a wedding or a bar mitzvah. Mr. Jerry might make some daring remark about preparing her for adultery, but the woman would giggle girlishly at the charming roué, Mr. Jerry, who felt sorry for them all. Most times, Jerry knew, they went through the beauty treatment just to revive their morale. They might be going out to a weekend movie or dinner at a Chinese restaurant. But often the bleached, teased heads would be wrapped carefully in kerchiefs—in styles that hadn't varied in decades—to sit in front of a television set. In any case, the beauty parlor became an unbreakable ritual—even an act of hope.

There was one category of woman who stood apart in the beauty parlors: the women who were upwardly mobile. Their men were "making it." The signs were unmistakable. The wife would complain less about the cost of ordinary food, but point out the expensive extras she was serving her family. She would sigh about the price of the beach club they had joined; about the trouble of taking the vacations they were between. She would flash the oversize diamond rings and, Jerry, please make the hair whiter than white. Her hair would be stripped and made the whitest shade of platinum, with silver tips. Often the price of arrival was parched, starved, and thinning hair. Her children would be riding new bikes, and the woman no longer bore the pained, martyred look of a wife who had to grind out the cost of baby-sitters or compute the cost of parking for a night in New York. It was understood that it was only a matter of time until they moved on. They would be buying a home in Woodmere or Syosset. Soon they would be gone and already a separation —like the imposed distance preceding death—was growing between them and the others in the courts.

Sophie Earomirski had accepted the limits of her existence, but not without some bristling. Her life had always been a struggle. As a young girl, she had had no special dreams, but there was vague ambition. Her father, George Satirion, was a cook at a series of restaurants, but he regarded himself as a chef. In the restaurants where George worked, speed was valued over subtlety. George Satirion was somewhat out of place. He read, understood, and quoted from the ancient Greek philosophers. And he accepted the life of respectable unimportance in Apartment 1-A of the twenty-four-family house on 34th Street in Long Island City. His wife was a sickly woman and the chores fell on Sophie and a younger sister.

On August 31, 1947, at the age of twenty-two, Sophie Satirion escaped the drudgery of caring for her mother and father and working in the garment district by accepting the overtures of Stephen Earomirski and becoming his wife. Sophie married into permanent disappointment. Her husband, a man much smaller than the generously proportioned Sophie, was an unpromising lithographer. He would be able to provide little more than the bare necessities, but at least he would be providing them for her own family. If Sophie did not complain openly about her fate, she did create a rich fantasy life for herself. Even her pregnancies— which were difficult—were embellished with dramatic textures in the retelling. Her friends and, later, a psychiatrist would say she was prone to exaggerate.

A circle of friends would learn to extract the truth by listening to Sophie and subtracting. The children came along and kept Sophie busy. In 1948 she gave birth to her first child, Susan. In 1952, after three days in the hospital, she gave birth to Stephanie. In 1955 she gave birth to Nancy.

124

As the children grew older, Sophie resumed her career. She worked at a series of part-time sales jobs, although she was determined that the business world would not dismiss her as a Queens housewife. In December 1961 she went to work for Saks Fifth Avenue —part of the reinforced Christmas sales force. Although she earned the equivalent of sixty dollars a week, the job was an education for Sophie. She was exposed to a class of people as remote from her world as the Habsburgs. The smart, rich jet-setters who browsed Saks insisted upon instant recognition of their class and station. They carried jeweled poodles and charged five hundred dollars worth of trifles with the insouciance with which Sophie would have ordered lunch.

"The salespeople at Saks develop the same snobbish arrogance as the customers," said one daughter of a store executive. "An identification takes place. It is perhaps unreasonable, but it is inevitable nevertheless. The salespeople began to think of themselves as possessing the taste and values of the chic customers."

Sophie stayed on after Christmas, but on February 1, after being turned down for a raise, she quit. She returned to Saks the next Christmas. This time she remained until June, leaving without explanation. She came back for the Christmas season and left permanently on December 31, 1963.

The pattern of Sophie's career was erratic. She would work for a while, claim that she was not appreciated, complain about her nerves, then suddenly quit. But she couldn't bear staying home either. On February 24, 1964, she went to work in the Better Boutique Accessories Department of Alexander's department store in Queens. It was closer to home, but there was less exotic appeal to the job, despite the name. She resigned over the telephone on July 27 without explanation.

Sophie became one of those women convinced that they are plagued by an unkind fate. She might have achieved some sort of success if it had not been for a series of bad breaks or unlucky coincidences. After all, she was not so very different from the grande dames of old wealth who shopped at Saks Fifth Avenue. She couldn't see the differences. If she hadn't let herself go and become overweight, she would have been pretty. People were always telling her that. If she could resist the temptation to heighten the drama of her life, people might take her more seriously. But Sophie Earomirski was helpless against her appetites.

On October 16, 1964, Sophie suffered one of her "accidents." This one was destined to interrupt and fatally flaw her career. She was working as a hostess at a booth at the World's Fair. Her job was to be charming to the public and develop leads for the home-improvement company that ran the booth. It was a pleasant, effortless position and she had been working there for two months. She had the advantage of being able to see all the exhibits at the Fair and of lunching in the dazzling variety of international restaurants. On that fall afternoon, however, at lunchtime Sophie reached down to retrieve the purse she had stored in one of the sample boxes. She lurched up and struck her head against a beam. It was a powerful blow that knocked her unconscious for half an hour. Later she would claim that a yellow mouse had scampered up her arm and made her leap, striking the beam with the left side of her head. She would explain with what she regarded as impeccable logic that a yellow mouse was perfectly plausible. There was a cheese display nearby and the mouse could have been coated with cheese. Hence the yellow mouse.

The accident would leave Sophie "nervous" and subject to long fits of sleeplessness and dizziness. She would be suffering one of her bouts of nervous insomnia on the night of July 13/14, 1965.

It was inevitable that Sophie Earomirski would notice Alice Crimmins. They patronized the same beautician, but Alice had star presence, while Sophie was lost in the assembly line of processed heads. She would pass Alice on the street and would notice Alice, but Alice would not recognize Sophie. They would shop next to each other at the supermarket, but Sophie would remain a stranger. Each encounter would register negatively with Sophie.

She would later claim that she could remember clearly an incident at the supermarket in early July of

126

1965, less than two weeks before the children disappeared. Sophie recalled that little Eddie wanted a ride on one of the plastic horses parked outside the supermarket. Alice became annoyed and cursed and cuffed little Eddie. Such behavior was uncharacteristic of Alice, and Sophie's memory might have been colored by the scandalous stories she heard at the beauty parlor. But she was sure she had seen Alice Crimmins cuff little Eddie.

About two weeks later, during her night of jittery insomnia on July 13/14, she was standing at her window trying to catch a breeze. The most dramatic event of her life was transpiring somewhere in the next court, where Alice Crimmins lived. And Sophie believed that she saw something.

27

The letter was dated "Nov. 30, 1966"—more than sixteen months after the event. It had been lost in the avalanche of mail inspired by the deaths of Missy and Eddie Crimmins. There has never been an official count—some of the letters came addressed to the District Attorney, some to a particular assistant directing one aspect of the case, some to the police. There were tens of thousands of letters over the years. Most were indignant. The public—usually a writer who signed himself/herself as "a taxpayer"—wanted to know why no one was apprehended in this most heinous of all crimes. What were the authorities doing? Other letters were written by fanatics who suggested that if the detectives would pray, the answer would come to them. Priests volunteered round-the-clock prayer. Nuns offered sisterly sympathy. Obscure religious sects posted thick envelopes quoting what they felt was relevant scripture—a portion predicting tragedy and holocaust meaningfully underlined. Some of the letters, from as far away as San Francisco and Singapore, were meant for Alice and suggested that she repent. A few contained prayerbooks, crucifixes, missals. They were stamped with slogans about "God is Love" and assured Alice that she would be forgiven anything if she repented and confessed.

Pathetic, lonely men and women also wrote Alice. They would usually begin by saying how sorry they were for her plight and that they understood her predicament. And then they would offer their love. The offers were very specific and they made Alice shudder.

Finally there were letters containing tips, and these the police sifted through. Most came from wives who made tormented, oblique accusations against husbands they didn't trust. Hundreds of men who stayed late at work were now under domestic suspicion of infidelity and, incidentally, collusion in a double homicide. The mid-1960s was a difficult time for married cheaters on Long Island. Wives suspected husbands of hustling cocktail waitresses, and husbands suspected wives of not belonging to a bowling league.

DD5: Checked on Frank Pomeroy, insurance agent, who hung around the Heritage House, where suspect Alice Crimmins was working as a cocktail waitress. Investigation was in response to a letter from Pomeroy's wife that her husband had been seen in the company of said suspect on numerous occasions. Pomeroy denied that he knew Alice and introduced us to his girl friend, Margie Knowland, his secretary, who swore they spent the night together at Howard Johnson's motel on night of July 13/14. She remembered incident because they had known of Alice at Heritage House, but had never met her. Margie Knowland's husband said his wife had not come home until 6 a.m. that night—he remembered because it was the final fight before their separation.

It became almost impossible to separate the crank

128

letters from those of people legitimately concerned. Inevitably, because of the crush of time, they all became lumped together. One of the dead letters buried in District Attorney Nat Hentel's file was painfully, reluctantly handwritten.

Nov. 30, 1966

Dear Mr. Hentel:

Have been reading about your bringing the Crimmins case to the grand jury and am glad to hear of it.

May I please tell you of an incident that I witnessed. It may be connected and may not. But I will feel better telling it to you. This was on the night before the children were missing.

But as the press reported that a handyman saw them at the window that morning, it may not be related at all.*

The night was very hot and I could not sleep. I went into the living room and was looking out the window getting some air. This was at 2 a.m. A short while later, a man and woman were walking down the street toward 72 Road. The woman was about five feet in back of the man. She was holding what appeared to be a bundle of blankets that were white under her left arm and was holding a little child walking with her right hand. He now hollered at her to "hurry up." She told him "to be quiet or someone will see us." At that moment I closed my window, which squeeks [sic] and they looked up but did not see me.

The man took the white bundle and he heaved it into the back seat of the car. She picked up the little baby and sat with him in the back seat of the car. This woman was then with dark hair, the man was tall, not heavy, with dark hair and a large nose. This took place under a street light so I was able to see it quite planly [sic]. The car turned from the corner of 153 St. onto 72 Road and out to Kissena boulevard.

---

* There was such a report, but it remained totally unsubstantiated.

Please forgive me for not signing my name, but I am afraid to.

Wishing you the best of luck.

A reader

P.S.—About one hour later I thought I saw just the man getting into a late model white car.

The letter came too late to help Nat Hentel. Back in 1965, Paul Screvane's ambition to succeed his friend Robert Wagner as Mayor was crushed in the Democratic primary by Abe Beame, who later lost to John Lindsay in the general election. Probably it had no part in the campaign, but political reporters close to Screvane knew he had been questioned by detectives about the Crimmins case. Even Mayor Wagner was indirectly asked some questions. Aides said he was not involved, and he was not bothered further. Naturally, it was unthinkable that either man was connected with the sordid mystery in Queens, but there were connections that had to be explained. The interviews with Screvane were never anything approaching official. A detective, sprinkling his sentences with "sir," asked if Screvane knew Sal LoCurto, a former Deputy Sanitation Commissioner. Of course Screvane knew LoCurto.

LoCurto was a close associate of Anthony Grace, was he not? Anthony Grace did a lot of work for the city and there were business and social connections. Yes.

Sal LoCurto owned a boat? Yes.

You went for a cruise on that boat during 1964? Yes.

Alice Crimmins was on that boat during that cruise. Did you know her?

There were many people on the boat, replied the would-be Mayor of New York. If he knew Alice Crimmins, it had nothing to do with his high office. Was he being accused of anything?

The detectives backed off. There was never a hint that Screvane—or any other important official—was involved in anything more than social contact with Alice Crimmins. Still, it was a matter to be checked.

Paul Screvane would never become Mayor. He

watched John Lindsay take power and Frank D. O'Connor become City Council President—the post Screvane had given up to run for Mayor.

O'Connor, a flinty Irishman, had made his reputation for rectitude when he was a private lawyer. He had solved the famous "Wrong Man" case in Queens and was regarded as a man above sordid motives. Although O'Connor was District Attorney when the Crimmins case broke, he had already turned over the functions of the office to his subordinates. He was preoccupied with his ambition—the run for the Governor's mansion, with a local stop at City Hall. Although Lindsay, a Republican, won the Mayoralty, Frank O'Connor, a Democrat, was elected City Council President. It was a measure of his popularity. The victory was also regarded by the pols as a triumph of media. O'Connor had made a series of effective television commercials, showing him in the street, which, he said, had to be made safe. The lesson would not be lost on his successor.

When Frank O'Connor resigned as District Attorney after his election, it fell to Governor Nelson Rockefeller to replace him. Rockefeller had his own ambitions. He was constructing a national base for a run for the Republican Presidential nomination for 1968. First he would require a secure home base. It was imperative for Rockefeller to maintain the warmest possible relations with the Republican subalterns throughout New York State. O'Connor's election was like the gift of an unknown rich uncle dying. For one thing, Republicans would finally get a shot at the job. In Queens—a Democratic base camp—only the primaries counted. Democratic candidates were elected for local posts with fateful monotony. The primary fights might become contentious, but the long knives were never drawn, for the Democrats kept the county and all the jobs like a trust. The young lawyers coming out of St. John's and Fordham knew that if they joined a Queens Democratic Club, attended the meetings, and paid the dues, they could get a crack at one of the 100 or so Assistant District Attorney posts in Queens.

Rockefeller felt that 1965 offered an opportunity to

break the Democratic hold on Queens. There were many worthy Republicans in the line of succession— men who would be helpful and grateful for the honor of serving as District Attorney, if only for a brief period. But what Rockefeller wanted was someone who could win an election in 1966. He was looking for a Republican who had charisma—enough charisma to carry Queens and keep Rockefeller loyalties alive until 1968.

To replace O'Connor, Rockefeller picked Nat Hentel, a plucky little attorney with a private practice who dangled cigars out of his mouth like Edward G. Robinson. Hentel was a clubhouse Republican, and the kind of man who made an effort to slur his diction and try to sound like a cop. He had a back-slapping way about him. He was small, but the impression he made was larger than life. He called the reporters "boys" and made certain that his friends were never "scooped." The "boys" on the afternoon papers were provided with a fresh lead to compete against the morning papers. Hentel was always available for television interviews. When he staged a raid on a "so-called Mafia little Apalachin" meeting in a Queens restaurant, he notified certain reporters before he informed precinct commanders. His public-relations assistant became the most important man on his staff. Hentel believed he would be reelected through the effective use of saturation publicity. If that meant sacrificing some of the dignity of the District Attorney's office, Hentel would become a populist. He was determined to get elected. From the moment he took office, he was convinced that a successful prosecution of the Alice Crimmins case would win him the election. He faced a deadline. He took over the job in January of 1966 and there would be an election in November.

28

When Nat Hentel became District Attorney, all the Republican lawyers in Queens came out of the wings. Anthony Lombardino could almost taste the opportunity.

Tony Lombardino, at the age of thirty-four, was a very hungry young lawyer. He had broken from the family tradition of Democratic loyalty, but not out of philosophical disagreement. Lombardino did not believe he could indulge himself in the luxury of conscience. The Democrats in Queens were fat and powerful and he would have to wait at the end of a long line for his chance. So in the late 1950s Lombardino joined the anemic Republican Party in Queens, where he was at least near the front of the line. "Tough Tony," as he came to be known, simply didn't have the patience that the Democrats kept urging on him. He was shaped like a barrel and his personality had the obstinate force of one: he would roll over opposition with the same purposeful determination.

On the morning after the children disappeared, Anthony Lombardino was driving along the Belt Parkway in his oversized Oldsmobile. He was on his way to Freeport, Long Island, to go fishing. A fleet of charter boats waited there for weekend fishermen; they would motor out before dawn, returning just after lunch, when the pails of beer were empty and the tubs of fish were full. As he drove, listening to the radio, he was alone in the car. *"Helicopters . . . dozens of detectives . . . hundreds of policemen . . . Mayor Wagner deplores . . ."* Lombardino was excited. The sun had just begun to flash off his hand jewelry—the gold watch, the pinky ring with diamond chips spelling "AL" on his left hand, a ring on the right hand in the shape of a huge gold crucifix. "Instantly," he would recall later, remembering the long drive to Freeport, "I wanted to be the prosecutor."

In January 1966, Tony Lombardino joined the staff of District Attorney Hentel, along with a flood of other young Republican attorneys. Lombardino was appointed to the felony trial part, where he began to establish a reputation as a flashy but effective prosecutor. He got along with the cops, even if his style did violate the esthetics of some of the older, more traditional Republicans. Lombardino did not have the Crimmins case, but he kept abreast of every detail. He made friends with the detectives dogging the killings. And he never let pass an opportunity to boast that only he could obtain a conviction.

Later, when police officials began to have doubts about the District Attorney's office—when they sensed a failure of nerve about pressing Alice Crimmins; when they became skeptical about the jugular intentions of the polite prosecution lawyers; when they began to suspect that someone would go soft inside the courtroom and hesitate—they would look for someone to drive the stake into Alice. The police knew that it would be a formidable job—going up against a woman who would be depicted as a pathetic victim, the mother of two dead children. It would take someone who could tear through the pretty layers of makeup and grief and bring out all the sexual tangents the police felt were relevant to their case. They entertained sharp doubts about the killer instincts of the mild, bespectacled attorney assigned to the case, James Mosley. They would have no such reservations about Tony Lombardino, who would sit in a bar across the street from the courthouse gulping Scotch sours and offer to put the nails in the coffin of Alice Crimmins.

Tony Lombardino was born just around the corner from respectability, on February 27, 1931, in a railroad flat on Furman Avenue in Brooklyn. Close by on Bushwick Avenue lived the doctors and judges and attorneys and dentists. Lombardino's father, Tony, was a clerk for the International Ladies Garment Workers Union. His mother, Christina, almost ruined her eyes as a dressmaker. Lombardino had two older sisters—Josephine, thirteen years older; Antoinette, ten years older—but it was clear that the family ambition rested with the son. He was expected to make the leap from working to professional class. It was an unspoken but powerful factor in his youth. Lombardino's grandparents had struggled to America from a fishing village on the coast of Sicily—Sciacca. The grandson believes that there is a genetic link in his past in his passion for fishing. There is nothing he enjoys more than spending the day catching a load of bass, cleaning them, and cooking them for dinner.

In Brooklyn, as a youth, Anthony Lombardino was taught pride. It was the pride of people who were at an ethnic disadvantage—Italians who could barely make themselves understood in English—but who had transplanted themselves to America convinced that centuries of European civilization would not be cast aside like an old language.

The Lombardinos would never accept charity. No matter how dire their finances, the money would be pooled and they would scrape by. On Saturday mornings Anthony Lombardino remembers seeing the old women in black scrubbing the three steps leading into the rented brick homes. In the vestibules he would smell the fresh linseed oil that the women stroked lovingly into banisters and paneling that they didn't even own. Recently he went back to the now rundown neighborhood and was moved to tears by the broken stoops and graffiti.

In 1941 the Lombardinos moved to a strange neighborhood in Queens. It was not much of an improvement—a forty-year-old semi-attached brick building—but it was their own. The first thing his father did was finish the basement, where they took all their meals. Their section of Queens—Ridgewood—was on the Brooklyn-Queens border, but already there were psychological differences in Lombardino's life. His cousins were laborers or butchers. None had ever finished high school. But his father made Tony understand that better things were expected of him. He would be a dentist. Or an accountant. Something.

At John Adams High School, Tony Lombardino applied himself. He played football, but had no time for girls. His grades never rose much above a C average, but his determination did not go unnoticed. He studied the clarinet and the saxophone because his father believed that some musical training helped a man appreciate the finer things in life. His father had played the violin at a silent-movie theater, where he met his wife.

In school there was a monitor system, and Lombardino experienced his first taste of prosecution. The cases involved talking, or stepping out of line, or some other school infraction. The penalties weren't harsh—an hour after class at the most—but Lombardino was proud of his high record of convictions.

When Lombardino was a senior, his grades began to improve. At the time, he planned to become a dentist. The title impressed him. He remembered the respect commanded by the men on Bushwick Avenue who were dentists.

Some time before Lombardino entered Hofstra College he changed his career plans—he was going to be a lawyer, a prosecuting attorney. It had something to do with pride and respect. When he was a kid, someone had stolen some fruit from a peddler. A cop had come along, twisted Tony's ear, and told him to get home. When he complained to his father, the latter had whacked him. He had to have respect for the police, even if he thought that an officer was being unfair. Some time later, in Queens, he heard someone call across the backyard that he couldn't go fishing—his son had been arrested and he had to go to court. Tony Lombardino was offended. Where was the shame?

"One of the reasons that I became a prosecutor was my belief that people were getting away with things," he would say later. "This is what's happening to society. 'I can't go fishing today—my damn kid got arrested!'"

When he was nineteen years old, Lombardino got in to see the trial of Willie Sutton. It was held in the

100-year-old courthouse in Long Island City, where the ventilation was poor and the wooden benches were hard. He was made to feel the sharp sting of the law in that old building. Here was weight and substance, and he would regret that he would have to practice the law in modern brick-and-glass buildings where there were concessions to comfort. The law, he believed, should be cold and stiff, as unbending as the time it had taken to draw up the code. But at the trial of bank robber Willie Sutton, Peter Farrell presided and Lombardino was impressed by the dignity and depth of this judge.

Farrell would preside at the most important trial of Lombardino's life. It would be almost two decades later, when the struggle against people's disrespect inside the courtroom had spread to the streets and homes. It alarmed both men. Lombardino and Farrell had become prisoners of hard memories of tightly run courtrooms and tightly checked passions.

There was a two-year interruption in his education when from 1953 until 1955 Lombardino served in the Army. He became a corporal and operated a landing barge, stationed at Fort Eustis, Virginia. "They told us that there was a WAC behind every tree at Eustis —only there were no trees." The nearest big town was Newport News. But Tony Lombardino didn't feel comfortable there and he would drive an 800-mile round trip for a weekend in New York City.

When he resumed college, it took time for him to regain momentum. He graduated from Hofstra with a C average, and when he took the test for Brooklyn College Law School, he was in the lowest percentage of those accepted. His father explained that the family had taken out loans, that they had mortgaged their home to put him through school. He was expected to do better. And he did. Lombardino began tape-recording his lessons and taking elaborate notes. He studied furiously on weekends and organized study groups. He took an accelerated course and never received a mark below B. He was graduated in the top ten percent of the 1957 class of 400.

In his senior year, as an indication of his newfound maturity, Anthony Lombardino also took a bride. The ceremony was held on a Sunday afternoon—a concession to the self-employed butchers and hairdressers who couldn't afford to take off a Saturday—at Our Lady of the Cenacle Church just off the Long Island Expressway. Lombardino wore a tuxedo. In the carefully structured society of Long Island Italians, he was considered to have "married down." His father-in-law was a maintenance man.

After the wedding Lombardino and his wife lived in his old room at his parents' home. It was a sensible thing to do. When he graduated from law school, he was advised to enter an important firm in some junior capacity. But he was impatient. Against the unanimous advice of his relatives, Lombardino and a classmate, George Faber, opened a general-practice office in Ridgewood. His father helped build bookshelves. His first case was a negligence claim, and with the two-hundred-dollar fee he and Faber and their wives went out to celebrate.

But after the brave beginning, business was bad. "I realized soon that other lawyers had political friends —connections—and status to recommend them," Lombardino recalled. "They had a *lot* of connections. It was a lot more difficult than I had anticipated."

In Queens the law worked within circles. Judges could assign cases to favored firms. Police could recommend defendants to grateful lawyers. Lawyers could pass along overloads to colleagues certain that the favor would eventually be returned. When a judge was to be appointed, political leaders were consulted. When an Assistant District Attorney was needed, the Democratic committeemen drew from a pool of talent that had demonstrated loyalty and could be counted upon in the future. Every job had a string, and every string was held by a county committeeman, a grand puppeteer who could make the borough dance with business. Companies that wanted to do business with the county were eager to employ ambitious young attorneys who could connect them to the puppet masters. It was an ancient system of sleight-of-hand.

Because the Democratic ranks were crowded, Lombardino joined the Douglas MacArthur Republican Club. It met on the first and third Thursday of every month in a Protestant church at Liberty Avenue and the Van Wyck Expressway. Tony had chosen carefully. The membership consisted mostly of old Con Edison workers, retired policemen, and middle-level bankers. Like Lombardino, they had sensed something stirring in the activities of Senators Robert A. Taft and Joseph R. McCarthy. Later the club would become affiliated with the Conservative Party, but in the early 1960s it seemed that the political movements could lead to a rupture of Democratic control of Queens. Lombardino wanted to run for an Assembly seat, but the old-guard members of the club told him he was too impatient, that he hadn't earned the right. During this period Lombardino became friendly with a young city councilman, Nat Hentel.

When Hentel was appointed District Attorney, Lombardino went to his district leader and said he knew Hentel and should be recommended for a post as Assistant District Attorney. Reluctantly the district leader passed Lombardino's name along to the county leader. In January, Tony Lombardino moved into an eight-by-ten-foot office on the second floor of the Queens Criminal Courts Building on Queens Boulevard. In his off-duty hours he volunteered to go on felony runs with detectives. He was just like a kid again—riding around in unmarked radio cars, carrying a 7.65-caliber Beretta on his hip.

Lombardino's office was across the hall from Assistant District Attorney Edward Devlin, whose door seemed to be always closed. Lombardino knew that Devlin was working on the Crimmins case, but he wouldn't be satisfied until he discovered what was going on behind the closed door.

29

Eddie and Alice Crimmins had been reunited in the fall of 1965. It was, for both, a marriage of convenience. They were being hounded by the police, and legal advisors had said that for the sake of appearances it should be evident that neither blamed the other. They moved into a three-room apartment in the Beechhurst section of Queens. The development known as Le Havre consisted of middle-income eight-story buildings with the pretensions that the name implied. They had been thrown up hastily in the 1960s, in time to cash in on the great white urban decampment. A gloss of paint and a foreign name, like the presumption of a royal title, were expected to lend distinction, but only made the development seem more rootless. There was even less sense of community than at the garden-apartment complexes of Kew Gardens Hills. Residents of the high-rises were perpetual strangers, nodding perhaps now and then at a familiar face, but seldom reaching under the smile. Social exchanges were rare and invariably accompanied by some sense of apology or shame. When the buildings had just gone up, a woman had flung herself to her death from one of the upper floors. The reaction to the suicide was strange. The management had some difficulty renting that particular apartment, as if the affliction were somehow communicable. But there was almost no curiosity about the reasons for the woman's plunge. Suicide was not an unthinkable alternative.

The Crimmins apartment on the third floor at 9–20

Air view of Kew Gardens Hills apartment development, foreground, where the Crimmins family lived *(N.Y. Daily News)*

Alice Crimmins and her two children, Christmas, 1964

Missy and Eddie Crimmins

Below left: Alice Crimmins escorted by detectives after viewing the body of her dead daughter *(N.Y. Daily News)*
Below right: Alice and her husband, Eddie Crimmins, later the same afternoon *(N.Y. Daily News)*

The funeral of Missy Crimmins *(N.Y. Daily News)*

The place where little Eddie Crimmins's body was found, five days after his disappearance *(AP)*

The Crimmins boy's body was discovered not far from the Van Wyck Expressway. Part of the New York World's Fair is in the background *(UPI)*

Anthony Grace, center, talking to Detectives Jerry Byrnes, left, and John Kelly, right *(N.Y. Daily News)*

Edmund Crimmins, Alice Crimmins, and lawyer Harold Harrison leaving the courthouse *(N.Y. Daily News)*

Joseph Rorech *(N.Y. Daily News)*

Above left: Assistant District Attorney Anthony Lombardino, left, and Detective Gerard Piering, right *(N.Y. Daily News)*
Above right: Medical examiner Milton Helpern *(N.Y. Daily News)*

Assistant District Attorney James Mosley, left, prosecutor Lombardino, center, and Queens District Attorney Thomas Mackell, right *(N.Y. Daily News)*

...e would justify the means. There would come ... when all the recordings were silenced by the ... of his conscience. He would eventually quit the ... Department in disgust at his colleagues' fascina- ...with spying. But in the fall of 1965 Phil Brady ...bsorbed by the techniques of detection. Like the ...precocious student in class, he plotted with geo- ...c precision where the microphones and tapes ...d be employed. He tried to ignore the business of ...was coming over the tapes. That was for the ... detectives—Jerry Piering, John Kelly, Charlie ...tia, Harry Shields.

...he assignment was to sit on Alice Crimmins. And ... after she took up residence in Beechhurst she ...med her extravagant sexual affairs. Eddie had gone ...k to work at Kennedy Airport. Alice became an ...cutive secretary for an official at a company in ...g Island City. A middle-aged man from Atlanta, ...asplanted by his company to New York, he had ... his wife and children behind. At first he was un- ...are of the history of the redheaded woman assigned ...his secretary. She was efficient and clever. He had ...ly to tell her once how a thing ought to be done, ...d it was done to perfection.

"I was always quick to pick things up," she would ...plain. "I never had any formal lessons, but I pick ...ings up."

...She could type with speed and file with care. She ...d coffee ready when it was needed. And she pos- ...ssed one of the rare gifts of an office assistant—the ...ility to anticipate needs. She reminded him to call ...me; to have his cleaning done; to cash a check. ...was an endearing quality that went beyond the ...unds of office loyalty. Alice Crimmins was unable ...separate her life into inviolate compartments. Her ...lings were open and often transparent, and she was ...y careful about other people's feelings. Once when ...was in a lesbian bar and one woman attached her- ... to Alice, she was as gentle and diplomatic as pos- ...e. She accepted a drink, but made it clear that her ...entation was purely heterosexual. The woman per- ...ed. In a burst of impetuosity, she declared her love ...Alice. Quietly, Alice held the woman's hand and

142

The all-male jury of the first Crimmins trial, May 26, 1968 *(N.Y. Daily News)*
Below left: Judge Peter T. Farrell *(N.Y. Daily News)*
Below right: Alice Crimmins with attorney Herbert Lyon, June, 1970 *(N.Y. Daily News)*

Alice Crimmins, right, waiting with spectators for a session of the second trial to begin *(UPI)*

Sophie Earomirski waving to spectators outside the courtroom *(N.Y. Daily News)*

166th Street was almost underneath Bridge. All day and night the thunde head could be heard. And from her was almost directly opposite the unma the bay where her children were buried look directly down into the parking lot restaurant where Tony Grace spent hi At any hour she could see whether his was parked outside.

The apartment complex was also ad from Whitestone General Hospital. The into the hospital on the same day that into her apartment. If the residents kep distance from one another's lives, the such intentions. Before the painters had the Crimminses' walls, ultrasensitive micr been planted behind each beam. Before t company finished connecting the two tele had been impregnated with multiple bugs. standard recording microphones that wo when a telephone was in use. But there sophisticated voice-activated microphones record every sound in the apartment. Alice her telephone was tapped, but she had no i depth of the surveillance.

Less than 100 yards away, in a corner of floor pharmacy of the hospital, detectives kep four-hour watch on the machines. They woul the listening post for three years, twenty-fo day, seven days a week. And they would n one incriminating statement.

The installation, maintenance, and trans the tapes were in the hands of Detective Philip Brady, a big, florid man who had be man since 1946. Before that, Brady had be sergeant in the Criminal Investigation Div U.S. Army. He was well over six feet a more than 200 pounds, and the effect of ence was softened by a creamy, toleran educated voice. He was, everyone agreed technician. He could bug or counterbug i situation. But he was a faithful Catholic he was convinced that he was in pursu told the lesbian that it was nothing personal, but that she simply couldn't handle that kind of relationship.

Alice took the same care with men. She worried about their needs and their feelings. The man she worked for had taken an apartment in Long Island City. There were a thousand confounding details, made more bewildering for him by the strangeness of the environment. Alice helped him buy furnishings. One night the man took her out to dinner. They slept together. Given her soft shoulder, the next stage was inevitable. It wasn't long before Alice had moved some of her clothing into his apartment. For a brief period they were happy. Alice would recommend shows, restaurants. She fell in love with the turn of the seasons, and for her it was again the springtime of an affair when the police interceded.

Harry Shields, Jerry Piering, Charlie Prestia, and John Kelly were furious. What kind of grief was that! So the detectives began a new tactic—an extralegal device to make Alice crack. A telephone call was made to Atlanta. The executive's wife was told the exact nature of her husband's new relationship. The woman was on the next plane north. She went straight to the apartment, where she found Alice's things. Methodically, with the police in a nearby apartment, she destroyed all of Alice's clothing.

Given the stagnation of the case, the detectives were ready to try almost anything. They were out to break Alice by harassment. They let her know that she was always followed, that her affairs would never be secret.

The executive was transferred home, his career blighted, his marriage wrecked. But Alice's composure hadn't cracked. She had never intended to damage the man's career. To her, he was someone who could comfort her, fold her in the protective cup of his arms during her lonely ordeal. To the police, she was a slut. Instead of grief, they read lust.

The field reports reinforced the theme. Piering would sit in his office long after dark reading the smudged detective reports. Alice had been out with this man; she had slept with a chimney-sweep. To him, the picture was an impossible incongruity. Soon after the children's burials Alice was seen again in her familiar

143

night spots. She was no longer a cocktail waitress—
she was a customer. The reports, in clipped police
jargon, delineated her movements, pinpointed her
whereabouts. Subject was seen entering Heritage House
in the presence of five men and two other females.
Subject consumed five whiskey Scotch mists, danced
several times with different partners . . . appeared to
laugh a lot. . . .

What was missing from the reports was a certain
tone, a kind of subtle understanding. Alice Crimmins,
in the fall of 1965, drank harder, danced faster, and
laughed with more abandon than she had done a year
ago. But it was a frantic diversion that was not so
identified in any of the police reports.

In their turn, the detectives visited the lonely bars
and spoke to the people there, enlisting them as allies
in the siege of Alice Crimmins.

He was the manager of a steak bar and Alice had once
been his favorite cocktail waitress. The steak bar had
had a different name then, but that wasn't unusual.
Sometimes a bar switched names for tax reasons.
Sometimes to elude creditors. Sometimes merely to revive excitement, like changing a dress. The Four Spoons
would open again in a month as the Five Aces. If you
looked closely, you could spot the same stains on the
carpet; there were the same aging bartender, the same
world-weary manager, the same tired singer at the
piano bar tapping out ballads in ragged reminiscence
of fashions that had already been beaten to death.
Even the suntans seemed pasty; expressions on the
bar veterans bore witness to all the sins Long Island
could offer—from the rings of housewife prostitutes
to child pornographers. The manager, in his velvet
dinner jacket, wore the mechanical smile of a man for
whom human appetites held no surprises. "I always
liked Rusty," he would say. "She glowed, know what
I mean?" It was no small compliment in the burnt-out
candescence of this world. "She could sit down with a
bunch of executives and liven them up. She was champagne. When I heard about this, I never believed she
had anything to do with it. I mean, I could never really

144

picture her as a mother, but all of these broads have kids home. They're all supporting a couple of kids. Her, though . . ." A few days after they buried Alice's last child, she was back at the steak bar, seemingly without any sign of grief or mourning. "I changed my mind about Rusty after that," he said with the shiver of someone who realizes that the people who come through his doors into daytime darkness are all strangers. "What kind of mother is that?"

Charlie Prestia was on duty at the listening post. He had gone through his second cup of coffee. The microphones across the road picked up the voice of Joe Rorech. It had been Phil Brady's idea to reunite Alice and Joe. He knew that they cared about each other, and in an almost paternal way he hoped that the solution of the case might even lead to some happy reconciliation. It was a vague and not entirely reasonable hope. But Brady was a man of infinite hope. So one day he gave Alice's new telephone number to Joe Rorech. Brady wasn't on duty when Rorech called and Alice told him to come over. In the listening post Detectives Prestia and Harry Shields waited breathlessly. The microphones were picking up voices—the familiar sounds of the early stages of seduction. Shields called Eddie Crimmins at the airport. Joe and Alice are at the apartment making love, Eddie was told.

At the listening post Prestia heard the telephone ring. It was Eddie.

"Are you alone?" he asked.

That idiot! thought Prestia. Now he'll give Joe a chance to get away. Why didn't he just get in his car and rush home?

"Of course," said Alice. "Who'd you think was here?"

Alice was lying. This was not new to the police. If she could lie to Eddie about a tryst, she could lie to them about the children. At least, that was how their reasoning went.

Eddie was still not certain. He received another call from the detectives telling him that Alice was lying, that she was shacked up right this minute, and that he'd better get home.

The voice-activated microphones in the apartment now picked up the conversation between Alice and Joe. "That was Eddie," said Alice. "I told him no one was here, but I don't think he believed me."

"You want me to go?"

"I think you better," said Alice.

The police in the listening post heard the hurried sounds of dressing, kissing, sighs of regret.

"We better do something," said Shields, seeing his chance at confrontation slipping away.

"What?" said Prestia.

Prestia and Shields left the listening post. And then Shields got an idea. When Rorech came out of the apartment, he found three flat tires on his car.

"Oh, Christ!"

Alice had come out to watch the departure with her dog, Brandy. Rorech couldn't find a jack. He ran to Alice's car to see if hers would fit. Brandy, meanwhile, began sniffing around the bush where Prestia and Shields were hiding. It was a frantic half-hour. Finally Rorech called his friend Detective Phil Brady, who lived nearby. Brady, guessing what had happened, showed up with a jack and a tow truck from an all-night garage.

Rorech's suit was torn, his manicured hands had been scratched to the quick, and Alice had to bite her cheek to keep from laughing. Brady and Rorech towed the car out of the neighborhood before Eddie got home. The two detectives hiding in the bushes learned gratefully, after watching Brandy circle and circle before picking a spot right in front of them, that she was female and would squat instead of squirting.

Joe Rorech and Phil Brady drank together in a bar, unwinding from the near miss. More and more, Brady was becoming disillusioned by the way his colleagues were handling the Crimmins case.

30

The meeting was set for the squad room of the 107th Precinct at six o'clock and the police brass began arriving fashionably late. A few minutes after 6:00 p.m. on November 9, 1965, the black limousines screeched in front of the Fresh Meadows Precinct, the drivers jockeying for positions close to the door, to fit the rank of their bosses. Tom McGuire's driver edged forward and back, keeping away the car of Joe Coyle, the borough commander. McGuire, known as Friar Tuck for his priestly manner and ample figure, bounded inside like a track star. His face was flushed with excitement. Inside, the detectives closest to the case were nervously mashing out cigarettes, wondering if this would be the break in the case. Only Jerry Piering circled cautiously, unable to accept any solution that didn't include Alice Crimmins. He took Phil Brady aside. "Look at this," he said, showing Brady the report of an interview between Alice Crimmins and Anthony Grace that had been taped. During the conversation Alice Crimmins had said she had come to believe that the children were "better off now."

He shoved it under Brady's nose as if that would settle all of the detective's doubts. Brady read the report and looked at Piering with his eyebrows raised, as if to say "So what?"

"If she were my wife, I'd kill her," said Piering.

Brady shrugged and waited for the commanders to assemble and begin the meeting. It was a refrain that he had heard often from the major detectives in the

147

case—"If she were my wife, I'd kill her." Brady shoved aside Piering's interruption. He had something more important to think about. The *Journal-American* had been contacted by a man who claimed he'd been hired to kill the Crimmins children. There had been more than a score of "confessions" so far—not unusual in a much publicized case. But there were details in this man's statement that couldn't be ignored. In addition, he was in the hands of a newspaper that couldn't be relied upon to sit on the story for very long. For the sake of prestige, it was imperative that the police have better information than the newspaper.

By 6:30 p.m. the police officials had gathered around the scarred wooden table. Coyle sat quietly, his cigar dangling expectantly, waiting for the subordinates to commit themselves about the suspect. The discussion started and then the lights began to flicker.

The desk lieutenant came rushing in. "It looks like a power failure," he said.

Coyle and McGuire shrugged.

"It's the whole city," added the lieutenant.

The meeting broke up as everyone scattered to take up traffic-control duty during the East Coast's major power blackout.

A few days later the suspect sat under the lights in the lieutenant's office at the 107th Precinct, repeating his "confession" for Piering and Brady and Jerry Byrnes.

"Tell us again how you got in," said Piering.

The suspect, a small, nervous man with wire-rimmed glasses, was a maintenance man in Manhattan. He said he had been approached by two strangers and for the unlikely sum of $500 had driven to Queens, slipped into the children's room, taken them out through the front door, and killed them both. Two men had helped him, he said, but he didn't know their names.

"OK," said Brady, who knew that the layout of the Crimmins apartment had been very carefully published —all except the details of the children's room, "now where was the double bed?"

The man skipped a beat in his story. By the far wall, he replied.

And what kind of lock was on the children's door? "It was a barrel-bolt lock," said the man.

The detectives turned away in disgust. There had been no double bed in the room. The lock was a hook-and-eye, not a barrel-bolt. They had been taken in for a moment by another crank. Newspapers were not the best detectives.

"Get him out of here," said Piering.

"What's wrong?" asked the man, bewildered, seeing his spotlight and moment of glory fading.

"Get that creep out of here."

Phil Brady was married to a perky little redhead named Ann, and he'd never been entirely convinced that Alice Crimmins had killed her children. It was not a popular position to take among his colleagues, and, for the most part, he kept his opinions to himself. He did his job—placed telephone taps where he was supposed to. The District Attorney, Nat Hentel, instructed him to put a bug on the telephones of the Assistant District Attorneys in the case, Edward Devlin and Nicholas Ferraro. The taps on the official telephones were for the sake of the record. It was the tap on Devlin's telephone that produced Brady's basic skepticism about the conduct of the case and about the guilt of Alice. In the fall of 1965 the cluttered fragments of the case were beginning to assemble themselves. The stories had been recorded. The alibis checked.

"What it boils down to," said Devlin decisively, "is the time factor. Alice says that she checked the kids at midnight. If the autopsy shows that they were dead at midnight, then . . ."

He let it hang there. The meeting turned to young Dr. Michael Baden, who was representing the Medical Examiner's office.

Dr. Baden felt the pressure. "I don't know if we can do that," he replied, squirming under the third degree. "I'm not sure we can pin it down like that."

"Well," said Devlin, "without some kind of evidence, we don't have a case."

There was another moment of silence and Baden felt the expectation fall on him.

"Let's get Dr. Helpern on the phone," said Devlin, nodding to Brady, who slipped out of the room and went to his listening post, a converted janitor's closet at the end of the second-floor hallway of the District Attorney's office. Brady picked up a headset and monitored the conversation between Dr. Milton Helpern and Dr. Baden. Helpern was arguing that it was impossible, absolutely impossible, to pinpoint the time of death with precision.

I know, I know, said Baden, passing the telephone to Devlin. Helpern repeated the medical truth—that the time of Missy's death couldn't be pinpointed before midnight. The closest they could come with scientific certainty was to estimate that Missy died sometime between 10:00 p.m. and 4:00 a.m.

Disappointed, Devlin hung up. It was early in the case and if they couldn't nail Alice on the time factor, there would be other wedges. Brady would later transcribe this conversation from the tapes and turn them over to the District Attorney's office. Later he would be amazed and conscience-stricken when Dr. Helpern testified in court that the medical evidence indicated Missy died before midnight. Of course, Dr. Helpern had been subjected to relentless pressure from police and the District Attorney's office.

After Brady retired from the Police Department, he tried to contact Alice's defense attorney to reveal his knowledge of the tapes. Three times he phoned Herbert Lyon, her second attorney, but the calls were never returned. For a time Brady kept a copy of the Helpern tape in his Flushing home. Later it would be reclaimed by the District Attorney's office, but he still kept a transcript of it. The tape itself was filed with the other stacks of details of the case. But that call echoes in Philip Brady's memory, even a decade later.

31

If Phil Brady thought his colleagues were showing a lack of professionalism, he was not immune from his own emotions. He did not like Eddie Crimmins.

On December 22, 1965, Brady stared out of the window of the hospital across the street from the Crimmins apartment and blinked in disbelief. There was Santa Claus on Alice's window. Red, green, and blue Christmas lights were strung gaily around the room. And he saw Eddie, as if nothing at all had happened in the past year, putting up a Christmas tree. The Christmas lights seemed obscene and inappropriate, but confirmed his feeling that Eddie was the more mystifying of the pair. It was then that Brady started keeping a private dossier on Eddie Crimmins. Every time he raised a suspicion about Eddie to one of his colleagues, it was brushed away as if he were a finicky accountant calling attention to some minor unpaid bill. Stick to the technical side, he was told. Keep up with the paperwork and tape transcriptions and cultivate your friendship with Joe Rorech.

And so Brady kept his private diary. The detectives in command had focused on Alice that first night and virtually dismissed everyone else. The newspapers repeated the official innuendo that both parents were under suspicion, and, indeed, in December 1966 the *New York Post,* the *New York Times,* and the *Daily News* would list Alice and Eddie as uncooperative witnesses. But Brady's suspicions had landed on Eddie. He was bewildered by the others' lack of interest. In

151

his routine canvass of the neighborhood shortly after the killings, Brady had found a woman who said she had seen a man standing near the children's window at 1:10 a.m. The man, tall and dark-haired, wore tan slacks and a dark shirt—clothing such as Eddie had been wearing that night. Her name was Maria Gomez and she'd been coming out of a friend's home a hundred yards away from the Crimmins house. Her companion, a married man who did not want to get involved in the case, said he had noticed nothing—a figure, perhaps, but he would never be able to identify the person. The woman was more willing.

John Kelly and Brady found Eddie Crimmins in a diner on Union Turnpike. Would he be willing to come with them and stand under the window? Kelly asked. A woman said she had seen a man standing there that night.

"I don't have to go," said Crimmins.

"It would help us," argued Brady, "if you would just put on your tan slacks and shirt and just stand there."

"I'm not gonna go," said Eddie, continuing his meal. "If you bother me, I'm gonna call my lawyer."

"Either you come with us," said Kelly firmly, "or else we take you."

Eddie went reluctantly. He didn't change his clothes. He stood under the window, but the woman couldn't be sure. He *looked* like the man, she said. But she couldn't be positive.

Brady thought, anyway, that Maria Gomez would make a terrible witness. She lived on welfare and the generosity of the men she took to her bed. He could imagine what a hostile attorney could make of her credibility.

But the things about Eddie that bothered Brady mounted. There was, for example, Eddie's alibi. Eddie claimed he had been in a bar at 12:30 a.m. watching a particular television program. When Brady checked with the station, he learned that the program had been interrupted by a bulletin about Adlai Stevenson's death. Eddie Crimmins knew nothing about the bulletin. Also, Eddie had been in the Nite Cap Lounge drinking gin-and-tonics later that night. Eddie had never before or since drunk gin-and-tonics. He invariably took beer. It was as if he'd been trying to make an impression on the bartender for an alibi.

One of the more puzzling aspects of Eddie's story was that he had told many people he had exposed himself to children in Kissena Park. He told the story to Alice, to a friend, Margie Fischer, and to Inspector McGuire. Eddie's later explanation—that he'd been trying to show Alice that he was as bad as she was—didn't sit well with Brady. Why would a man invent such a story? Why would he drill holes from the basement to Alice's bedroom in order to hear her bed squeak when she was with other men?

"Look," said Piering, "he's a schnook!" As if that would explain it all away. Brady wasn't satisfied and found a sympathetic superior officer, Wolfgang Zanglein. He prepared a five-page single-spaced document outlining certain facts about Eddie.

Eddie had not been to see his children for two weeks until the day before they disappeared.

Eddie had a key and access to the apartment.

Eddie had a more important motive than Alice, since she had custody and was not likely to lose it.

On the day before Eddie was to take his lie-detector test, he went to the public library and read everything he could about the subject.

There were more subtle things that Brady told Zanglein in one of several all-night conferences. Eddie had seemed almost pathologically curious about the injuries on his children's bodies. He didn't seem to show the normal revulsion that Alice felt. While Alice cried, Eddie had wanted to know every detail about the bruises and whether a cause of death could be ascertained.

His fascination with the case seemed to Brady less like an aggrieved father than like a man keeping track of police knowledge. And when he said that Alice was innocent, it sounded like an obligation—as if really he wanted the police to keep after her.

Finally, there was the business of the telephone calls. For some time Alice had been getting strange calls. Sometimes the caller would just hang on, saying nothing. Sometimes there was a brief, although almost incoherent conversation. A few days after the children died, Alice phoned Eddie and said they should bring in the Federal Bureau of Investigation.

"No," said Eddie laconically. "The police are handling it."

"But don't you think the FBI could do a better job?" said Alice.

"The police are handling it," said Eddie.

Brady listened to the tape of this conversation. He played it again. The voice seemed familiar. He wondered if it could be the same voice that Alice was receiving at home. He contacted Lawrence Kersta of Voice Prints Labs, Inc., in Somerville, New Jersey. Kersta, who had invented the process of tracing people through the use of voice prints, said Brady's information was too sketchy to be traced.

"Couldn't we make a composite tape?" asked Brady.

Kersta said it was possible, but the results would probably be useless since it would be impossible to maintain a "chain of evidence." There would never be anything incriminating against Eddie. His faulty reactions and strange patterns would be attributed to nothing more than normal variations of human behavior. In Alice's case, each item became a weapon. But with Eddie the investigators put things into a different perspective and dismissed them.

Brady arranged a reunion between Joe Rorech and Alice late in 1965. They met one night at Chez André's on Northern Boulevard. Brady was with his wife, Ann. It was a delicate maneuver. They stood in the dark at the huge egg-shaped bar sipping whiskey that flooded their reserve. André's, nestled behind a moat of hedges and protective trees, was an almost perfect rendezvous. The people who worked there were bred like eunuchs to discretion. The parking-lot attendants had seen women go home with strange men while their husbands dined clandestinely in another room. More than just a cheaters' bar, André's was the last word in Long Island's elegant game of musical mating.

By midnight Joe and Ann and Phil and Alice were feeling glowingly mellow over the rediscovered friendship. The whiskeys had softened the bad memories and *Pal Joey* was playing on the television over the bar—a nostalgic whisper of the past. And then Alice broke the spell. "Eddie's home by now," she said. "I better call home."

Phil Brady remained at his post at the bar, knowing he could hear the taped conversation the next day. The conversation with Eddie was brief, although charged with unstated tensions.

"I'm out here at André's having a drink with Phil and Ann Brady," said Alice.

"Who else is there?" asked Eddie.

"No one," said Alice.

"I'll be right over."

Alice didn't say a word when she came back from the telephone. She picked up the conversation and her Scotch mist. About twenty minutes later Brady looked toward the door and saw Eddie. Joe Rorech was hidden behind Brady. Without turning, Brady delivered the warning: "Eddie's here!"

Rorech didn't say a word. He slithered off his chair—as Brady recalls, it was as if his body suddenly shed its bones. He slid down to the floor and crawled on all fours the long way around the bar. The only problem was the bill, which Ann Brady goodnaturedly paid.

Brady was impressed and amused by Rorech's bizarre escape. The reunion, it seemed, had been successful. For the rest of the night no one said a word about the spare drink on the bar in front of the four.

32

Alice Crimmins worked under her maiden name, Alice Burke. But her past and all its associations followed her. The pattern hardly varied. She'd get a job—as a secretary or receptionist, once as a travel agent in Manhattan. After a few weeks, just long enough for her to settle comfortably into a new environment, her employer would receive a pair of official visitors. Sometimes they would spare Alice the embarrassment of an office visit and see the boss at his home.

One such visit was to a large house in a Westchester suburb. There were fountains on the expanse of lawn and a maid to escort the two detectives into a den. Another servant asked if they wanted drinks and they said no, not wishing to diminish the solemnity of their visit. The business executive came in smiling, extending his hand. He was wearing a smoking jacket and an ascot. He apologized for shunting them into the den, but he had guests and dinner was waiting. John Kelly said he understood. As he flashed his detective's shield, he noted that the man paled momentarily. The shield always had the same effect. Even the most innocent people, perhaps experiencing a flicker of some remote guilt, were stunned by the show of force.

"Sit down, gentlemen," said the executive.

The detectives made themselves comfortable, having established themselves. Kelly lit his thick cigar.

"What's this about?" asked the executive.

You have a girl working for you, began Kelly. You know her as Alice Burke.

The man nodded, absorbing the information, unclear about the implications.

Her name is really Alice Crimmins, continued the detectives. Maybe you've heard of her.

The name would always jar some tabloid memory. The executive waited.

We think she killed her children, the detectives said. The man waited. Was there something else?

We just thought you should know, said the detectives. "Is she charged with a crime?" asked the man.

The detectives said no, but they had no doubt that she had been involved in the murder of the two children.

"She's a secretary," said the executive. "A good one. What do you expect me to do?"

Maybe you don't know what kind of person she is, continued the detectives. Maybe we haven't made ourselves clear.

Yes, said the executive, rising. You have made yourselves completely clear. Now, if you'll excuse me, I have dinner guests.

In the squad room of the 107th Precinct there was consternation. This had never happened before. Every time they went to one of Alice's employers and told what they suspected, she was fired. Or quietly asked to leave. But now they had, in effect, been told to go to hell.

"He was the only stand-up guy in the case," said Phil Brady.

As winter folded over the investigation, the detectives had exhausted the usual investigative techniques, but a solid case still eluded them. They believed they possessed the seed of the answer—but there were blank spots. Gaps. All the inferences seemed to lead to Alice Crimmins. Her frustrating denials and cold silences were maddening.

Nat Hentel had to worry about the election. If he allowed this case to dribble away, he risked being dismissed at the polls as an impotent prosecutor. He faced a formidable adversary, State Senator Thomas Mackell, a widely popular Democrat with a bank balance of friendship all over Queens. Mackell was an organization man who glowed with the reflected blessings of the Kennedys. He had been one of the first state politicians to endorse John Kennedy for President and Robert Kennedy for Senator. He also enjoyed the reputation of being a hard worker with dependable loyalties. In the clubhouses they would speak affectionately of his common touch and his fine Irish voice. And it went without saying that Tommy Mackell was a good family man. He was devoted to his wife, Dorothy. Perhaps a little too devoted, since Dorothy had an amusing innocence and could blurt out mistakes and then Tommy would trail behind her tolerantly repairing her gaffes.

During the early stages of the campaign Mackell boasted that he would make the Crimmins case his first order of business. The culprits would be behind bars in his first season in office, he implied. The case was no mystery in the Mackell household. The night after the children disappeared, Mackell's wife poked him in the chest and said there was no doubt in her mind—the mother did it. She based the judgment on intuition—and, of course, the reports that the mother would not appear in public without makeup. Mrs. Mackell had developed something of a reputation among friends as an amateur sleuth. Her hunches had the eerie insight of a Miss Marple. The Mackells' apartment in Rego Park was across the street from Alexander's parking lot. Late at night Mrs. Mackell would stand at her window and count the cars in the lot, picking out the ones that were stolen. She had been right often enough for the local precinct to send a car around to check. Her husband had learned to accept his wife's hobby with a certain amount of good-natured kidding, the way some men shrug helplessly at cold remedies. Still, Mackell did not dismiss his wife's hunches out of hand.

When the gossip coincided with Mrs. Mackell's hunch about Alice Crimmins, the official viewpoint hardened into virtual certainty. "A great little detective," Mackell would say with a trace of condescension. And yet the police version and Mrs. Mackell's hunch were based on the same foundation—an attitude; an

158

unsettling defiance in the stance of Alice Crimmins; the way she took sex like a man, as an appetite to be satisfied without entanglements; her dismissal of faith like another casual lover.

The detectives working on the case sensed Nat Hentel's vulnerability, and they used it. Each subject in the case—from the maid to neighbors—was isolated and the dossiers began to grow like a forest.

The police enlisted Margie Fischer, the upstairs neighbor. Phil Brady fixed up a tape recorder inside her wicker handbag. She was asked to meet Tony Grace at Ripple's. What did the cops want to know, she asked?

Pump him, she was told. Get anything you can out of him. Margie kept the date and had a long, rambling meal with Tony Grace. They spoke passingly of Alice and agreed that everything would have been different if Tony had gone over that night.

Her assignment completed, Margie Fischer drove home along Queens Boulevard. Along the way, she stopped to pick up a man. The tape recorder was going all during their brief encounter. It amused the men of the 107th squad.

33

One morning in early December 1965 John Kelly and Phil Brady sat across a desk in an office of the Fresh Meadows Precinct. Spread over the table were stacks of dun-colored folders, each containing a file on a principal in the case. Like two chemists, they stared at the folders, knowing that one or more contained the right formula to solve the case. They were reluctant to start, knowing the complexity of their puzzle. Kelly puffed on his cigar and Brady smoked cigarettes as they sipped coffee to postpone the ordeal. For the moment, the subtle rivalry between the two detectives was forgotten. John Kelly had entered the case late and Brady felt proprietary misgivings. Kelly had been touted as a golf expert who could use his hobby to wedge himself into the confidence of Eddie Crimmins and Joe Rorech. But Phil Brady played golf, as did a dozen other detectives on the case. Brady and Shields and Prestia had worked as a team on Queens homicides and there was resentment of the hotshots from Brooklyn, the Bronx, Manhattan.

It was natural enough. Detectives are, after all, human. Even within the home borough, someone was always feeling left out. The thousand little details that create the mosaic of any case have multiple authors, each convinced that it was his tile that fleshed out the picture. Men who have been partners for years have broken up over misappropriated credit for solution of an important case.

With Brady and Kelly, the antagonism was not a smoldering one. Brady believed that he had better access to the people in the folders, despite Kelly's seemingly urbane understanding of the world of Joe Rorech. Brady's asset was his priestly manner—an ear that absorbed confessions with the natural suction of a sponge.

If there were tensions between Kelly and Brady that morning, they could at least agree on the humorous flaws of the man running the case, Jerry Piering. And there *were* comic aspects to Piering's frantic attempts to cover every part of the investigation. Piering regarded himself as the compleat detective. He would, for example, install his own recording machinery, even if all the tapes did come out blank. He would take his own photographs, using expensive telephoto equipment, even if the pictures were blurred and out of focus. On his days off, he would follow witnesses, although they would often turn around and smile at him.

Some of the cast of characters had settled comfortably into their stories as if moving into a familiar home: For a time there had been some mystery about Carl Andrade, the slightly overdressed waiter at the Surrey Steak House. He was one of Alice's more important lovers. They had slept together more than fifty times. And yet, whenever he was questioned, the detectives had a feeling that an element was missing, that he was concealing some ingredient of his story. Alice had called to ask Andrade to intercede with her maid, Evelyn Linder Atkins, when she learned that Evelyn was going to testify against her at the custody hearing. Why, the police wondered, would Andrade have any influence with Evelyn? Then they learned that Andrade worked with Evelyn's future husband, Teddy Atkins, at the steak house, where Teddy was a chef. Andrade had been born in Jamaica, a fact known by very few, including Teddy, Alice, and Evelyn. One week before the disappearance, Andrade had come to the apartment house to talk to Alice. They had sat on the lawn about midnight and discussed strategy for dealing with Evelyn and her damaging testimony. The detectives were convinced that Andrade was not involved in the disappearance and that there was nothing sinister about his protectiveness.

Anthony Grace, the middle-aged millionaire, left a trail of gratuities in his wake, like a careless oil tanker. He was a crude man, but he could always retreat behind the barricades of his money and his important friends. There were lapses in the folder on Tony Grace. An implicit decision had been made early in the case that certain names would never appear in writing—names like Bob Wagner, Paul Screvane, Sal LoCurto. More than one detective had been sharply reminded of Inspector Michael Clifford, transferred to Brooklyn for his clumsiness. Phil Brady was not convinced that Tony Grace was sacrosanct. He set that folder aside; he would come back to it.

There was a slew of folders on minor actors, all with their own pet positions to protect—a neighbor afraid of having an affair exposed and a marriage ruined; a welfare recipient unwilling to jeopardize her income.

The file on Alice Crimmins had spread to multiple folders. Phil Brady reread his own transcriptions of the tapes he had placed on Alice's telephone. If someone

161

was to approach Alice, Brady felt it should be himself —the president of the Holy Name Society in his parish and a teacher of confraternity. He came to believe that Alice could be brought around to cooperating if only she was approached in the right spirit. A settling feeling of forgiveness seems to bathe everyone that Brady touches. No one seems beyond his understanding.

Alice had sensed this quality. When she had stopped talking to almost all of the policemen in the case, she would still call Brady. They were chatty, private calls, a substitute, perhaps, for her lost lovers. Although he never forgot his role in the case, Brady was upset one day when he saw Jerry Piering listening in on an extension to one of his talks with Alice.

Brady learned to keep his sympathies private. The others in the case had reached a level of such bitterness that his own views struck his colleagues as naïve, even a betrayal. Almost alone, Brady suffered in parallel isolation with Alice. He knew her defiance had its limits. Sometimes, alone in her car when she thought no one could see or hear, she would scream out her grief. In public she never dropped her insolence. If it would shock the police to flaunt her lovers, then she would parade them wantonly. The police, according to Alice, had committed the ultimate betrayal by not looking for her children's killer, and so she felt justified in almost any kind of reprisal. The detectives who listened to every sound from her apartment heard a one-dimensional refrain:

"Fuck me! Fuck me! Fuck me!"

The words were recorded by literal-minded police typists, and repeated in a kind of latrine fascination. Sitting in their carpeted offices after telling the secretaries they were not to be disturbed, the prosecutors and detectives listened to the tapes from Alice's apartment with a mixture of anger and confusion. Jerry Piering's face would flush in frustration.

Kelly would sit with his reaction clouded behind a puff of cigar smoke. It was strange. Alice knew very soon that her telephones were tapped and that her apartment was bugged. And yet:

"FUCK ME!"

What were they to make of it? It had become an all

too familiar cry. Sometimes they heard Alice say she felt a pang of guilt about what had happened to the children. That was enough for Piering—to him, she was confessing murder. No matter that Brady pointed out she had made the same assertions of guilt feelings months before the murders. In February, five months before the deaths, she had spent a weepy night with Joe Rorech, telling him she was a bad mother and felt guilty about it. When she said it in December, after the children were dead, Piering regarded it as a confession.

For Brady, Alice's feelings of guilt were tragically attached to lost innocence and some uncanny lapse of faith.

But as the grave-faced detectives and prosecutors sat in the District Attorney's office listening to the tapes, they began to accept Jerry Piering's view; they took Alice's flesh need as the technical explanation surrounding the bones of their case. Phil Brady's liturgical explanation was dismissed.

Brady heard pain instead of pleasure. Alice Crimmins, he had come to believe, was appealing to her lost God.

34

If Phil Brady was going to help Alice Crimmins, it would have to be an oblique assist.

"What've you got?" he asked Kelly, who had been reading a single file for more than an hour.

"It's your notes on Joe Rorech . . ."

Brady had conducted one of the first interviews with Rorech. He had gone to the man's home and passed himself off to Gloria Rorech as an insurance adjuster. If there was one brittle character in the case, it was

Joe Rorech. Kelly read the notes of Brady's long interviews with Rorech.

The notes covered the familiar story of Rorech's strange behavior the Tuesday before the children disappeared: he had met his cousin and a friend at the Steak Pub in Huntington in the early afternoon and had consumed six vodka-and-tonics. There had been no elaborate plan to his day. He had gone home, where he consumed a few drinks, then had begun his restless nighttime meandering. He met Bob Rorech and Dick Nevins at the Bourbon Lounge of the Heritage House. They had not wanted to make a late night of it—all had told their wives they would be home by midnight. But Gloria had come to expect little of her husband's promises, and was coming to think of herself as a minor Catholic martyr. Her husband was out drinking, by then, Scotch and water. Joe had called Alice, and he told Brady how calm she had sounded. Trying to entice her out, he had described a singer, Anne English, and said she was "wild and sexy," words designed to lure Alice from her nest. But Alice had been stubborn. He'd kept drinking after that and admitted he had been "stoned."

Brady's notes indicated he should check with the telephone company to see if Rorech had used his credit card—692–5515 Code K 123—to phone Alice. He would also check American Express credit card number 001 033 171 8, issued to Joseph Rorech, Jr. In the interview Rorech said he never paid in cash. There was also a note to check with the singer, the bartender, and the drummer at the Bourbon Lounge.

Brady's notes: "He says that she has told him of several calls she received at night when no one was on the phone when she answered. She suspected her husband of making the calls. . . . She also said to Rorech that she left the house after midnight on many occasions to check the whereabouts of her husband, Edmund, visiting the bars and other places he used to frequent, checking for him personally and for his car. He [Rorech] has, on several occasions, ridden with Alice about the area where Edmund lived before his present address to determine the whereabouts of his car, and she was not satisfied until she saw the car in the vicinity of the house and to be assured that Edmund was not out and in a position to check on her. . . . Relates that on one occasion Alice told him that she was going to take the children to a farm upstate where she and her husband used to go for vacations. He says that she spoke to him of this on the telephone two or three weeks before the present incident. . . . Alice had told him that Edmund had tapped her telephone and he described the manner . . . Ed had drilled a small hole in the wall adjacent to the telephone, and had inserted wires in pinholes made in telephone wires, whereby he was able to listen by throwing a switch in the bedroom."

This incident had upset Rorech. He was jealous of Alice's dates with her own husband. And Tony Grace. And Carl Andrade. And all the others. His vanity had been punctured. He was described by one former associate as a "penny millionaire," and this seemed to fit a man of such intense hopes. Brady noted that Rorech was easily wounded and found it almost intolerable to be brushed aside for someone as unpolished as Anthony Grace. It was as if he could barely understand the insult. Tony Grace left bigger tips than Rorech did; he even gave five dollars to Evelyn, the maid, when he came to call. Tony took Alice to the Capri, Ripple's, Mancini's—superior restaurants that were now slipping out of Rorech's economic reach. And when Tony got tied up on business and was late for their regular Friday-night dates, he would send a taxi to pick up Alice.

Brady's notes on Rorech's mood rose and fell like a temperature chart as Rorech rubbed open cuts and threw in some spite. "She didn't care for the children that much," Rorech told Brady. "Not until recently, that is. She'd work all night and sleep all day. She'd leave the maid with the kids. Of course, she'd always tell Evelyn where she was—she'd tell her what motel and under what name she was registered. But in the past few months her entire attitude had changed. Once we were at a motel and she was crying uncontrollably, berating herself for the type of mother she was. Normally, she was extremely unemotional."

Brady noted that Rorech's business was becoming

a shambles. Desks were empty. Bills were piling up. Alice was his obsession. She said she didn't sleep with Grace. Rorech told Brady he believed her. Brady believed that, didn't he? asked Rorech.

Rorech dribbled out little hints that would scatter the attention of the detectives. Did they know she had worked as a hostess in a Manhattan restaurant in March? She had met a man at the restaurant who used her as a model afterward. At least, she said it was as a model. Rorech had always suspected that it was a job closer to being a hooker. Brady was emotionless as he recorded Rorech's outbursts. Rorech softened. Alice had never showed any sign of active hostility toward the children. She and Eddie had shared a fantasy that they would one day own a farm where they would live peacefully with the children. The vacations on the farm had been a blissful interlude in her endless bickering with Eddie, and she had looked forward to a life upstate. If there was any danger of losing the children, she had told Rorech, she would run away. She would go to Canada, or Europe, or simply disappear. She didn't want her children to grow up in the strangled world of Eddie's and her mother's church.

Rorech paused. Look at Tony Grace, he told Brady. Grace was always introducing Alice to important politicians and gangsters.

What to make of this bleating, jealous lover? "We always had the feeling," Brady would recall, "that he had a lot more to tell, but we had to find the right questions to ask." It was like trying to figure out a combination lock.

"Let's see if we can get him to take pentothal," said Kelly. If Rorech had secrets to tell, truth serum might be a short cut. Besides, by December 1965 Rorech seemed ripe to fall apart. He was tens of thousands of dollars in debt. He had written worthless checks for thousands of dollars. He was drinking more and more. Nassau County authorities could have indicted him on dozens of counts of fraud. But the New York City detectives and the Nassau County police had an unwritten agreement that they would leave Joe Rorech free to assist in trapping Alice Crimmins. He was a man on a very thin string.

When Rorech first started getting into financial trouble, he hired a young former Queens Assistant District Attorney, Donald Manes, to handle his affairs. At first it seemed a straightforward legal tangle. Rorech's business failures were resulting in lawsuits. There was also a messy situation about a girlfriend who was suing him for sodomy. Eventually the charge was thrown out.

When Rorech's financial troubles became enmeshed with a double murder, Manes decided to turn this client over to one of his partners. Manes was, at the age of thirty-one, very ambitious. He sensed trouble in Rorech—even his checks to the law firm weren't reliable. Later Manes would become Queens Borough President and a candidate for New York Governor. His real ambition was the Mayoralty of New York, and a client like Joseph Rorech could jeopardize such ambitions. Long after Manes left the law firm of Martin Baron, Donald Manes, and Harold Harrison, Harrison would still be mired in the swamp of the Crimmins case.

35

Throughout the case, Harold Harrison did not understand that the stakes had changed completely. He was afflicted with the misconceived overconfidence of a man who knows his rights. It was as if his client had been picked up for speeding and Harrison, the attorney, were indignant about rough treatment by the police. What Harrison failed to grasp was the difference between the routine tidiness of textbook law and the emotional turmoil produced by the murder of two children. There were procedures to chart behavior, but professional detectives were inclined to bypass fussy technicalities under what they regarded as extreme pro-vocation. The truth was that the greater pressure was for a solution, and if they were rude in the process, it would be dismissed as well-intentioned zeal. Short of searing brutality, they could treat a client as they wished. Harold Harrison's knowledge of the law was sound, but flawed by artless naïveté. He would have been better served by an instinct for survival.

For Harrison, Joe Rorech represented an interruption in the endless list of divorce cases and petty crimes that made up his dreary practice. Harrison was a Queens lawyer—a prisoner of a stagnating backwater of the law. In his world there were no dazzling legal precedents. The courtroom victories were, in reality, little more than cajoling an indulgent Assistant District Attorney into downgrading a felony case into a mis-demeanor.

There were a hundred like Harold Harrison who anchored like fishermen around the Queens Criminal Courts Building. They practiced the law, but not in the sense of someone driven by the passions of Brandeis or Blackstone. Their law was a bitter compromise between loyalty to a client and the sensibilities of the District Attorney's office. It was smart, if you intended to keep alive a private practice, to mitigate the court-room antagonisms by buying lunch or drinks after work . . . by reiterating at convenient moments that it was all really a game, wasn't it? The smug young as-sistants in the District Attorney's office knew that they had the upper hand and could manipulate lawyers like puppets. In Manhattan young assistants would be scouting important firms for jobs, but in Queens they were career prosecutors. In Queens, prosecutors could cut off court-assigned cases, shutting out fees for mis-creant firms that depended on them to survive. It went without saying, but the lawyers knew they had to go along with the District Attorney's office when it counted. When it was important for the public image of the District Attorney, for example.

Harold Harrison usually knew how far he could go. At thirty-six, he was grateful for his profession and often said that if he hadn't been a lawyer he would have been doing something menial. Harrison was a mutation of New York's tenements. His father, Louis, had been a cab driver—one of a generation of self-executing men who willingly sacrificed themselves so that their sons could have that cloak of respectability, a profession. The idea of the law was implanted urgently and early, and if he dragged his feet, Harold went along. He came to the law at night, after working cabs and cargo during the day and sleeping on the subway to Brooklyn College.

Harrison was a barrel of a man. He seemed more comfortable working up a sweat tossing cargo than in a strangling shirt and tie. An aptitude test once showed he had a proclivity for police work. He even took the test for the FBI, but his mother was horrified at the prospect of her son carrying a gun. There was always a tinge of regret about the lost opportunity, and as an attorney Harold Harrison would still carry a pistol. In his Bayside house he maintained a bed for special detectives who needed to sleep near the station house.

If Harrison had an abiding sympathy with policemen, he knew he had been faithful to that elastic code of ethics of those who call themselves attorneys. He would protect his client past the point where others fell away. There was substance under the glib surface. Harrison might boast about extravagant gambling trips to Vegas or the islands, but he was sensible enough to hoard a valuable coin collection like a postponed annuity. (The police and the District Attorney's office were not displeased when the principal characters in this case later retained Harold Harrison to protect them.)

Harrison did not require an elaborate briefing. Jerry Piering and George Martin had breakfast and lunch with Harrison on a more or less regular basis when his connection to the case was only tangential. Harrison was a man who always spoke just below a shout. And in a place like the Pastrami King—a frantic delicatessen across the street from the courthouse where judges, court attendants, lawyers, police, and defendants shouted at one another with their mouths full of spicy food—it was not uncommon for his remarks to be picked up three tables away. The incestuous proximity produced an atmosphere thick with drifting pieces of information. Eavesdropping secretaries would go home and spread Piering's hunches across Queens like a virus. At first the phenomenon was misunderstood. The District Attorney's office came to believe that someone was passing along secrets to Alice Crimmins. The mundane explanation, that high police secrets swirled together with common table gossip, was too uncomplicated to accept. Instead, authorities searched for plots, intricate connections, compromised associates. There were transfers, inter-office bugging, and threats of reprisal. Security became tighter. Later, however, when the spawning route of the rumors became clear, the District Attorney's office found that the trickle of information worked against Alice. Security was relaxed and some rumors were deliberately leaked into luncheon conversations.

In December 1965, however, when Harrison became Joe Rorech's lawyer, Piering and Martin began to avoid him. In hallways of the courthouse, spotting Harrison, Martin would whisper "Cancer" and walk right by him.

Harrison was unruffled, even flattered. It was the first time he had considered himself dangerous. He was still Piering's and Martin's attorney; later the question of conflict of interest would become hopelessly tangled when Joe Rorech brought Alice Crimmins to Harrison as a client. Harrison would, at one point, be representing Joe Rorech when Rorech turned against Alice Crimmins. Harrison would also be handling legal affairs for the detectives prosecuting Alice.

But at the time Rorech came to Harrison, he was only another of Alice's long list of boyfriends. There was nothing complicated about it, except that Rorech's alibi was flimsy.

"Have you got anything to hide?" asked Harrison.
"Nothing. But they want me to take truth serum."
"Are you certain that you have nothing to hide?"
"Positive."
"OK," said Harrison, "let's take the tests."
Harrison's tactic was to drive straight through a challenge, daring the police to prove anything against his client. He won a wide range of concessions from the District Attorney's office, which would give up

more and more to entrap Alice Crimmins; like an addiction, the habit was bound to grow more expensive. Harrison was happy with the agreement. The District Attorney's men agreed that nothing said under the influence of the drug would be used against Rorech. Also, Harrison would get to see the test results first and delete whatever he felt could injure his client. It was clear to Harrison that the prosecutors were not interested in Joe Rorech. They merely wanted to pick his brain, not target him as a suspect. Harrison's obligation was to Rorech, not Alice Crimmins, and so he felt safe agreeing to the deal.

The authorities had no intention of being bound by the agreement. Harrison could select the doctor, but they would wire the room thoroughly to record anything Rorech said.

On December 6, 1965, at a laboratory on Main Street in Bay Shore, Long Island, Joe Rorech took the first of two sodium-pentothal tests. Dr. John Murphy administered eighteen cc's of the drug. The results of the test filled two pages.

> She went out with Mayor Wagner, Paul Screvane and hoods through Tony Grace, who is a New York contractor.
>
> She lived in a small apartment in Flushing. I was giving her $10–$50 a week. Tony was giving her dollars too.
>
> She said she didn't have any sex with Tony, but I felt she did.
>
> I was having sex with her too—three times a week for nine months. I stopped seeing her because her husband threatened a custody action. I went out with Alice's roommate Anita before Alice.
>
> Through it all I kept up sex with my wife. I always look for an outside girl. It flatters my ego. I realize I have to buy love. I still want to go out and have been going out with others.
>
> I don't necessarily go out with women for sex. I look for excitement and enjoyment.
>
> Alice—I felt sympathetic for her—no compassion for her—no love affair—but sex with her was fantastic. She would blow me—so would [my] wife . . .

171

I love my wife . . . way too much drinking—half quart of scotch a day, half home and half outside.

At this point his narrative, more like rambling, was interrupted with a question. He was brought back to the night of July 13/14:

I saw her two times—once she delivered shirts to me—once for cocktails. I think she liked me. She said she couldn't care less about her children. She didn't show them any affection but towards the end. She told me I satisfied her like no other man ever did. I loved her kids. They loved me. Maybe I like Missy a little better . . .

He had apparently confused the question and was still going on, and so the question was driven home again.

I phoned her that night at 10:30 or 11 p.m. or 11:30. I missed seeing her. I thought she was calmer than in months because she knew she was going to lose the kids. Her husband had so much against her.

He was interrupted with another question.

Did the kids get in the way of seeing her? Definitely not. I didn't want to lose Alice.

Alice said she had a meeting and might meet me later. I called her back at 2 a.m. from the Bourbon House—no answer. I was still dying to see her. I wanted to have sex with her. She wasn't home—there was no answer. I went next door to another bar— Club House West on Jericho Turnpike near the new Wantagh–Oyster Bay Parkway . . .

I feel like crying—love my wife so much. She deserves more.

There was a little scribble of his initials after this page of the transcript.

Eddie's body was found five days later—badly decomposed—probably intentional. Missie was strangled, probably accidentally with a scarf. She was found the next day in woods many miles apart. She was half a mile from home. The kids had to go with somebody they knew. Eddie was about a mile in the opposite direction. Both were in underbrush in woods —but not buried in the ground.

Papers said Alice was hysterical when the children were found. The husband works as a mechanic for TWA—good job. He was great in bed. Nobody knows why she left him and I know her better than anybody. She was very shy about undressing. She always wore her diaphragm.

Her meeting that night had something to do with the custody. She told me but I can't remember who.

That ended the first session, but the police were unsatisfied. Joe Rorech, they were convinced, was holding back. They dropped vague hints about exposing his triple life. Often Rorech would attend private parties at Club 82 in the East Village of Manhattan, known for its female impersonators. One of his friends, a man who called himself Hans Crystal, dressed like a woman.

"I don't think you should take any more tests," Rorech was told by Harrison, who felt his client had cooperated enough. He didn't know of the pressure that Kelly and others were bringing to bear about Joe's New York City life. They wanted to "turn" Rorech, make him an informer on either Alice or Eddie. In either case, they wanted Rorech as an agent. At a conference at the 107th detective squad room, without the advice of his attorney, Rorech agreed to take another sodium-pentothal test.

"There are a couple of very puzzling aspects to your answers," said Kelly. First, there was this business about Alice saying she was to meet another person. She might have been attempting to deflect Rorech's advances or he could be lying. Truth serum is not infallible, so he could even be lying about the second call. Neither his cousin, Bob Rorech, nor his business partner, Dick Nevins, had been present at that attempted second call at 2:00 a.m. when he got no answer. In addition, it had seemed that Joe was showing self-pity during the first session. He claimed he

didn't care for Alice, and yet he boasted that only he
satisfied her. He threw in important names. All in all,
the test was inconclusive. Eleven days later Dr. Murphy
injected twenty cc's of sodium pentothal into Rorech's
left arm.

She wouldn't exactly tell me who she was seeing
when I first called her. She was hedging. I wanted to
see her, but she was going to be busy . . . The whole
thing has been a headache. It could have gone on
better. I just have to do these things and she was
really good. She went for me.

At 11:30, she was nice, friendly, chit-chatted. I
was never in love with her. A tramp in her own way,
but very lovely, just chit-chatted. She said it was
very, very important.

I hope and pray to God that it's not her. She didn't
want Eddie to go live with her husband . . . Why did
she give me the brush off? I presume it was money.
She never asked for it. She wouldn't tell me why she
was separated from her husband . . .

She told me to call back to 2 A.M. I expected to see
her.

Another question.

What did she say at 2 a.m.? I wish I could remember—chit chat. She was at home. I don't think she
had anybody there. She does not make a habit of
bringing women or men into her place . . .

No, no—she wasn't home at 2 a.m.—was 11:30
call.

I'm sorry I got involved with her. She positively
told me who she was going to meet that night. I think
it's Eddie, her ex-husband. I think she was going to
meet Eddie. She told me to call about 2 a.m. but that
it would be too late to go out . . .

I went home about 4:30 from Holiday Inn motel
in Plainview.

I don't know why she wanted to meet her husband.
She hated him. He had been putting pressure on her
recently. He constantly threatened to take the children
away from her. She feared the children would be-

come like her husband. . . . I never met him. No, I'm sorry, I did meet him when I was going out with Anita before Alice. It took eight months to switch from Anita to Alice. Anita was mad and wanted to kill us both.

Gloria [Rorech's wife] is wonderful—has them all beat except Ginger [another girlfriend]. Why do I have to go out.

I tried to destroy myself financially a long time—it could have been self-punishment. I let my business go to pot because of women.

I became Catholic just before marriage in 1949 to make her happy. You should meet Gloria. They don't come any better. You'd love her.

I called Anita a few days ago at her office. I'd have a drink with her. I get lonely. She chit-chatted with me. We're going to meet next week. I have to call her again. She's exceptionally good-looking. . . .

She's a secretary. She was very friendly with Alice. Alice wanted to take off on her own. Alice didn't hear from her for a year. Maybe I think Alice called her to cover me up because of the custody business. Alice didn't want Tony Grace to know about me. She was going out with Tony. I didn't want to think she was going to bed with Tony. She covered herself good.

He initialed the last page of the transcript. What were the police to make of this weepy, contradictory statement? The glimpses into his heart were carefully hedged and protected against exposure by self-serving rationale. She didn't sleep with Grace, he would rather believe. And even if she did, it was only because he paid her more. Anyway, Rorech didn't love her. He loved Gloria.

The police found it very difficult to accept anything he said. At one point he claimed she was there for the 2 a.m. phone call. Then he denied it. But he finally gave details.

If Rorech's defenses had been lowered by the sodium pentothal, it was clear that some of them could not be reached by drugs. As a witness, Kelly and Brady de-

175

cided, Rorech was unreliable. But that did not mean they couldn't make use of him.

Was Rorech willing to turn double agent? He had very little choice. He needed to buy time. The bills were starting to come in—$357.25 from Lord & Taylor, unpaid; a $1431.89 judgment for Texaco, Inc.; a $15,001 judgment for Mutual Associates. There would be other judgments in Nassau and Suffolk courts for unpaid bills—$412.60 from the Long Island Pool Co., Inc.; a $13,147.59 judgment for the Franklin National Bank; $938.25 for American Express Co. The Huntington Savings and Loan Association would win a judgment against Rorech and his wife of $30,000, foreclosing the mortgage on his Dix Hills home. The judgments would total $56,748.51. The world of Joseph Rorech was crumbling like a stale cake.

36

Alice Crimmins was being isolated. One by one, the people close to her were being transformed into police agents. They would agree, under relentless pressure, to allow their homes, their telephones, and sometimes their persons to be wired for sound. It was all done on the premise that the detectives were only trying to solve the murders of two innocent children. The target of all of this attention was Alice Crimmins. No one had to be told—not even her mother, Mrs. Burke, who allowed Phil Brady to install a microphone in her telephone. (This device never worked satisfactorily. The only usable transcriptions the police were ever able to obtain were conversations between Alice's mother and the dog Brandy inside the apartment.)

Joe Rorech had effectively been "turned" and would

take Alice to motel rooms where recorders had been planted to trap her into some kind of admission. What Rorech didn't know was that even as he acted as a double agent, others were taping his conversations. The people he met socially and in business were often wired for sound and would lead him in strange verbal dances. While he checked on Alice, he was being covered. There was no way for those involved to know where the circle began or ended. Margie Fischer would check on Grace, who checked on Alice. Detective Phil Brady was wired when he spoke to Margie Fischer. Jerry Piering recorded the briefing sessions with Phil Brady. The only person in the case not actively engaged in police spying was Alice Crimmins. She was not ignorant of it. Early on, in the midst of a conversation with Joe Rorech, she found strange wires poking out of her mother's telephone. And so her talk began to take on a kind of indirection. Gradually, she accepted a third presence whenever she spoke.

In such a world, it was not odd that nothing said could be absolutely trusted. Who could tell what was a coded reference to something else? Who could say for certain that something said to a second party was not in fact meant for a third party? Words were judged for prosecution purposes alone. Every sentence took on multiple layers of meaning. In the winter of 1966, during a telephone conversation with Rorech, Alice talked about her exhaustion, but said hopefully that the case appeared to be near solution:

RORECH: I don't believe it.
CRIMMINS: If only they were. The only thing is they're ready to solve it, but I'm afraid they are trying to solve it by me. I don't like that.
RORECH: I don't like that either.

The language is vague enough to convey several meanings, but the police singled out one meaning. Alice was eager to have the case solved, but she was afraid she was the target of the solution.

If there was one sorry hinge in this encirclement, it was the conscription of Anthony Grace. Alice trusted him more than any of the others. She trusted her

177

brother, John Burke, but she knew that he was co-operating with the police. However, she didn't think her brother would provide them with material of any value. But Tony Grace had become more than a lover—he was a substitute father. She had confided in the Bronx contractor as she had in no one else.

Detective Brady wanted to warn Alice that Tony Grace wasn't the friend she thought he was. One cold night he sat alone at the listening post in Whitestone Hospital. He had just ended a telephone conversation with Grace. In a kind of man-to-man fashion, Grace had delivered heretofore unuttered confidences. Alice was merely a proficient tart, he told Brady, but nothing more. Her hopes of eventual marriage, he said, were idiotic. He had no intention of getting married again, especially not to someone like Alice Crimmins.

Brady brooded over the conversation. He thought of Alice, exposed on a battlefield surrounded by snipers. In Alice's apartment the listening devices picked up noises, movement, but no conversation. Assuming that Eddie wasn't home, he started across the street. In his pocket was the tape of Grace dismissing the relationship with Alice. When Brady knocked on the door, Eddie answered. Brady, who had expected Alice, was shocked. He fumbled for a moment and made up an excuse for the visit. They had a drink together until Alice got home and then Brady left. He couldn't very well play Tony's tape with Eddie present. So the warning he had intended to deliver was filed somewhere in the back of his mind.

At the beginning of the investigation Anthony Grace had intended to keep as much distance between himself and Alice Crimmins as possible. His first real interrogation was held in the privacy of the detective command center at the 102nd Precinct on August 5, 1965. Harry Shields and Jerry Byrnes were present, but the questioning was handled with obsequious politeness by Deputy Inspector Thomas McGuire.

MC GUIRE: For the record, will you give me your pedigree?

GRACE: Yes, Anthony Grace . . . G R A C E, Bronx, New York. KI 7-6321. Business telephone IN 1-3000.

178

MC GUIRE: I assume that's the number you called from the boat at the time of the cruise?

GRACE: Yes. We called that a couple of times. Yes. Or that call is either one of the two.

MC GUIRE: Tony, I have already had a chance to speak with you briefly.

GRACE: Yes.

MC GUIRE: As I indicated in the talk with you and with Mike LaPenna, your attorney, we are not concerned with your activities or with the activities of anyone— we have spoken with a thousand people in connection with this investigation and I hope you understand that context. I think I explained to you before these are all police officers. . . . [At this point McGuire gently introduces the officers present and then brings Grace back to the night of the disappearance, when Alice called him at the Capri bar in the Bronx.] I want to go back over that, Tony, and make sure. I know I spoke to you before, but I would like to know how you fixed the time as 11 o'clock. Could you be wrong or is that an approximate . . . if it is . . . is that an approximation?

GRACE: No. I'd say not because we left there a little after 11:30 to go out and eat.

MC GUIRE: Where?

GRACE: We went to the Ripple's.

Grace left, he said, with the owner, Tony Gordon, and three women known as "the bowling girls." McGuire's questioning proceeded with exceeding tenderness, considering that Grace had been caught lying— in his previous statements he had claimed he had never left the Capri. But he was a man of substance and standing. The names that McGuire dreaded mentioning were the names of people to whom he owed his job.

MC GUIRE: If somebody said you were in Ripple's earlier that night who would be right? Who would be wrong? Would you be correct or would they be correct? Here is why I'm asking you and I will be very frank with you; you see our information is that you were in the area of 10:30 in the Ripple's. Would that be wrong?

179

GRACE: That would be wrong. Yes. I will tell you why it
would be wrong.

MC GUIRE: We have information to that effect. That's
what I'd like to hear.

GRACE: It's got to be wrong. But here, I'll work it backwards. I left the office around 8:30. Near 8:30. I
picked up my wife. We went to dinner . . .

MC GUIRE: At the Capri?

GRACE: No. We went to the King Cole. We finished
having dinner around 10 o'clock or so. I asked her if
she wanted to stop off for a drink at the Capri. She
said she had better not. I said OK. She said to drop
her home. So I dropped her off. She asked for a paper
and then I took her home. I must have got back to the
Capri around quarter to eleven. I had two or three
drinks there. Then they wanted to eat and we left there.
So it had to be around 11:30.

There was no accusation in the questioning. It was
all well-mannered—someone had made a mistake and
they were only here as gentlemen to rectify time and
circumstance. It was not the way they questioned Alice
—at her they pointed fingers, her they called a liar.
With Grace they continued talking about the trip to
Ripple's.

MC GUIRE: Well, Tony, you went there with three . . . as
you indicated and as I have spoken to you, with three
bowling girls. Who were they?

GRACE: I only know their first names.

MC GUIRE: You know only their first names?

GRACE: Yes.

MC GUIRE: What were their first names?

GRACE: One was . . . Let's see now, there's five of them
in all.

MC GUIRE: This was a Tuesday night. Go ahead.

GRACE: I think one is Sylvia. One is Marie . . . that's all
I know them by.

MC GUIRE: Who drove your car?

GRACE: Sylvia drove over. She wanted to drive.

MC GUIRE: I understand you wouldn't let her drive again,
by the way.

GRACE: She's a fast driver. As a matter of fact, going

over Tony Gordon got a little bit upset and he took the wheel coming back.

MC GUIRE: Because of her driving?

GRACE: That's right.

MC GUIRE: Are they all married?

GRACE: Yes. They're all married.

McGuire struggled to frame his next question. He was faced with Tony Grace, sitting with his back braced, his defenses alert, his protective devices at his fingertips. McGuire moved with care.

MC GUIRE: Let me ask you something, Tony. I know you'll be frank. I'm sure you will give us . . . You know in my first meeting with you I spoke with you and Mr. LaPenna. I have spoken with Charlie Fellini here and we are only concerned with what will furnish us the truth about the death of these two children. That's the only thing we are concerned with, and I have explained it to you before and I am repeating myself, but I don't mind repeating myself because it's something I want to emphasize and I don't mind repeating myself.

GRACE: Well, Lieutenant [here Grace reminds Deputy Inspector McGuire of their relative positions in life by instantly demoting him], as I said to you before, I'm not going to lie about it. If there is anything I can do to help you I will be glad.

MC GUIRE: That's what I like to think, because I can't see why any guy wouldn't tell us the truth about two innocent children and that goes particularly for you, Tony. You had an association or a friendship—you pick the word—with Alice?

GRACE: That's right.

MC GUIRE: Despite that . . . I don't know whether you have a deep affection for her or that she has for you. . . . Regardless of that, in view of the circumstances now existing today with these two children dead, I still will expect the truth from you.

GRACE: That's what I'm going to give.

MC GUIRE: I really mean it.

GRACE: Yes.

MC GUIRE: But one consideration of this as far as the police are concerned . . . we have spoken with almost a thousand people in connection with this including your own friends who were here this morning, and I have told them I expect them to be telling the truth. If this case goes . . . remains unsolved . . . if this case continues . . . this is not a threat, it is just an observation . . . we are not squeamish . . . I'm not squeamish about using any means in order to arrive at the truth. Now, I have refrained from any public exposure of witnesses in this case . . .

GRACE: Yes.

The threats were there, however, just under the surface politeness.

MC GUIRE: It is the policy that I use and everyone in this room has been using, but if the situation reaches a point where because of problems that we are constrained to put witnesses before the grand jury . . . if we do so, of course, it will be far beyond my province to safeguard their identity.

GRACE: I know.

MC GUIRE: I mean, I'd like you to know.

GRACE: I know.

It was not necessary for McGuire to spell out what he meant. Tony Grace knew he could not shield his relationship with Alice and he would have to expose those parts of his life where his dignity was invested. He was vulnerable to the kind of scandal against which there is no defense. He could salvage his power and his higher friends, but he was in for more than a dollop of shame. He seemed to sag a little in his chair as he endured McGuire's questions about his affair with Alice Crimmins.

Yes, he had helped Alice when she was served with custody papers. She had asked for legal help and he complied.

GRACE: I think I called Sal LoCurto [then Deputy Sanitation Commissioner], who used to be my attorney in my construction business—not personal, but in the construction business.

MC GUIRE: Yes.

GRACE: And, actually, he couldn't handle the case . . .

The other lawyer recommended by LoCurto was Michael LaPenna. Grace had spoken to Alice four or five times about the custody battle. McGuire wanted to know about Alice's attitude. Had she been desperate?

GRACE: Well, she once told me that in her separation agreement that he couldn't take the children. I naturally had not read the agreement and I am not a lawyer and I said, Rusty, I think you are wrong.

MC GUIRE: Of course she is wrong. If they could prove some way that she was an unfit mother that agreement is vitiated.

GRACE: I think it was a Friday night she called me and Sal came to the office this Friday night and we went to the doctor's office in Whitestone for an injection. That's the night we went to Ripple's—Sal and myself alone and nobody else. We were there awhile and I told Sal I had spoken to Rusty and she told me that in her agreement the kids couldn't be taken and I told her I thought she was wrong, but anyway would he mind talking to her. I called her from the Ripple's. I think this was about two or three Saturdays before it happened and Sal spoke to her for about 20 minutes I think. I don't know what they talked about. I wasn't near him. I walked back to the bar. I think he told her that if she were unfit they could take the children away.

MC GUIRE: As a result of that in your meeting with her after that . . . what was her attitude about the children?

GRACE: Well, Inspector, from the time of the custody struggle I didn't see her very much. I think I only saw her once or twice. I didn't know when the custody issue took place or what she was served, but I stayed away from her. I didn't want to get involved. I didn't think I saw her but once or twice—at tops three times—during that period. I talked to her almost every other night or so. I thought I shouldn't see her and she shouldn't see me. In other words, if she wanted to go out for a night she should consider the children. We didn't discuss it very much.

And yet she had called several times on July 13. But Grace said he was involved in business and then took his wife to dinner and forgot to call Alice back.

MC GUIRE: The point I'm trying to make, Tony, is that there is something odd here. There is this custody struggle with these children and you are a friend of hers—a close friend of hers. She has quite a bit of affection for you, from what I gather. Which is all right, but I know that you were the person she would confide in. What did she say to you at 11 o'clock?

GRACE: Well, Inspector, like I said before, I don't remember. Here's what happened. She first called me and asked me what had happened—why I hadn't called her, so I told her I had problems in the office. I don't remember whether I told her what the incident was or not. I don't remember that well enough. She asked me what time I got through—what I was doing—when I was going to leave and who was there. I said I was going to have a drink and then going to leave. She wanted to join me for a drink.

MC GUIRE: She said she wanted to join you?

GRACE: She said she wanted to come over and have a drink with me. I said where are you?

MC GUIRE: That night?

GRACE: Yes. I said where are you? I thought she might be in the neighborhood. She said I'm home. . . . I think she said she was painting the foyer or something. I told her she couldn't come over for a drink because I was leaving. I think the last thing she asked me was if the bowling girls were there.

MC GUIRE: Who?

GRACE: The bowling girls. I said no, but they were there, and frankly that's all that was said. It was a very, very short conversation.

MC GUIRE: Well, how did she sound? Did she sound desperate, as though she was anxious to meet you, or what?

GRACE: The other inspector [Michael Clifford] asked me the same thing. I can't remember any disturbance. She was a little angry that I hadn't called her. I explained I had a problem. I don't remember whether I discussed it or not, and that went over all right. And then when

I told her the bowling girls weren't there that seemed to go over all right, too . . .

MC GUIRE: Let me refresh your recollection. I'll give you a loaded question. Did she mention that she had any trouble with the children that night. That one of the children was acting up—that she had to slap them?

GRACE: No. Not a thing. She didn't mention the children at all. Didn't mention them.

McGuire turned to the subject of the winter cruise when Alice had gone off and left the children with the maid. That cruise had led directly to the custody suit.

MC GUIRE: On the day before she had been speaking to another person [presumably a high city official also on the cruise], as a result of information we have obtained in connection with this investigation. She talked about the cruise. You are familiar with that cruise? You know the cruise? You know the cruise I'm referring to? We have all the records on that. I guess you know that we have checked that.

GRACE: I put her on the cruise.

MC GUIRE: I know you did. I know you are very frank about it.

GRACE: I told you everything about that. [In fact, Grace had locked her in a washroom until the boat had sailed.]

MC GUIRE: Did she discuss the cruise and the fact that this could put her in a bad light about the cruise and the fact that she left the children and went on a cruise with three men? And we know, of course, how she spent the time on the cruise. We checked that. I wouldn't want any double talk on that, particularly if there were conversations about that. We know exactly what happened on the cruise and that would be important in the custody struggle.

GRACE: Yes.

MC GUIRE: Did she discuss the substance of the information on that in order to assist her in the custody struggle? I can see that would be a source of concern to her if information and affidavits of information were presented, showing that she left the children in their residence. The maid gave the children to her husband and here she is going on a cruise with three men and sharing

185

quarters with two. Did she discuss that with you on that night or any other night to help her retain custody? If she did I would like to know.

GRACE: That was discussed but I don't recall whether she brought it up or I brought it up.

MC GUIRE: Would you endeavor to suppress that? Why would you worry about that?

Tony Grace took a swallow of water and wiped the moisture from his forehead. One of the detectives excused himself for a moment out of sheer disgust. The detective had come into the room with some regard for the weight of Tony Grace's wealth. But the life of high merriment was in fact a dreary round trip into bars where, for a price, you could have liquor or women. One seemed to matter as much as the other. The self-contempt spread outward.

The questioning continued.

GRACE: I was involved in the cruise . . . and for that reason I think she told him [Eddie] about the cruise and Mike LaPenna told me what the other attorney had said. I told her again they couldn't take the children away from her because they were all lying and this and that.

MC GUIRE: Who said this?

GRACE: She told me that.

MC GUIRE: She knows they're not lies. She was talking through her hat.

GRACE: She told me that . . . She mentioned that some . . . in other words what Mike LaPenna had told me . . . he didn't tell me everything . . . but he told me some of the things the other attorney had said to him about one of the things was that he came to the house to serve papers . . . She got very upset about it. So I told Sal LoCurto I didn't believe it. So I brought it up to Mike LaPenna and Mike asked him point blank and he finally admitted she had [gotten] a coat of some sort. I told her the truth could be damaging. She said she left the children with a maid. I said you don't leave children for one or two days or even overnight without proper care. If it gets into court it's rough. Something was mentioned about the custody.

MC GUIRE: Tell me. I have spoken to you and I have spoken to LaPenna away from the office. I hope Mr.

LaPenna appreciates it and I think he does. I am going to ask you a very frank question. Of course you know it would not be proper for me to discuss the extent of our evidence or what we have. We have information which at the proper time will be properly utilized. But you are a close friend of Alice—as I have said before there is no one here who is not a veteran police officer . . .

GRACE: I know.

MC GUIRE: It is the same as if you are talking to me alone. We have no intention in any way, shape or form and no one is going to force you to discuss it at any time and it is not going to be discussed by the police . . .

GRACE: I believe you.

MC GUIRE: I want to ask you a question. You have of course discussed this with Charlie Fellini [a developer of the Freedomland amusement park], and Sal LoCurto. What happened to those children? I know your association with respect to her. These are two innocent kids here.

GRACE: That's right.

MC GUIRE: These are two innocent kids. It is not a pretty picture. I will show you a worse picture. [He is showing pictures of the dead children on morgue slabs.] That's a little girl looking up. Have you ever seen a more horrible picture than that? These are two wonderful innocent kids. Tony, I have never met you before now. You are not a friend of mine. You are not an informer. I don't want to know about narcotics and gambling.

GRACE: Yes.

MC GUIRE: I couldn't care less. But I think that you, as a man, as a person . . . I think I am entitled to know—when I say that, I mean the police are entitled to know if you know anything further.

GRACE: Inspector, I can't help you at all.

MC GUIRE: You are not involved in the death of these children?

GRACE: Definitely not.

MC GUIRE: Then you are not involved? Is that the truth?

GRACE: Positively, no.

MC GUIRE: If you are not involved, then . . .

GRACE: Yes?

MC GUIRE: If you are not involved then I think the Police

Department and the people, and, as a man of conscience, I think the Police Department is entitled to know it.

GRACE: Inspector, I wish I could help.

MC GUIRE: Have you discussed this?

GRACE: I have discussed it many times.

MC GUIRE: You saw these children? You knew them?

GRACE: Not too well.

MC GUIRE: You've seen them?

GRACE: Beautiful kids. I saw them at the dedication of the Verrazano Bridge.

MC GUIRE: Have you considered the possibility . . . I want to tell you something. This is not in the press. These children were not sexually abused. This little girl was not sexually abused. The opinion about the boy is not provable, but a warranted one. This is not a case of a degenerate taking one child. You are a very sensible and responsible person. You wouldn't be in the position you are and the friends and associates you have in this. What do you think happened to those children?

GRACE: Inspector, I discussed it again and again with many people—my friends. I tried to point her out. I tried to point him out. I tried to point out anybody else. I tried to point out any of their friends. I can't figure anything out. I will be very frank with you. I can't figure out how any parents—him or her—I never met him—could harm children. These children were out of this world. I only saw them four or five times. I can't see where either of them would have any advantage to gain. First of all, it would have been temporary. I'll give you my idea—if it happened to one of them accidentally, what about the other one? If either one of them is trying to hide something, it's a mystery. I talked with Charlie. I talked with Sal several times and I can't figure it out. I can't point a finger at her or him or I can't also find a reason for it.

MC GUIRE: Let me tell you something, Tony.

GRACE: Yes.

MC GUIRE: I have talked to you now and you are not under oath.

GRACE: Right.

MC GUIRE: I can say at this time—it's not within my province to indicate any of this—I think the Police Department has been more than fair with you and everybody else connected with this case.

GRACE: I think so.

MC GUIRE: I would like to think that if you did come up with an answer—if there is an answer which presents itself to you—without being an informer—I would like to know that this information would be forthcoming—I would not care how—to the Police Department.

GRACE: You can depend on that. I wouldn't care. Inspector, I wish I could help. It's a terrible thing. I've gone with a lot of girls. . . .

MC GUIRE: That's not our concern.

GRACE: I'm not in love with Rusty. I never was . . . I still go with other girls.

The detectives in the room joined in the questioning now, pressing Grace about whether Alice could have gone looking for him that night, hammering at the eleven o'clock call, probing at Grace's feelings about Alice Crimmins.

GRACE: When I heard that her husband was around the house—I don't think I was around the house since February—in other words I heard that she was separated from her husband and he was happy where he was. As soon as I heard that he was around the house, I said, "Fine, I don't go to her house again." I would tell her to take a cab. . . . I'm not going to stick my neck out. This is during the custody period. I mean, it's nonsense.

She talked about her husband to Grace and he advised her to go back to Eddie, he told McGuire.

GRACE: I told her several times that she ought to go back to her husband—that she was young and all that kind of stuff and that the way she was going she would end up in the gutter. I figured that to myself. I didn't say that to her. She said that her husband was never home and she was home and all that stuff. It didn't look good. But the thing that occurred to me was that there was something wrong with him. I think I mentioned it before.

MC GUIRE: Did she indicate that she thought he might have

189

been queer? If he were, any woman would be disturbed with her marriage.

GRACE: I never met the man. I can't really say whether he was or not. She said he was never home during her marriage. I don't know whether that's true or not because who do you believe?

Grace conceded that he paid for Alice's cruise and plane fare home. Margie Fischer and Alice Crimmins not only went to the *bon voyage* party and then got trapped on the boat, but met the men from the cruise when they returned and went to the Crossways Motel with the men for a welcome-home party.

MC GUIRE: OK, Tony, I'll be in touch with you.

Tony Grace had become a police ally.

37

"Queens . . . is a borough of New York City and it has over 2,000,000 people. But it is a very small place. It is a collection of small towns that spill into each other and the people who live in the towns that spill into each other, when they get in the subway for the ride to their jobs in Manhattan, always say that they are 'going to the city.' "

—*Jimmy Breslin,*
the Oracle of Queens

In the winter of 1965/66 the rats started moving back into Flushing Meadow Park. The World's Fair had packed up its international condiments, along with the exotic nomads who camped around its fringes for two years and then, like birds who irresistibly follow some distant scent in the wind, migrated in search of the action . . . to Montreal, or to Tokyo, or to Houston.

Measured by thermal charts, it was a mild season. But a field of ice crawled inexorably over those parts of Queens where the Alice Crimmins case had frozen into an obsession. Alice was free, or at least not under any direct police constraint, enjoying some measure of anonymity in her new address and her maiden name. During the day she worked in a variety of secretarial jobs under a succession of vinyl wigs. She undertook a course in Speedwriting, but the discipline bored her and she dropped out of the class, devising her own method of symbols and scrawls to take quick dictation.

At night she would drink herself into a numb sanctuary, mumbling to whatever companion that the children were angels in heaven now—it was something she remembered, some dim priestly consolation that came out under the alcohol—that the children were better off, Monsignor Schultheiss had told her, they were angels in heaven now. In a voice husky with whiskey, Alice would repeat her litany—they wouldn't have to endure the scorn of people who watched for every deviant sign.

The police had set up a sound room in the basement of Alice's apartment house, and the taping never stopped. Somewhere in the endless spools of Alice's life during that period is recorded the plaintive half-wish that her dead children were now "angels in heaven," looking down at her plight in sublime pity.

There were, of course, for Alice, the men. It was not a small consolation to the police, but between the summer and spring the lively flash of her smile had curdled into something sad.

The detectives had done all that could be expected and more. The traps had been baited and set. The friends and relatives had undergone relentless questioning and acquiesced in whatever entrapments were asked of them. No move that Alice made went unwatched, no sound unheard. And yet it all came to nothing. The frustration was teeth-gnashing. The neighborhoods had been canvassed and recanvassed. The whereabouts of anyone remotely connected to the case on the night of July 13/14 was recorded in the more than 2000 DD5's—detective reports—that accumulated faster than any one person could read. Again and again detectives went back over the same ground, talking to the same people. Those questioned were asked to rack their memories for something that would help the police. It might seem too silly to bring up, it might seem totally insignificant, but the police were begging for some forgotten sound, some second sight.

Under that kind of pressure, there would always be

someone who remembered something . . . something perhaps real, perhaps imagined . . .

There were random possibilities that presented themselves to the police—promising leads that would dissipate but had to be checked out carefully. A fifteen-year-old boy with a troubled history seemingly committed suicide two weeks after the killings of Missy and Eddie. He had been a problem in school and had told a teacher that he was responsible for the deaths of the Crimmins children. The teacher said the boy had confessed to a priest.

He was a tall youth who always wore a baseball cap. He had been born brain-damaged and was a familiar figure in the Kew Gardens Hills neighborhood, although he lived in Elmhurst. From the night of the murders, however, he didn't leave his room except to see his teacher and the priest. One day, in the basement of his Elmhurst home, he blew his head off with a twelve-gauge shotgun. The police quickly dismissed it as accidental, although in order to pull the trigger of the gun with a twenty-six-inch barrel, the boy would have had to use his toe. The police went through the motions of an investigation. They spoke to the teacher. The priest invoked religious privilege and the detectives were willing to drop it. The boy was the son of a police officer and no one wanted that kind of scandal connected to the department. The official report would give "Accidental" as the cause of death, and any attempt to link it to the Crimmins case was rejected.

There was another hopeful lead. A janitor from a nearby housing project had disappeared immediately after the killings. The man had a history of erratic behavior. He once had attacked a woman in a supermarket, threatening to "get her kids" for some forgotten insult. The man was found in Detroit that winter after a long binge. He was in a hospital ward for recovering alcoholics. A doctor watched as the detectives questioned the man.

"We want to talk to you about the Crimmins case," said one of the detectives, and the man started to tremble violently. The detectives exchanged meaningful looks, as if they had both detected an unmistakable sign of guilt.

"He's a drunk," whispered the doctor, noting the detectives' heightened interest. "He's been shaking like that for days."

The detectives bore down on the man's story. He had left New York two days before the disappearance. He had gone to his sister's house in Philadelphia, then drifted on a stream of cheap wine, landing, finally, in a Detroit hospital ward.

The man's story checked out. The sister in Philadelphia said he had been with her on July 13. She remembered reading about the disappearance and asking her brother if the location was anywhere near where he used to work. And so he was eliminated from the list of suspects.

The time for a breakthrough was past and a kind of plodding inevitability settled over the case. Veteran detectives know that if a case isn't solved within the first few weeks, it is likely to be dismissed or forgotten. The fickle public wants fresh outrages on the front pages and the commanders are slaves to the public.

There were weekly update meetings at the 102nd detective command headquarters for Queens. But the silences became longer and more painful. Inspector Joseph ("The Clam") Coyle, the borough commander, would sit back in his chair, chewing on his cigar, reproachfully waiting for his subordinates to announce the breakthrough.

But there was seldom anything new. They could drag out a tape on a new lover, but the men around the table had already grown tired of playing tapes. At first they had fascinated the police as if there were some mysterious clue in the fierce couplings. At the early weekly meetings, doors were guarded for security. Shades were drawn, as if the sound itself could be seen. Only those closest to the case were allowed inside the room. The tape hummed for a moment as the machine found its voice, and then there was the jangle of a telephone.

Alice's voice was light and, as always, seductive. The man on the other end asked if she were busy and she said no, come over. Bring Chinese food, she said.

What kind? asked the man. Any kind, she said, I like any kind.

They skipped over the sounds of preparation: cleaning glasses, putting away clothing, straightening pillows, setting a table, freshening her makeup. Then the man came in. She had drinks ready, in her thoughtful fashion. They had dinner, laughing a lot, refilling their glasses. Only the men crouched over the winding machines in hidden compartments seem to brood about the dead children; at least, that is what they told themselves as they listened. After dinner Alice and her date had more drinks and there was that awkward pause before someone made a move, one way or the other. "Let's dance," said Alice, turning on a record player.

"When she moved against you," explained a man who had once fallen under Alice's charms, "it was a unique experience. It was as if every surface of her body strained for some sensual interface. There was a kind of melting that took place; she dropped all her inhibitions." It had been several years since the encounter and the man was still awed by it. "She reached down to touch me and then she was pulling me in the bedroom. The thing I remember is that there were no lights in the entire apartment. It was black. She disappeared into the bathroom and left me on the bed. I was naked when she crawled in beside me—and she was also naked."

He was a middle-aged man and had known many women under many circumstances, but the memory of that single night still burned like a pilot light. "I can't describe what it was like. I can say that she was an animal, but that demeans it. She was all over me. Touching. Crying. I still had possession of myself, mind you. I was thinking about the lights and the darkness. But I'm certain, I'm positive, that she didn't have another thought in her head. She was possessed in a way that I have never seen another woman sexually."

The sounds coming from her—the cries and whispers of passion—"Fuckmefuckme, oh, please fuckme"—rolled into perfect circles on the tape machines.

The man who went through the experience with Alice Crimmins that night he brought the Chinese food was

195

shattered. "I guess she was a nympho," he said, then re-gretted the description. "No, I can't say that. How can I say that? But you have to appreciate, here I had just gotten through dinner with this perfectly controlled person; this person who cleaned every dish almost before it was dirty, and I was overwhelmed. I have my own normal passions. But I've thought about it a lot ever since—what it must have been like to reach that level. She was on an entirely different level—screaming, whispering, scratching, pleading, whimpering. It was as if the whole experience was orgasmic—a continual climax. Afterward we got dressed—again in the dark—and she pecked me on the cheek goodnight."

At first, when Inspector Coyle asked them, "Where is your proof?" they would play him the tapes, watching his face for some sign of agreement, a raised eyebrow or at least some bawdy laugh. But Joe Coyle was called "The Clam" because his feelings and thoughts were hidden under layers of defenses. Where is your proof? he would ask with his eyes, but all they had were their suspicions and the miles of tape.

For the hard-core—Jerry Piering, Bill Corbett, Jerry Byrnes, John Kelly, and Harry Shields—the tapes were solid evidence of guilt. These men were Catholics and there was a blurring between their religious and pro-fessional dogmas. All cases are susceptible to solution; if they didn't crack the Crimmins case, it was a failure in understanding the testament of their work. What they had to do was seek some sign of guilt; and Alice Crimmins provided that, but in the religious sense. They would play the tapes and hear the guilt and eventually became confused about precisely which guilt they were accusing her of.

And Alice did not help herself. When John Kelly asked her out for a drink, she went, impervious, taunt-ingly indifferent to his intentions.

By late summer Joe Rorech was urging Alice to get a lawyer, since the police surveillance was intense and hostile and she was obviously the target of the inves-tigation. Rorech suggested that she hire his own at-torney, Harold Harrison, since they were on the same side and it would save money and duplication.

So on September 27, 1966, Alice Crimmins walked into Harold Harrison's office at 89–02 Sutphin Boulevard, across the street from a complex of civil and surrogate's courts. It was a cool day and Alice had on a sober hat and a pink coat, adding an extra glow to her strawberry hair. And when she entered the sober law offices, she created that special murmur that comes to scandalous women. Harold Harrison was at the door to meet her. He held her chair. He lit her cigarettes. Did she want something to drink? They sat in the office of his partner, Martin Baron, a guarded man who could not resist Alice's spell—she was wearing a tight dress with the incongruity of a little-girl collar, and that face! It was a face that sucked a room of attention.

She carried herself with the pride of someone unapproachable, someone enduring an unspeakable wrong. Harrison asked her a few preliminary questions, until he realized that he was on trial. Under her half-lidded gaze Alice was making her judgments. She knew many men like Harold Harrison; perhaps too many . . . men living on the lip of success in white-on-white shirts, men who threw nothing less than a twenty-dollar bill on a bar . . . men who would extend themselves to impress her. She could manipulate such men, charm them into granting her wishes. She preferred this kind of relationship, now that she had found herself abandoned by men of larger ambition. She would choose men she could control rather than the fickle men of convenient loyalties.

Alice Crimmins answered Harold Harrison's questions, asserted her innocence, and made clear that there were aspects of her life that would remain closed to Harrison. She would not be badgered again. Her sex life was private, or, at least, as much of it as she could control. She closed her eyes against all the intrusions of the past year.

Alice had decided to hire an attorney because of an incident that took place on September 9.

Rorech had picked her up at the Westbury station of the Long Island Railroad, having reserved a room at the Kings Grant Inn.

He was armed with a bottle of Scotch and a bottle

of champagne, but first they stopped for a drink. At the inn, Alice disappeared into the bathroom for her ablutions. She had bathed and was in the process of shaving her legs when she saw a headline in a copy of the *Long Island Press:* "Thirteen Top Hoods Arrested in Queens Restaurant." She covered herself, came out of the bathroom, and lay on the bed reading the story.

During the last desperate months of his incumbency, Nat Hentel had resorted to supercop-style prosecution to steal the thunder of the apparent front runner, Tom Mackell. The raid on La Stella Restaurant on Queens Boulevard was supposed to be an example of his fearless brand of law enforcement. To his friends in the press corps, Hentel privately confided that the raid amounted to a "little apalachin," since he had caught thirteen mob figures having dinner together. The story never reached Hentel's expectations, but it did fascinate Alice Crimmins as she sat on the bed of the Kings Grant Inn. There was one name she had heard before that bothered her, a name that had come to her through Tony Grace, Rorech would later testify.

When Rorech got home that night—or, more precisely, in the early morning hours of September 10—he called Detective Phil Brady.

He told Brady everything that had happened . . . how he had attempted to comfort her and how Alice had said that the children were "better off where they are; you'd understand if you were Catholic." Brady stayed on the telephone with Rorech for two hours. He hammered at the story. Had Alice said anything really incriminating? No—she had just read a name in a newspaper that had triggered memories of the children.

Brady persisted: Damn it, Joe, if there is anything you're holding back . . .

Rorech swore he was holding nothing back. The only thing that had happened at the motel was that Alice had become upset by the newspaper story, and then sad over her children. She had never made any incriminating statements.

"I recall the conversation and my questions to a great extent," Phil Brady would say after he retired from the police force, "and I asked if she had said anything as to how the children died. He said no, she hadn't. I emphatically asked if she had implicated herself in any way on several occasions, and he said she had not."

38

The Alice Crimmins case had by now spawned Byzantine suspicions in the Queens criminal-justice system. The police didn't trust the District Attorney because they were convinced that Nat Hentel was out for a quick kill merely to get himself elected, and didn't have a real stomach for the case. The District Attorney's staff did not trust the police because it suspected that information was being held back by them; the Hentel loyalists believed that the police wanted Tom Mackell—a former cop—to get credit for cracking the case.

All of this was compounded by an intricate network of subplots within both staffs and outside. Inside the Police Department there were detectives who believed Alice Crimmins was the key to the solution. Anyone who questioned that point of view was cut off from the inner councils. Neither side trusted the informants, and when people were wired and the tapes malfunctioned, it was always regarded as deliberate.

There were jealousies and divisions within the District Attorney's office as well. One prosecutor who wanted the case sought out the hard-core detectives. "If I were prosecuting Alice Crimmins, I'd have her behind bars in a hurry," boasted young Anthony Lombardino. Lombardino was being indoctrinated into the fine points of prosecution by Eddie Devlin, a sixty-year-old attorney who had worked as a prosecutor for more than a dozen years.

Nat Hentel was dissatisfied with the progress of the case. If he could say something concrete about it to the press before election day, his chances might be enhanced. Hentel told his chief assistant, Howard Cerney, to find out what the hell was going on out in the field.

One morning in July, Cerney visited Devlin's second-floor office in the Queens Criminal Courts Building. Devlin had just completed the three-month trial of a murder case and was clearing up a few motions. He smiled at Cerney as a man might before packing up for a vacation. Devlin didn't have much intention of coming back. He knew that Tommy Mackell would be the next Queens District Attorney, and although he was a lifelong clubhouse Democrat, Devlin wouldn't work for him. Mackell had publicly announced that his assistants would not be able to hold outside jobs, and Devlin made the bulk of his income from his private law firm. Hentel had winked at Devlin's moonlighting, but Devlin knew that under Mackell he would have to quit.

"We got a job for you, Eddie," said Howard Cerney, and Devlin could see little Nat Hentel standing behind Cerney. "We want you to take over the Crimmins case."

Devlin laughed as if Cerney had made a disgusting joke. Not me, he said. I'm going on vacation. Besides, I got a job—breaking in that fellow across the hall. He was pointing to the eight-by-ten office of Anthony Lombardino.

When Devlin returned from vacation in August, Hentel and Cerney told him he had to take over the Crimmins case.

Devlin hesitated. "What've you got on the case?" he asked Hentel.

"I have no idea," replied Hentel.

That month Eddie Devlin reluctantly assumed the criminal-prosecution responsibilities for the Alice Crimmins case. At first glance, he might have seemed a bad choice—he was not graceful, in the sense that he spoke with a kind of Flatbush lilt; in a courtroom his mind sometimes fogged and sputtered at surprise; and he dressed with almost fanatic blandness. And yet there was something reassuring in the grandfatherly effect of his theatrical senility, and there was undeniable trustworthiness in his face, terraced by years of experience and honored by a sparse patch of gray hair.

A Queens juror would find it hard not to identify with the plainness of Eddie Devlin. If the case ever came to court, Devlin would provide a devastating counterpoint to the flourishes and legal guile of the firm of Baron and Harrison.

But before he could convince a jury, Devlin had to convince the police. The meeting was staged with conspiratorial secrecy at the 102nd Detective Command Headquarters. The cops wanted Devlin on their turf. They had ears inside the District Attorney's office and they knew Devlin's opinion of them.

"Sloppy," he commented after reading the reports and going over the crime scene. "There was no effort to protect physical evidence, and the detectives focused on one suspect."

He read through the stacks of paperwork and found nothing of prosecutorial value. Oh, it was rich in gothic detail about every aspect of Alice's sex life. But, my God, they hadn't even photographed the interiors properly. They had lost the blanket that Missy was found in. No one had saved the crucial piece of evidence that would have proved what Alice fed the children that night—the discarded box that had contained veal or manicotti, depending upon whom you believed. Piering even claimed to have seen a plate of leftover manicotti in the refrigerator, and that hadn't been preserved. Devlin knew it all had started as a report of two missing children, but there was no excuse for this unprofessional carelessness. Even the fingerprinting had been botched. Technicians had dusted the window and bureau, the bed and some toys, but none of the crucial surfaces—walls and doors outside the children's room.

So when Devlin and the detectives met in late August, their opinions of each other were mutual. Inspector McGuire was present, as were Jerry Piering and

John Kelly. Devlin had come to find out what evidence the police had beyond the reports, but before he could speak, Jerry Piering stuck his finger in Devlin's nose.

"You're not trying to make this case a political football, are you?" said Piering, more accusing than questioning.

Devlin tried to calm the men down, but Piering kept pacing and saying that they weren't going to allow this case to be mixed up in politics.

"What about if I talk to Rorech?" said Devlin.

"Stay away from Rorech," said John Kelly. "He is ours. We've been cultivating him and we don't want anyone to spoil it."

Devlin was in a curious dilemma. He was certain that the police were holding things back—perhaps even mystery witnesses that they would introduce later—but he was helpless against the tactic. He was given a free hand by Nat Hentel in one area: Tony Grace. Devlin brought in "the bowling girls," trying to double check Grace's story, that he had been occupied the night of the murder. And he talked to Tony Grace.

"Oh, the stories this guy used to tell about this dame," Devlin would recall years later, laughing. "But he never sold her out. He never said she did it or had anything to do with it."

Devlin's other major contributions centered on certain telephone calls. They were always muffled affairs from men trying to imply their importance. "I am the attorney for Mr. Such-and-such, a very happily married man," the calls would invariably begin. "We would appreciate, if my client is to be questioned in connection with this Crimmins matter, a phone call to my office instead of a subpoena to his home."

"If your client is such a happily married man, how come he was dipping Alice?" Devlin would reply mischievously.

He lost count of the number of such calls, and he began to be impressed by Alice Crimmins' energy.

By the fall, after the "little Apalachin" bust, Nat Hentel came to Eddie Devlin again. "Have you got a case?" he asked.

"Nothing," replied Devlin.

Hentel was desperate. Even if there were no case,

he would make a public announcement that there would be some activity on it "soon." The implication was that he was going to call a grand jury to hear evidence and possibly present indictments.

On the first Tuesday of November, Nat Hentel became a lame duck. He was trounced by about two-to-one at the polls by Tom Mackell—who was already being called "Tough Tommy."

Hentel decided to convene a grand jury. "What've you got?" he asked Devlin again.

"Nothing," said Devlin. "But maybe the sight of the grand jury will make her want to open up. Maybe it just might do the trick."

39

The detectives who had attached themselves to the case with such zeal began to display a disproportionate clout. For a while they tolerated within their midst those they considered "nonbelievers"—that is, those policemen unconvinced of Alice's guilt or complicity. But when the leaks remained unplugged, when they began to feel embattled and isolated—developing symptoms dangerously close to paranoia—they decided to enforce ideological unity. In late 1966, after the believers felt that the District Attorney's office had betrayed them, the nonbelievers began to be cut off from the case.

When Deputy Inspector Wolfgang Zanglein started to have second thoughts about the target of the investigation, he had to take his suspicions to Detective Phil Brady. The others—Piering, Kelly, Shields, Byrnes—were a "closed corporation." Zanglein and Brady discussed other possible suspects. The inspector had held a secret meeting with Nick Farina, the former detective broken to patrolman because of his relationship with Alice Crimmins, and had devised a scheme to approach Alice in a totally different manner. Zanglein's first step was to re-establish official contact with Alice. He planned to have Farina transferred to the precinct where Alice worked. There would be a chance encounter on the street, perhaps one thing would lead to another. Zanglein also wanted to approach Alice himself and try to convince her that not all the police were certain she was guilty.

Brady set up a series of meetings. At first they were tentative "drinks" or "dinners," at which Zanglein would be accompanied by a policewoman and Brady. It was a way of getting to know and trust each other. Alice still hoped the police would solve the case, without implicating her.

One evening Brady invited Alice to his home. Zanglein showed up about 11:30, wearing a turtleneck sweater and carrying a bottle of Chivas Regal. It was a famous night. Three detectives in the basement were taping the entire session—which lasted until 4:00 a.m., as Alice and Wolfgang drank their way through the first bottle and sent one of the detectives scrambling home for another. All it produced for Zanglein was a massive hangover and continuing doubts about Alice's ability to commit murder.

Shortly afterward Zanglein was transferred. The plan to reintroduce Nick Farina and Alice Crimmins was forgotten. Brady would be taken off the case later, convinced that he and Zanglein had been removed because of their skepticism about Alice's guilt.

At the same time that the hard-core believers were dealing so effectively with what they regarded as traitors in their midst, they felt that they themselves were embattled. Anthony Lombardino, by now a trusted member of the inner circle, noted that the number of full-time detectives assigned to the case began to dwindle—from twelve to ten to eight to six. Jerry Piering had to work on the case on his days off and was given "shit" assignments.

"We had some idea that a call was placed from some important people to lay off the Crimmins case,"

Lombardino would recall later. He could never trace the source of it, but he was certain that major pressure was being exerted to protect Alice Crimmins.

The grand-jury system has one great advantage—it is removed from the professional interests of police and prosecution. A Queens grand jury is composed of twenty-three men and women drawn from the community, who sit in an oak-paneled room on the fifth floor of the Kew Gardens Courthouse and listen to the proposed case presented by the police and an Assistant District Attorney. There is a presiding officer, but the grand jury can decide to ignore the strictest interpretations of the law and vote indictments on instinct or feelings. The rules of evidence before a grand jury are looser, more flexible than those in a regular courtroom. There is a certain unpredictability about grand juries, and experienced prosecutors are always apprehensive about the system. The term "runaway grand jury" usually applies to people who are moved by passion, rather than by narrow interpretations of the law. Another purpose of the grand jury in the case of Alice Crimmins was to take the heat off Nat Hentel. If he presented his strongest evidence and the grand jury failed to indict anyone, Hentel would be off the hook.

In November 1966, against police advice, Hentel threw the problem of Alice Crimmins into the lap of the grand jury. In effect, he was saying, we haven't been able to crack her; maybe you can.

Piering, Shields, Kelly, and Detective Walter Anderson from the District Attorney's staff appeared before the grand jury, presenting whatever fragments and solid nuggets of proof they possessed. Joseph Rorech testified, without seeming to add anything except a bit of mystique. On Thursday, December 1, Nat Hentel called Harold Harrison and requested that his clients Eddie and Alice Crimmins be present the next day after the lunch break.

In the morning Eddie Devlin told Nat Hentel something that the District Attorney already knew: "There's no case." But Hentel had other reasons for calling

205

Eddie and Alice Crimmins to face the grand jury. "You can't tell what's going to happen in there," he said to Devlin.

Alice and Eddie spent the morning at the office of Harrison. "You don't say a word," said Harrison; they were to take the Fifth Amendment.

Under normal circumstances, a lawyer whose client is the target of an investigation will advise him/her to cooperate as little as possible. The Fifth Amendment to the U.S. Constitution was designed to protect citizens against self-incrimination. In a textbook sense, Harrison was correct. But in the emotional climate of Queens he was terribly mistaken.

Harrison was smiling as he escorted his clients through the empty fifth-floor corridors. Several days before, Hentel and Cerney had taken Harrison aside and offered Alice Crimmins any kind of immunity if she would tell who had helped her dispose of the children. Harrison read that as a sign of desperation by the District Attorney. When he informed Alice of the offer, she still denied any knowledge of the case, but was fetched with the idea of ending the harassment. "Who do you have a grudge against?" she asked Harrison jokingly. "I'll name him."

Alice's and Eddie's appearances before the grand jury were brief. They refused to answer questions on the grounds that answering might tend to incriminate them. When Harrison came out into the corridor, he found that Nat Hentel had assembled a platoon of reporters and photographers to play witness to the Crimminses' lack of cooperation.

"As a parent myself, I am shocked by the whole thing," said Hentel, turning into the microphones. "People in this area are still worried about the safety of their children. My feeling is that if they had cooperated we would have solved this case a lot quicker. Now we will have to subpoena more witnesses."

Alice's head was buried in a Garbo-style floppy hat, her powder-blue sweater-dress hidden under a brown coat. Her husband, in a snap-brim hat and thin tie, hovered protectively around his wife, fending off interviewers. The corridor became a madhouse. Hentel, playing it for all he could get, turned to Harrison.

"We want their cooperation in solving this case. After all we are the People's attorney."

"My interest is in these people," cried Harrison, drawn against his will into a media contest. "I won't do anything at their expense. My clients have been called suspects in this case."

Wherever they turned, radio microphones waited like an encircling army. Then Howard Cerney joined in. His voice was lower, trying to sound restrained. "The reason that we asked them to come here is because they have more information than anyone else. The mother was the last to see the children."

"They are here to assist us to find out who took them," said Hentel.

Harrison's voice was out of control now: "Who put the telephone-taps order out for them? *You* did."

Cerney: "No we didn't."

"They've been bugging them! They've been tapping them! It's an inquisition!" shouted Harrison.

Eddie Devlin joined in with the question that was implicit in the whole drama, but that had so far been unspoken: "Aren't they interested in finding out who committed the crime?"

It was a simple question, free of the complexities of the past seventeen months, striking the precise nerve of the case.

"They're interested in being left alone," replied Harrison lamely.

Harrison led them out of the building. "We helped them already," said Eddie, sounding a little too apologetic. "We want to know how come they haven't found the killers of our children."

The grand jury would expire without returning indictments. But Devlin's single question—"Aren't they interested in finding out who committed the crime?"— would haunt the headlines, capture the evening television news, and stick tenaciously in the minds of people who lived in the borough of Queens.

40

Thomas Mackell looked older than his fifty-three years, his body swollen from eating his way through all his political campaigns. But when he took office as District Attorney in January 1967, it was with sincere gusto. He was like a man enjoying a Fourth of July picnic, winning every event from the one-legged potato race to the beer-drinking contest. When he laughed, it was with pure, untroubled glee.

Tommy Mackell was a Queens success story, and his pleasure seemed unmarred. His parents were immigrants from Ireland; he was graduated from All Hallows High School on the day his father died. The coincidence lent a tragic coda to his saga, an oral history that would unspool for his cronies over drinks in the aftermath of a long day. Mackell studied at City College at night, while working during the day as a relay tester for Consolidated Edison. The juxtaposition was important for him. His college degree was complemented by an authentic test of hand. Before receiving his law degree from St. John's University School of Law in 1942, he worked in the subways. That same year he joined the Police Department, where he served for ten years. In 1954 he was elected a State Senator, and although he became a powerful man in Albany, he never lost contact with the people of Queens—the people who still lived off the punched Con Edison checks. And he never forgot that he was a blue-collar child.

The election of Mackell was only to fill the unexpired term of Frank O'Connor. In November he would have to run again for a full four-year term. And so he came in on the gallop, facing the same dilemma as Nat Hentel—a looming election. Of course Mackell had all the advantages. The police were ready to cooperate with the former cop. And he brought with him a specialist—an imported gun hired from the staff of Manhattan District Attorney Frank Hogan. James Mosley and Tommy Mackell were as different as the Manhattan and Queens District Attorneys' offices. While Mosley seemed quiet and understated things, Mackell had a Texas-size imagination. Where Mosley was reserved, Mackell had a talent for instant intimacy. At first the combination seemed promising. Mackell might swoop over the landscape, blurring fine details, while Mosley plodded behind, worrying over every point. At the age of thirty-eight, James Mosley had an unbroken record of fifteen homicide convictions in Manhattan. Of course, an indictment in a major case in Manhattan—until recent political trials—usually meant a conviction. It was common knowledge that Manhattan prosecutors didn't go into court unless they had defense-proof cases. In point of fact, the conviction rate was better than ninety percent. Manhattan never overindicted.

But James Mosley was coming to Queens—a place where rumors were treated like Balkan curses; where one could never be certain whether the whispered conferences at lunch were political plots. And there was an undercurrent of resentment at the superior implications of Mosley's appointment. It was all very different for Mosley, trained in the sterile law laboratories of the Manhattan District Attorney's office, where points of law were recited and mulled over with Protestant detachment.

Mosley, a tall, droopy, professional man, seemed miscast in the frantic new environment. He had a tendency to treat people with exaggerated formality—this among people perpetually hoarse from screaming at each other. Mosley's questioning technique was calm and polite. He would call a man "Mister" until the moment a jury pronounced him guilty of something. The subdued presence was a handicap. Some people saw each tentative stammer as a statement of superiority. Instead of uncertainty, they saw vanity. In the hectic Pastrami King, where members of the staff snatched quick sandwiches washed down with Doctor Brown's soda, Mosley stuck out like a motionless stone. He couldn't seem to master the technique for holding the bulging sandwiches together—and some of the investigators concluded that such a man could not handle the mysteries of Alice Crimmins.

Mosley was brought to Queens to crack the murder of the Crimmins children. Tom Mackell hoped that the sophisticated Manhattan perspective would reveal some elusive avenue for prosecution. But when Mosley examined the information, he found a vast, formless mess. He was accustomed to the fastidious logic of Manhattan trials. If there was a case against Alice Crimmins, it was still developing, and so Mosley was thrown into the trial of a mobster. It was a rude introduction to the frontier style of Queens courtrooms. Mosley bungled the trial badly. He seemed nervous in the courtroom and was never able to muster the drive necessary for conviction. His style was dry, compared to the flourishes of the local talent. The defeat was a huge disappointment, but Mackell was willing to write it off as opening jitters.

Mackell's victory did not result in wholesale firings of Republican holdovers, and Anthony Lombardino was building up a reputation as a "son-of-a-bitch" inside a courtroom. Assigned to the felony trial part in the District Attorney's office, he compiled an impressive winning streak. The word was passed in the men's detention pens and over coffee in the police precincts —where gossip often overlapped—that this new man, Lombardino, was one tough hombre.

Lombardino would never settle for obscurity. He carried himself like a star, strutting around the courthouse, boasting about his latest conviction. "Tough Tony" was bound to be noticed. One day when Lombardino turned from the bench to face the audience with an overdrawn dramatic gesture he noticed Detective John Kelly in the second row of the courtroom.

The next day Detective Bill Corbett sat in the second row. When Lombardino moved to another courtroom for another case, Detective Jerry Piering sat in the audience. By now Lombardino understood that he was being scouted like a talented high-school pitcher. He had gone to some lengths to be noticed, and he was pleased that the Crimmins team had picked up the signals. When John Kelly asked him to lunch, Lombardino coyly played out the seduction. Kelly picked an obscure table at Luigi's, a place where serious business could be discussed safely. Lombardino found himself sandwiched between Kelly and Jerry Piering.

"How would you like to be the Alice Crimmins prosecutor?" asked Kelly.

"It seems like a closed corporation," replied Lombardino.

Kelly smiled. Piering spoke, bending over the table. Jim Mosley was a muddled failure, said Piering. It would have to be someone who would not be afraid to attack Alice Crimmins in a courtroom. It would have to be someone who would not be afraid of mercilessly shredding away Alice's dignity, someone who would viciously assault her character.

"We want a successful prosecution," said John Kelly.

"Well," said Lombardino, a forkful of pasta poised under his lips, "I'm your man."

No one told Mosley about the luncheon meeting in Luigi's. He was left alone to continue the technical work of assembling a case. Lombardino was brought into the investigation under the oblique guidance of the detectives. He began attending the weekly briefings at the 102nd Precinct. Kelly or Piering or Corbett would escort Lombardino into the squad room and introduce him around, and soon the presence of the squat prosecutor was taken for granted. Later the detectives would be able to promote Lombardino's inclusion in the prosecution team by claiming that he was familiar with all the details of the case.

At the end of each briefing session, the men would cast paper ballots on whether or not to indict Alice Crimmins for murder. "No one wanted to go in with a loser," said Lombardino later.

The hinge upon which the case turned was Joe

Rorech. "We knew that unless we got Joe Rorech to crack, it would be thrown out," Lombardino would say.

Mosley had been handling Rorech, and the police investigators agreed that he was doing it all wrong. When Rorech appeared for questioning, Mosley would offer him a seat. He would speak softly. "Rorech knew he could take Mosley," Lombardino would recall.

But Piering and Kelly would take Rorech aside and warn him about "Tough Tony." "Oh, you don't want to meet Lombardino; he's a son-of-a-bitch," Kelly told Rorech.

By the time Lombardino was ready to meet Joe Rorech, he had been accepted as Mosley's partner. Tom Mackell had agreed to Lombardino as the cruel half of the classic Mutt-and-Jeff routine (a questioning tactic in which one person acts tough while the other befriends the subject). Lombardino was convinced that Rorech was terrified of the encounter. The contractor was dragged into Lombardino's office by detectives. Lombardino stalked heavily around the room, then burst into a sudden rage: "I don't want to hear any of your bullshit. I'll put your ass in there [jail] with her [Alice]." Rorech continued to dribble out information selectively, but his aplomb had been breached. He was genuinely afraid of Lombardino, who was theatrically playing a madman.

If Lombardino played one role with Joe Rorech, he played quite another with Milton Helpern. He rinsed the Brooklyn accent out of his speech and appealed to the doctor's emotion through intellect. The campaign to get Dr. Helpern on the prosecution side was relentless. "We had a constant string of meetings with Helpern," Lombardino recalled, "to bolster him."

Lombardino was nervous about Helpern. He was never certain how well the doctor would hold up as a witness. Finally, after one long session, Dr. Helpern agreed. "OK, OK," he said. "I'll put my entire background on the line that this child couldn't have been alive when she [Alice] said she had taken her to the bathroom."

At that moment Lombardino felt a thrill of exhilaration. He believed that he had enough. Everyone, presumably, had forgotten an earlier statement of Dr. Helpern saying that the time couldn't be pinpointed before 4:00 a.m. He had said this on the telephone and it had been recorded on Detective Phil Brady's tape.

Ideally, detection is a pure science which marches forward irresistibly toward a solution. Fixed ideas and prejudice, like enemy fortifications, are trampled by logic. In a typical case, the police are confronted with a crime. In the police academies, future detectives are taught that they must keep open minds as they match the strands and threads which will lead them to the correct solution. (For "solution," read "suspect.") In textbook conditions, this is accomplished without passion. Dispassion is crucial in criminal investigations because emotion can cloud judgments, throw up phantom clues, create solutions out of paranoia. In a complicated and sensational criminal case, investigators face a hundred blind clues that can lead to a hundred possible solutions. It is a lot like being in a room full of mirrors, where only one of the images is real. In the Alice Crimmins case, the police began with a solution and worked backward. It would become a classic example of investigative inversion. There had been token efforts at other solutions, but the police became obsessed with reconstructing Alice's guilt. The clues and the evidence were read with the single purpose of establishing her guilt. By the time James Mosley came onto the scene, he was caught up in the great retreat.

As Tom Mackell went through the disarray of Nat Hentel's departure, he came upon a stack of mail. He turned it over to Mosley, knowing that his baffled assistant was having problems in bolstering the case against Alice Crimmins. "Maybe you can find something in there," said Mackell.

Mosley put the stack aside. He had set up an interview with Alice Crimmins' mother. Alice Burke was driven to Queens by detectives and seemed almost shrunken with fear as she walked through Mosley's basement command post. It was an environment that inspired dread. Security was as tight as at an army

213

headquarters. Everyone had to be accompanied by a detective. Even unfamiliar detectives had to show credentials at two checkpoints.

Mrs. Burke, a small, timid woman, arrived in a black dress. She was still in mourning for her dead husband and grandchildren, and she bore herself with a kind of perpetual grief. Her hands, scorched raw by a lifetime in soapy pails, fluttered up and down, nervously covering and uncovering each other, as if she were ashamed of the dishpan scars. She was, in fact, so intimidated by the official confrontation that she wet herself at the first question and sat through the ordeal trying to reassemble her dignity. It started at 2:00 p.m. on May 15, 1967, and lasted a scant ten minutes. The notes on her visit to Mosley's office suggest little profit:

Mrs. Burke was questioned about Alice Crimmins' friends—about whom Mrs. Burke knew very little—not having met any of them except a woman she knew as Marge—Alice brought Marge to Mr. Burke's wake where Mrs. Burke met her for the first time.

Questioned about having found money on Alice—negative—a recollection that Edward [*sic*] Crimmins found money on her [Alice].

Questioned about the cruise that Alice took—no knowledge of whom she went with—never found out.

Questioned about how Alice and Edward were getting along since reconciliation—

Answer: no personal knowledge—neither one said much except that they were getting along well—Edward refused to comment to Mrs. Burke regarding this.

Mrs. Burke had no personal knowledge of Alice's activities, either prior to separation or after reconciliation.

Mrs. Burke questioned about Tony G.—never met him—never heard of him.

Mrs. Burke questioned as to whether she was financing the legal fees—Answer, no.

Mrs. Burke questioned whether she had any knowledge of Alice's extra-marital activities recently.

Answer: No, except that Alice told her recently that she had gone out with her last employer. It was

214

suggested by the District Attorney that there was more to this relationship than one date.

Mrs. Burke questioned about her opinion of what happened on the evening in question.

Answer: Alice told her she had looked in on the children and they were all right—could not remember the time.

Alice Burke had obviously assumed a stance of non-cooperation with the authorities. Her answers bore only a literal semblance of the truth. She could not help knowing the extent of her daughter's affairs, and yet she refused to acknowledge it officially. She had chosen to remain blind to the gossip and rumors swirling around her.

She had pledged to pay for Alice Crimmins' defense. Her husband had left a $15,000 life-insurance policy and she had been making monthly withdrawals from the Bronx Savings Bank, living off the capital. Eventually, in 1968, she would withdraw the entire balance —$10,394.52—to give to Harold Harrison, her daughter's attorney. It would close out the account. But as she sat in Mosley's office fighting for control, she told him that she was not paying.

41

"Sentence first—verdict afterwards."

—Alice in Wonderland

Dear Mr. District Attorney:
I know who killed the Crimins kids, but I'm not gonna tell. Ha. Ha. Ha. Ha. Ha.

Signed:
Guess Who?

There were bushels of letters; there were tissue-thin wisps of notes full of fretful sounds, from people who never slept and embroidered stray noise into the flesh of demons. Such people lived on every block, peeking out fearfully from behind lace drapes, pouring out their nightmares now that someone, at last, would listen. The detectives were deployed in teams of two, listening to all the dreadful details.

"They all want to give you tea," a veteran detective would recall after spending a hundred afternoons listening to a hundred accusations. A milkman with a sour disposition would surely warrant investigation, one smiling grandmother told the detective. A man wearing a black hat and carrying a wolf's-head cane was planning to kill a lady on 72nd Drive, the woman said with the certainty of a bishop. But she had taken precautions—installed extra locks and varied her schedule. She had read somewhere that was a good means of defense against assassination.

"Very good," said the detective, pretending to sip from the delicate china cup. "You can't be too careful. But, if I'm not being too presumptuous, what has this to do with the Crimmins case?"

"Don't you see?" she said. "It's so plain. He couldn't get to me, so he took the children!" She swallowed the remains of her tea with a glint of triumph. "Would you like a biscuit?" she asked.

"Do you know the man's name?" asked the detective.

"You just find a man with a black hat and a wolf's-head cane and you'll have your killer," she said with an impatience that implied she couldn't do *all* the police work herself.

"Thank you very much, ma'am," said the detective, trying not to look at his partner. They heard the clicks of four locks after them as they left.

"When you become a policeman," the detective would recall, "you get a special glimpse inside people. People who look perfectly normal walking down the street or in the supermarket, they have these really far-out, secret lives. They sit in their apartments and dream up the most incredible stories about each other."

In the course of their careers, policemen become accustomed to the bizarre fantasies of the people they guard. "You try not to become too turned off to it," said the detective, "because every once in a while you come up with something genuine."

In the Crimmins case it was necessary to answer every cry of wolf. The paucity of evidence was such that the investigators had to trust that one of the alarms would turn out to be authentic. So far, the police had only a few of the ingredients necessary for a successful prosecution. They had opportunity—Alice had been alone in the apartment with the children. This was, in fact, their strongest fact against her. They appeared to have proof that Missy's death was a murder. But the Medical Examiner had fluctuated, hemming and hawing so many times that they were never certain his testimony would stand up. Nick Ferraro, later to become the Queens District Attorney, was a young assistant when the case first broke. He left the job in December 1965, and up until that time Dr.

Helpern was still hedging, refusing to be pinned down about a time of death. "Helpern flip-flopped all over the lot," said Ferraro, who became a State Senator before coming back to the District Attorney's post.

That was before young Tony Lombardino started working on Dr. Helpern.

So, by now the police had the fact of murder, although there was doubt even about the strangulation, and opportunity. They could conjure up a motive with the custody suit. What they needed, what the case cried out for, was someone credible who could connect Alice Crimmins to the act.

In March 1967, James Mosley came across the anonymous letter from the woman in the window who had seen a woman carrying "what appeared to be a bundle of blankets . . . under her left arm. . . ."

Mosley knew that if he could find that woman and she made a credible witness, they would have a case against Alice Crimmins. It might not be a case strong enough to convict her, but the police and prosecutors were convinced that if they could crack through Alice's elaborate defenses, she would tell them the entire story. Each step became another bit of pressure to make her break, leading to a further step.

Tony Lombardino was also certain he could use Joe Rorech in a pinch. Rorech could be made to say incriminating things about Alice. Rorech could be made to do almost anything, Lombardino was certain.

The immediate problem was to find the letter writer. It took several weeks—a long time, considering the clues in the letter. Handwriting experts concluded that the writer was a woman; they could tell that by style and the flourishes of the handwriting.

From the evidence of the letter, the woman had a window that faced 72nd Road. She was in one of the upper stories, since the letter said that the people had looked "up" when she closed her window. The woman had a view of 72nd Road, but she could see that "The car turned from the corner of 153 St. onto 72 Road and out to Kissena boulevard." Only eight buildings fitted all the criteria. The police went to the garden apartments' management and got samples of tenants' handwriting to compare with the letter. Out of forty-eight possibilities, they had the letter writer—Mrs. Sophie Earomirski of 72–21 153rd Street.

Just before noon, on June 13, 1967, Detectives William Corbett and Harry Shields knocked on the door of Apartment 3-A. The door opened, held back by a chain.

"Police," said Corbett.

Corbett and Shields sat with Sophie Earomirski for hours. They wanted to make certain they were dealing with a serious person. "I knew you would find me," she told Corbett.

It was amazing. Sophie Earomirski had been interviewed by the police almost a dozen times about this case. "I spoke to her myself three times," said Detective Phil Brady. She had never uttered one word about staring out the window on the night of July 13/14.

"Why?" asked Corbett.

"I didn't want to get involved," she replied.

"Why now?"

"My conscience was bothering me."

It was staggering, and the detectives went over her story again and again, trying to poke holes in it but not really wanting to lose the one link that directly connected Alice Crimmins to the case.

James Mosley was going through a routine piece of paperwork when Corbett telephoned. Anthony Lombardino was standing over his desk. "What?" he heard Mosley cry in a voice he had never heard before. "You gotta be kidding!"

Corbett was telling Mosley that they had found the letter writer. "How is she?" asked Mosley.

"A little shaky," replied Corbett.

"Well, don't press it now. Get back here," said Mosley.

John Kelly was summoned from the golf course; Piering was pulled away from the dinner table. Mosley, meanwhile, went to Tom Mackell's office, to which Corbett and Shields had spirited Sophie Earomirski. On his rich desk Mackell had spread a rogue's gallery of photographs. Could you recognize the woman you saw from your window that night? asked Tom Mackell.

Sophie Earomirski, sometime saleslady, sometime neighborhood character, was beginning to appreciate her own importance. Detectives and prosecutors hovered around her in anticipation; she could sense their hunger. Suddenly her hand stopped that of Thomas Mackell, the District Attorney of Queens. She pointed a finger accusingly. "That's the woman I saw that night," she said in a dramatic voice.

"Are you certain?" said Mackell in half-disbelief that such an important witness could suddenly appear in his office so casually.

"That's the woman!" It was a photograph of Alice Crimmins.

"It had to be the most satisfying moment of my career," Mackell would later recall.

But someone else was even more gratified. James Mosley, who had virtually botched every opportunity since coming to Queens, who had gone from Manhattan hotshot to Queens laughingstock, had been vindicated by Sophie Earomirski.

James Carroll Mosley, father of four, graduate of parochial school and Fordham Law, counter-intelligence agent in the Army, had found Detectives Piering, Kelly, and Byrnes waiting on his doorstep when he moved into his new office. He'd barely had time to put his key in the lock before they were filling him in on the background of the Crimmins case. But time after time Mosley blundered in their eyes. The pressures made him appear foolish, and he would sometimes drink away his lunch hour in Luigi's.

Mosley's greatest fiasco took place the day he tried to break Joe Rorech. Here was a chance to redeem himself, restore stature to his role. On March 21, 1967, Mosley had Detective Phil Brady arrange an interview with Rorech in one of his own watering holes —the Red Coach Grill in Nassau County. It was a late lunch date and began pleasantly enough. Mosley washed down his steak with beer; Rorech with his customary Scotch mists. Lunch drifted into dinner and they moved to the bar. Brady lost count of the drinks, but by evening the moods had reversed themselves several times. Mosley tried being friendly. Rorech was impenetrable, giving his normal evasive answers. Mosley became angry. Finally, he lost his patience.

"OK, put the cuffs on him, he's under arrest," said Mosley, turning to Brady.

The detective leaned over and whispered to the Assistant District Attorney: "But we're in Nassau County."

"I don't give a damn. Put the cuffs on him, he's going in as a material witness."

Brady kept his head. He walked over to the telephone, called the Third Precinct, and asked for assistance. Mosley was, after all, a District Attorney and did have some authority even in Nassau County. A pair of county detectives arrived and arrested Rorech on Mosley's word. He was handcuffed and taken to the Third Precinct. Meanwhile, the bartender, who had been alerted beforehand by Rorech, called Harold Harrison.

Harrison received the call at home at 11:00 p.m. By 11:30 he was talking to a sergeant, then a detective in the Third Precinct. Finally he spoke to Mosley, who was forced to back down. Rorech was not *technically* arrested, he told Harrison apologetically. They had just wanted to bring him in for questioning, since he was to testify before another grand jury in May.

At 11:40 p.m., after everyone had regained composure, Rorech called Harrison from another bar and said he had been released. When Rorech went before the grand jury on May 12, he had in his possession a paper signed by Mosley conferring on him "immunity for crimes other than homicide in the event that any statements given by Joseph Rorech revealed his guilt of any other crimes."

Mosley never quite recovered from the humiliation of being bested by Harrison and Rorech. As he passed out of earshot, he always thought he could hear people laughing behind his back.

Understandably, Mosley played his moment of triumph to its limits. None of the detectives and attorneys who gathered around his desk on June 13 knew why they had been summoned. Mosley built up the suspense as each new arrival appeared, explaining gravely that he wanted to make this announcement just once. John Kelly, fresh from the golf course, felt foolish in his Hawaiian shirt; Piering was unshaved. By 7:00 p.m. they all had assembled. Mosley waited until everyone was seated, then said quietly: "We got the letter writer."

There was no way to react to such news but with silence. It had been so long. The room was filled with files and index cards, some stretching back two years, growing yellow and dog-eared. Some cards had had to be stapled together—lives had been disrupted and changed. There had been marriages, divorces, and re-marriages. In two years, girls become women, boys become men, memories fade or harden. There were files and charts and maps of the area, with the witnesses tracked and filed as to their whereabouts during the crucial hours of the night of July 13/14, 1965. Legal questions and arguments could be diagrammed and plotted like ancient syllogisms. The case could be measured by the 2500 DD's—reflecting the 2500 formal interviews. It could be tabulated by the cases of liquor consumed by the men trying to fit into Alice Crimmins' world.

But there was no way to calculate the emotion that had gone into it all—the passions, the venom, the sense of impotence. Hours staring at pictures of dead children; time spent at home brooding about whether some crucial clue had been ignored or missed; random moments looking at a wife in a quite different fashion; trying to pay as much attention to the live children as to the dead pair.

More than two years and too many hours and men to count had come down to one hesitant woman.

42

**"I wish Queens never asked ques-
tions!" Alice thought to herself.**

—Through the Looking-Glass

There were no more paper ballots. These men had gone
through two grand juries with less than a case. But
Mosley, in his methodical fashion, wanted to review it
all again, step by step, as much to reassure himself of
the structure of prosecution as to convince the men
around the conference table. He dragged out the charts,
the lists of witnesses, constructing a textbook chain of
evidence.

Mosley outlined his plan like a general organizing
a battle. The detectives would have to deploy their
forces, without, of course, alerting the enemy. Surprise
was an important factor. He felt confident, planning
the attack.

Lombardino didn't notice when the lights went on in
the office as it became dark outside. He didn't notice
until they were turned off at dawn when the curtains
were opened.

"Well," said Mosley finally, like a general who didn't
feel comfortable without a two-to-one advantage, "do
you think we have enough? Should we try for another
indictment?"

"Enough!" cried Lombardino, exhausted by Mosley's incurable hesitancy. "Enough!"

"OK," said Mosley, "then let's see a show of hands."

The arms went up like salutes—everyone wanted another crack indicting Alice Crimmins.

Lombardino looked through the window and thought with satisfaction of the morning when, driving on the expressway and listening to the news bulletins, he had dreamed vaguely of prosecuting the killer. He stretched and realized that he was famished.

Only one man left the room haunted by doubts. It might be a case strong enough for Queens, it would probably result in an indictment, but inside his professional soul James Mosley knew that the Manhattan District Attorney's office would never proceed on such uncertain evidence. Cases of circumstantial evidence had been brought to fruition in Manhattan, but the circumstances had always been convincing. Mosley did not believe there was sufficient evidence against Alice Crimmins to obtain a conviction.

Anthony Lombardino went home to breakfast. He had already outlined the argument he would use before the jury: Alice had killed her daughter in a fit of anger, then had got someone else to dispose of her son. He would not suggest who, for she would not be charged with her son's murder. Lombardino would tell the jury that Alice had killed her child because Missy got in her way. It was a weak argument, but he had presented it powerfully in Mosley's office. The thing was, he never believed it himself. Even when he got before a jury and presented the argument, he didn't believe it.

Five years later, looking back, he would say: "To this day I know it's weak. I don't know if she did it. It still seems unlikely. I can't believe it. I can't even believe the story I told the jury. I don't even believe it now."

The guardian of the basement command post that summer was forty-eight-year-old Audrey Montoy, a career member of the District Attorney's staff—a woman who probably knew more secrets than any of the senior assistants, but regarded each secret with the sanctity of something heard in a confessional. She was faced with an impossible job. The activity in and out of Mosley's suite was constant and she had all she could do to keep away the probing reporters. Witnesses were brought in and reminded of their testimony. New charts were drawn, showing with geometric precision the lines of guilt leading to Alice Crimmins. What Mosley lacked in tangible evidence, he tried to compensate for with overwork, demonstrating that only Alice could have had the motive and opportunity to slaughter her children.

Still, Dr. Milton Helpern refused to say that Eddie's death was a homicide. One could infer homicide, based on the circumstances that his sister was found apparently murdered in almost identical conditions. But the logic broke down under close study.

"OK," said Mosley, "we just go for an indictment on the girl."

"You'll stand by what you said about the girl?" asked Lombardino. "You'll stick by the statement that Missy must have been dead by midnight?"

Dr. Helpern, the world's foremost forensic pathologist, nodded his head, burying whatever doubts lingered, becoming a partner of the District Attorney's office. Helpern had, through the years since Missy's and Eddie's death, been under relentless siege by the office—from the supplication of Nick Ferraro to the understated puzzlement of Eddie Devlin, to the academic probings of James Mosley, to the urgency of Tony Lombardino. Dr. Helpern, Lombardino reported to Mosley, would perform his duty.

Anthony Lombardino was like a man trying to keep a thousand puppets dancing—this one had become reluctant, that one had moved away, someone else's memory was slicing away the details. None of the witnesses were more important than Sophie Earomirski. Without her, there was no case. Lombardino assigned Policewoman Margie Powers to stay with Sophie, who had to be pampered and reassured like a reluctant opera star. For Policewoman Powers it was not an unwelcome assignment. She had disliked Alice Crimmins from the beginning—from the first moment she had laid eyes on her that second morning after the disappearance, after Missy had already been found dead. Alice was busy putting on her makeup before submitting to another round of police questioning. That moment stood out for Margie Powers—a woman who was supposed to be in the ultimate stages of grief and anxiety (her son was still missing) was more concerned about her appearance!

Margie Powers did not keep her observation to herself. She made it plain with the expectation of distaste that she believed the gesture deserved. It was passed along to other police and thus, reinforced as the observation of a woman, spread through courthouses and lunchrooms and bars. Wherever anyone went in Queens in the latter part of the 1960s, the name of Alice Crimmins would conjure visions of a woman more concerned with her makeup than with her dead children.

Even with the full-time assignment of Margie Powers to Sophie Earomirski, Lombardino found himself spending more and more time stroking Sophie's doubts. Her husband had opposed her coming forward. Lombardino appealed to his civic duty, his patriotism, and showed him photographs of the dead children. Lombardino suppressed his Vesuvian temper and overcame the doubts of Mr. Earomirski. Mr. Earomirski knew his wife; he knew her tendency toward overstatement, he was afraid that she was jumping into something serious, something over her head. But Lombardino realized that without Sophie Earomirski there would be no indictment—the case would be thrown out by the first judge to review the evidence.

Everyone involved was attacked by nerves. Twice, grand juries had heard the evidence and failed to return indictments—in December 1966 and in May 1967. Harold Harrison was telling reporters that his client was being persecuted, and there were indications that reporters were becoming bored with the official obsession. They would print the ritual stories about imminent breaks and mystery witnesses, but without any second effort or follow-up stories. And Mackell was coming up for re-election.

On September 1, 1967, James Mosley went before a fresh grand jury to present the Alice Crimmins case.

He did it carefully, without undue fanfare. He brought in Joe Rorech, and this time Rorech told about the second telephone call to Alice Crimmins at 2:00 a.m. when there was no answer. Then Mosley laid the groundwork for Sophie. He brought in lighting experts, who testified that it had been possible to distinguish things at a certain distance that night. Sound engineers told the jury it was possible to hear conversation in the middle of night and that the mall acted as a kind of echo chamber.

And then appeared Sophie Earomirski, the mystery witness. It was hard to distinguish Sophie from her escort, Margie Powers—both were overfed. But the newspapers had been full of tantalizing hints about the mystery witness, and her entrance was watched with undisguised fascination.

Until the 1940s the names of witnesses who appeared before a grand jury were a matter of public record. But there had been a period of mob retaliation against grand-jury witnesses, and after Abe Reles was thrown from his window at the Half Moon Hotel in Coney Island before he could testify and Arnold Schuster was murdered after testifying against bank robber Willie Sutton, the New York state legislature conferred secrecy on the names of witnesses. The price of such protection helped District Attorney Tom Dewey, but it was a great hardship to defense attorneys, since the identity of the accuser would not be known until he appeared in open court—too late for serious background investigations to be undertaken. In the Crimmins case, Sophie Earomirski's medical past was thus protected against Harold Harrison's army of private detectives.

On the first Thursday in September she testified before the grand jury for forty-five minutes. "Keep it down," Lombardino had advised her, knowing the woman's impulse to embellish.

"How did I do?" she asked Lombardino after her appearance.

"Beautiful," he said, sounding more like a dramatic coach than like the attorney for the People.

This time Mosley could see the grand jury clicking in his direction. The arched questions, questions starched with skepticism, had turned into hushed, respectful requests for fleshing out with details. The detectives who testified—Piering, Kelly, and Byrnes—added their own incriminating punctures. But by the time Sophie Earomirski told about seeing Alice cross the mall carrying the bundle of clothing—presumably Missy—the grand jurors were ready to act. The pieces of the puzzle had fallen into place.

Late on September 12 the grand jury voted an indictment against Alice Crimmins for the murder of her daughter, Missy. And then James Mosley, Jerry Piering, Jerry Byrnes, Harry Shields, and Walter Anderson walked across the windy lanes of Queens Boulevard to Luigi's, where they drank the night away. More than two years had been invested in this case by most of these men, but somehow the celebration lacked dimension. Tomorrow they would arrest Alice Crimmins. Tonight the liquor let them down.

Piering and Byrnes shook off the effects of the whiskey and called for the assistance of a policewoman. Policewoman Lillian Smith met them at the courthouse at 6:00 a.m. Byrnes drove, Piering sat next to him, and the policewoman was in the back of the cruiser.

"We are going to arrest Alice Crimmins," said Jerry Piering simply as they drove to Beechhurst. The police cruiser remained in ambush for more than an hour, and a few minutes after 8:00 a.m. Piering nudged his partner. Alice was leaving for work.

"Actually, I've always been a very happy-go-lucky person," Alice would recall years later. "I'd always have my door open; have people dropping in. I'd always walk out with a kind of expectation. A new day; a new beginning. It was always an invigorating thing, to walk outdoors on a bright summer day. Until that day, that is. I've never been able to walk out without looking in both directions since. I never open my door any more unless I ask who it is. I've become a more closed person."

Byrnes waited until Alice Crimmins reached her car, then pulled the police cruiser into a blocking position. Alice was behind the wheel, but had not yet closed the door. She had grown accustomed to sudden police attention over the years and was not overly concerned.

"What do you want?" she asked.

"You have to come with us, Alice," said Detective Byrnes.

She didn't understand. During the time she had dealt with the police, they had always *asked* her to come with them. It had never been a command. "I have to what?"

"You have to come with us," repeated Byrnes.

"I want to talk to my lawyer," Alice said, beginning to yell. "I'm not going anywhere without talking to my lawyer."

"The grand jury has indicted you for the murder of Alice Marie," said Piering, showing her the warrant for her arrest.

"I don't believe it," she said through clenched teeth. "I'm not going anywhere." Her hands gripped the steering wheel as if it could hold off the police and the warrants.

Piering pleaded with her not to make a fuss because the neighbors were watching. Byrnes signaled for Policewoman Smith, who spoke calmly through the door. "Don't make me use jujitsu," said the policewoman. "I've had quite a bit of training."

Alice got out of her car and followed the trio of police to their cruiser. She asked if she could tell Eddie, who was upstairs asleep. Piering said she could make one telephone call at the Fresh Meadows Precinct.

And then Piering turned in the front passenger seat and suggested that it would have been so much easier if she had only told the truth from the beginning—that is, confessed. "But you did everything the hard way."

"Drop dead," said Alice Crimmins.

They were all waiting at the 107th Precinct—the inspectors, the detectives, the District Attorney. Alice phoned Eddie and told him to get in touch with Harold Harrison.

Harrison didn't need a telephone call to tell him that his client was under arrest. He was listening to the radio while shaving when a bulletin was broadcast that Alice Crimmins had been indicted for the murder of her daughter and was being arraigned at the Fresh

Meadows Precinct. Harrison telephoned the precinct that under recent Miranda rules as laid down by the U.S. Supreme Court he was instructing the police not to question his client. Joseph Coyle told his men not to utter a word to Alice, but when the police tried to process her, she balked.

Harrison, who lived less than a mile from the station house, was soon there. He took Alice aside and advised her to go through the formalities—he would try to have her free as soon as possible. She signed the fingerprint card that she had spurned moments earlier. She submitted docilely as the police took her pedigree:

NAME: Alice Crimmins
AGE: 29
ADDRESS: 9-20 166th St., Beechhurst, Queens
OCCUPATION: Secretary
ADDICTIONS: None

The routine was simple. Assistant District Attorney James Mosley asked that bail be set at $75,000. Harrison argued before Supreme Court Justice Charles Margett (whom he had clerked for when he graduated from law school) that his client was no risk and would not flee. Bail was set at $25,000, and by late afternoon Alice was free to go home until the case came to court. At first the police assigned a policewoman to shadow her, their contention being that she was in danger since she was involved with another person; the policewoman was there to protect her. Harrison made some angry telephone calls and said it was another instance of police harassment.

The question of bail caused controversy. Piering argued that a night in the slam would crack Alice's crust. She had already had a fainting spell in a courtroom antechamber before the proceedings. Alice was now officially accused of killing her child. It was another turn of the wheel that was supposed to make her crack.

Alice's defenses were infinitely complicated. She would say later that the persecution had become a form of grief for her dead children. "You see," she would explain, "I never got a chance to grieve for my child

. . . I never got a chance to grieve. From the first I was a suspect, and so I got angry. That became my grief."

In a hidden compartment of her purse Alice carried a picture of each of her dead children. When she was certain she was alone, she would take them out and weep. But never in public. "I wouldn't give them the satisfaction."

During the next few months Harold Harrison was invited for informal chats with one Assistant District Attorney after another. He knew the encounters were not casual. Each of the officials made it plain that Alice could have immunity, never spend one day in jail, if she would name the person who assisted her in killing the children.

"She says that she didn't kill her children and doesn't know anything about it," Harrison replied each time.

Meanwhile, each side was mobilizing for the courtroom test. The District Attorney's office had the head start, notifying witnesses of the impending case and warning them against speaking to the agents of Harold Harrison.

Harrison employed a variety of services. Among them was Superior Investigations & Claims Services Inc., of Brooklyn, which tallied Joe Rorech's various debts and creditors. The chief investigations were conducted by Victor Lederman of Massapequa Park; aside from poking around Rorech's past, he dug up material about neighbors and potential hostile witnesses. A thick dossier on Dr. Milton Helpern was compiled, establishing, if nothing else, that his achievements were broad and widely recognized. Harrison also employed Stanley Rivkin and a man who went by several names—Sam Poulos, Sam Gianapoulos, and Sam Spade. It would become Sam Spade's honor to be arrested during the course of his inquiries on a petty-larceny charge—he allegedly took housing records in an overzealous effort to find the "mystery witness." The charges were dropped, but Sam Spade would live on in the legend of the case as the indomitable private eye— a man who knew no limits in his grasp for the vital evidence. The truth was a little less dramatic. The arrest so shook him that Sam Spade retreated into virtual hiding, dissociating himself from Alice Crimmins.

The investigations were scattered and wasteful. The advantage lay with the prosecution, which knew precisely what evidence was going to come out. Meanwhile Alice had conferences with her attorneys.

"I wanted her to have her hair done in a certain way," recalled Marty Baron. "You know, subdued. I wanted her to wear subdued clothing and quit her nighttime activities. But Alice was a strongheaded woman. Things had to be done her way. She kept saying that she wasn't guilty and she had nothing to be ashamed of."

Harold Harrison waited a few months, then moved for a dismissal. The Assistant District Attorney, unsure of his case and hoping for further proof, kept asking for more time, but as 1967 slipped into 1968 the courts became impatient with James Mosley. He would have to move for trial or drop the case. In May he moved.

A famous confrontation took place one day between Harold Harrison and Anthony Lombardino. Harrison said that Lombardino had no case and that it would never go to the jury. The smugness bothered Lombardino, who passed word to the presiding judge, Peter Farrell, asking if it were true. The word came back indirectly that from the evidence he had seen, Farrell was ready to dismiss the charges. At that moment Lombardino knew he had to break Joseph Rorech completely.

43

Above all, there is the consideration of dignity. A courtroom is intended to ratify the dignity of people. The notion is implicit in the presumption of innocence. Whatever acts are committed outside the courtroom, the "day in court" cleanses and elevates the participants to immutable standards of behavior. Guilty or innocent, what matters is the ceremonial fanfare. The ritual is crucial. The court attendants stand guard like vestrymen with grave eyes, enforcing respect. Smoking, talking, and even frivolous reading are forbidden—a reminder of the singular and serious purpose. On the rear wall of the largest courtroom in Queens, where Alice Crimmins would stand trial, was the familiar motto: "In God We Trust." Indeed, the effort to evoke the feeling of a cathedral was not accidental: rich wood paneling and portraits of former judges lining the walls. The double doors leading from the hectic corridors to the hushed courtroom were a sobering barrier. As spectators passed from the throaty informality of the hallways to the chamber, there was a blast of something like awe. No one was immune. It was a place where people came to find their own dimensions; where raw passions were tamed; where the aggrieved quietly sought what people have always sought—justice.

In the most important sense, Alice Crimmins would stand trial inside and outside the courtroom. She was pronounced guilty in thousands of inadmissible conversations that took place in supermarkets and beauty

233

parlors. It was a judgment that was a reflex of fear. In Queens, where troubled husbands and wives clung together because of fear of transgression, it was possible to resolve doubt with a clear declaration of Alice's guilt. If it was not possible to eliminate a bothersome mystery, there were some who could at least deny it.

In the second week of May 1968, Alice Crimmins naïvely went to court seeking vindication. It began on May 9, a Thursday, in the huge ground-floor courtroom of the Queens Criminal Courts Building—a room that came to be known as "The Hippodrome." The relentless chorus of housewives began assembling before dawn. There was Nellie Saladino, a tiny, white-haired professional baby-sitter from Ridgewood who had difficulty concealing her bristling anger. Santa Ienna would hurry her husband and two children through breakfast, then take two buses to be at the courthouse early. Alice Bagnell would sleep in the corridor to ensure her place in line. They would form an unofficial club, taking turns reserving places for one another, bringing lunch for their friends, having them over for dinner. They shared an obsession and were willing to undergo hardship and ridicule and would gladly postpone every other event in their lives to bear witness. In the club they spoke in a shorthand of mutual understanding. "A mother," Alice Bagnell would say to the bobbing heads around her, "to do such a thing!" and the nodding heads would change direction and wag horizontally in disbelief.

The beginning of the trial was delayed for two days by Huntley Hearings—a contest to determine if statements made to police were admissible. It became clear that Alice had made no incriminating statements. On Friday, May 10, the spectators were back outside the courtroom, munching sandwiches and chocolate, afraid to lose their places in line. They carried newspapers like scorecards and had already begun to recognize one another and form groups—the courtroom buffs, retired people, who dissect every move and countermove like chess masters, an overlay of dispassion coating their voices the housewives with angry eyes, suspicious of everyone, afraid each question or comment was some attempt to help Alice; men in leather jackets and folded arms who had closed their minds. And there were the truly detached viewers—bearded young law students who read textbooks as they waited, like monks guarding against contaminating sin.

They all had their reasons. For Santa Ienna, the bruising lines, the inconvenience would all be worthwhile if the trial could provide some answer. "I want to know why," she said evenly. "I've made dinner every night, breakfast every morning. I've made all the sacrifices. I've got two kids. And I want to know why."

"All rise."

The decorum inside the courtroom is deceptive. The place seethes with unexpressed emotion. The judge enters quickly, hurrying to his perch high above the courtroom. He wears his position like the stars of a general and is uncomfortable outside the symbol of his rank.

Peter Farrell was the oldest active judge in Queens. At this time he was sixty-eight years old and had been a judge since 1943. Farrell, the eighth of nine children, was a staunch Roman Catholic. On the walls of his chambers were plaques from the Knights of Columbus. On his desk, in almost equivalent rank, was a portrait of John F. Kennedy. Farrell was a lifelong Democrat and had obtained his judgeship through hard precinct political work. He did not agree with the modern trend of de-emphasizing partisan identification for judges. He found nothing incongruous or compromising about attending political dinners and working for the party's candidates. A graduate of Fordham Law School, Farrell first dreamed of entering politics, but the dream changed when one of his four children died during an absence, so he decided to seek a career closer to home. Farrell was regarded as a hard-nosed judge of the old school, fighting what he himself felt was a losing battle against a lost generation. "We used to give out stiffer sentences," he would say ruefully. "We gave them ten to thirty years for robbery—and people did the time. We're all off base."

As senior judge, Peter Farrell assigned the Crimmins case to himself. It had been scheduled for another judge's chambers—Paul Balsam's—but Farrell by virtue of his position was able to pluck the case away. In most criminal courts there is a concept known as "judge shopping." That is, defendants postpone and delay until a friendly judge appears on the calendar. In Queens, however, Peter Farrell was able to overrule the four judges underneath him. The prosecutor's office was happy to let him, for they regarded him as someone who would be friendly to their side.

As she passed through the gauntlet on the first day of jury selection, Alice Crimmins' face was hidden under her favorite floppy hat. She walked by the crowd, close enough to touch, but there was something uncanny and unapproachable about her. She came and went unmolested. With demure little gestures, as if she were masking an impolite cough, she popped peppermint Life-Savers into her mouth as she walked between her lawyers. Alice Crimmins was always conscious of her breath and hated to offend with human odors.

Among one segment of the press there is a sloppy tendency toward lazy identification. From the first, Alice had been "the attractive 26-year-old red-headed cocktail waitress." Only the age would click off the passage of time. As the trial began, she was again the "attractive red-headed cocktail waitress," locked forever in that description. If Alice had been a cocktail waitress for only a few months, it didn't matter—that was her permanent rank. Because she had once been red-headed and beautiful, it went unnoticed that she now required dyes to keep up her appearance. And in the three years since the death of her children the pressures had taken their toll. She was still attractive, but she no longer looked young.

The case on trial was indictment number 1619, brought in the year 1967. On the right-hand side of the courtroom sat James Mosley and his itchy young assistant, Anthony Lombardino. Lombardino kept playing nervously with the prosecution files, set out in precise, military-like rows. Lombardino had trouble keeping the excitement out of his voice, and Mosley would remind him not to smile so much.

At the defense table Marty Baron and Harold Harrison positioned themselves around Alice Crimmins. They would always try to fit little Alice between them.

Although they understood that there were metal parts to her personality, there was something fragile about Alice. It was a quality that brought out tenderness in some men. As she sat at the defense table, no one could say what went on behind the strained smile of appreciation.

"There is a . . . a detachment as you sit there; you can't believe that they are talking about you. At least, I never did. It's a very strange feeling—all the things I had done in my life, and there they were, all brought out, all distorted. It never was really like that. It was never like what they made it out to be."

The potential jurors filed in and took their places, unable to keep their eyes from Alice Crimmins. The spectators, even the judge found themselves searching the expression, the aspect of the defendant, as if these would yield an answer.

During the jury selection it is possible to detect the broad outlines of attack and defense. Lombardino conducted the questioning of the prospective jurors. Blunt, almost crude, he left no margin for subtlety in his bulldog style. "There's no place for sympathy in a case like this," he would tell the jurors, virtually daring them to admit to such a weakness. A tremor ran through Alice Crimmins as she listened to his first probings. She turned to Harrison and whispered in a high, vulnerable voice that seemed out of place in the great courtroom, "I don't like that man."

That was precisely the reaction Tony Lombardino was after. He wanted Alice to hate him.

The prosecution had a profile for its ideal juror: he would be male, middle-aged, of lower-middle-class standing. He would be a man who had to struggle to make a living. A man with a family and a live morality. Roman Catholic. In effect, someone who would start out with a grudge against Alice Crimmins.

Harold Harrison did not have much hope of getting *his* ideal juror. He had consulted a psychologist, who recommended that he find a successful young liberal with a touch of skepticism. Such people were rare, and on juries virtually extinct. A successful person could

237

always evade jury duty, pleading the crush of important business.

Cases are said to be settled by the time jury selection is completed. That kind of traditional wisdom among attorneys goes unchallenged because it is impossible to prove or disprove. But it's also said that cases are decided by the choice of judge, the apparel of the lawyers, the quality of the free lunches provided by the state, or even the confluence of planets in their orbits. Still, the jury renders the final verdict. If the jury system works, it works best when truly dealing with peers. People on the fringes of society invariably have a tougher time. In early May, as the process of jury selection began, it seemed that Harrison and Baron had already been defeated. The first man selected, Carl Boyer of Forest Hills, a retired Civil Service employee, set the pattern. The jurors were an accurate reflection of a certain segment of Queens—a linotype operator from Flushing, a milkman from Arverne, a garment worker from Flushing. There were importers, electricians—none young, none women. The defense used up its twenty peremptory challenges merely trying to weed out those people with an obviously closed mind.

Women could get off jury duty simply by claiming that they had children to take care of, and the matter was not pressed. All the women on the prospective panel asked to be excused, saying they believed Alice was guilty. In the late 1960s few women elected to accept jury duty. Jury names were taken from voter-registration lists and young people usually were slow to register. The pool of potential jurors consisted of middle-aged men with a decided blue-collar tilt.

From the standpoint of the prosecution, an almost perfect panel had been picked—men wedded until death to a morality that would become the central question of the case. One man on the jury, however, did not fit the prosecution profile. This was Lewis Rosenthal, at forty, the youngest man on the panel. Rosenthal lived with his wife, Vera, in a two-story green-shingled house in an ethnically fluid part of Jamaica. He was an importer who had been born in Saxony in Germany and barely escaped the Nazis. First he had moved to Israel, where he fought as an officer in the

238

War of Independence. But in 1953 he had come to the United States to collect a small inheritance. Here he had met the woman he would marry, and stayed. When Rosenthal was picked for jury duty, he was upset; it would be a disruption of his business and personal life. Balanced against the inconvenience was Rosenthal's strong sense of duty. He had always had a deep respect for the American system of justice—the fairest in the world, he was convinced. That faith would become a casualty of the trial.

Rosenthal was surprised when he was chosen for the Crimmins jury. He wore a beard. It was neat and well trimmed, but in 1968 a beard was to many people a statement of rebellion. When he was chosen as juror number nine, another surprising thing happened to Lewis Rosenthal: he was not unhappy about serving. The first flinch of self-pity at being forced to participate in something unpleasant was replaced by an undeniable delight. An introspective man, Rosenthal found himself stretching his beliefs under questioning. He was not lying, but he was taking liberties with the literal truth, telling the prosecution and defense lawyers what they wanted to hear. "Suddenly," he would recall, "I wanted to be picked. It was a subtle thing. Wouldn't it be nice to be picked—to be important?"

In the Jamaica neighborhood where Rosenthal lived, Alice Crimmins' trial was the most urgent topic of conversation. He would hear a pleasant buzz in his wake when he went shopping—"He's one of the jurors in the Crimmins case!" Being a juror in such a celebrated trial brought a certain local status to Lewis Rosenthal, but it was something he didn't quite trust.

As the jurors took their places, one by one, in the box, Alice Crimmins wondered whether these men in narrow ties and inexpensive suits, precisely the people she had defied, would be able to understand her. She wore a prim black dress with a collar, her only concession.

During the selection process Anthony Lombardino had implanted the prosecution theme, asking each juror if he could accept the contention that a mother could murder her own child. Again and again it was repeated, reinforced every time a prospective juror, pausing to punctuate the enormity of the response, said: "Yes . . . yes, I could."

By the time the full jury was seated, Lombardino, by the simple repetition, had all but wiped away whatever natural sympathy a mother might have. For some he had created the corollary—that Alice Crimmins was not a real mother, but a mutation.

The jury knew that they would be together for a long time. Most had served on juries before and, understanding the signs of a lengthy trial, began to pace themselves for the ordeal. At first Lewis Rosenthal listened carefully to the judge's instructions and took strict care not to read or listen to anything about the case. Gradually the diligence was eroded as he noticed the other jurors reading and talking about the case and growing more and more careless about the judge's orders. Was it always this way? Rosenthal didn't know, but he noticed that the court correction officers who guarded them were careless and blindly ignored the jurors' abuses.

As the trial began, Harold Harrison finally devised a strategy of sorts. He didn't have any real plan to counter the prosecution because—aside from knowing that there would be a mystery witness, hearing hints that it would be a "woman in a window"—he simply was not aware of the strength of their case. But in his direct, almost childlike way, Harrison would try to create some sympathy for Alice Crimmins. As he passed a reporter in the hallway on his way to lunch that first week, he clutched Alice's elbow and said in a stage whisper: "Be careful, remember your condition." When the reporter asked if Alice was pregnant, Harrison was coy. "Use your imagination," he said. To other questions, he retreated behind a theatrical "No comment." Eddie was let in on Harold's tactic, and when he was questioned by reporters, he said: "Isn't the husband the last to know?" an inadvertent homily usually applicable to another kind of secret.

The next morning the *Daily News* headline on page five said: "Strain Hits Mrs. Crimmins; She is Reported Pregnant." By that afternoon, however, the *Long Island Press* had aborted the story: "Mrs. Crimmins Isn't Awaiting the Stork."

Harrison's tactic backfired. Reporters felt betrayed and would no longer trust him. Publicly humiliated, some reporters wrote off the Crimmins defense team as capable of supporting any lie to enhance their case. The regular courtroom reporters would not be so easily misled again. Whatever Harrison told them would be weighed against that first cheap trick. At the prosecution table, Tony Lombardino was delighted. In a stroke Harrison had destroyed his own credibility and enhanced the District Attorney's. Lombardino winked at his friends in the press corps—he couldn't help gloating, saying he had tried to warn them.

But if Harold Harrison's public-relations efforts were clumsy, it was a measure of his desperation. His cause, he was beginning to discover, was not a popular one. In his own legal firm, Donald Manes was remaining as remote as possible. Manes, who had first brought Joe Rorech to the firm, did send a note to Harrison suggesting that his partner remind the jurors that people were innocent until proven guilty, and that he should avoid letting anyone be picked for the jury who was related to a policeman.

After the first few moments of Lombardino's opening statement, there was no more mystery—it was to be a slugging match. James Mosley would sit at the prosecution table looking slightly bewildered while his partner delivered the blows.

"We won't produce motion pictures of her doing it," said Anthony Lombardino, his voice thick with contempt, but there would be ample proof under the law to convict Alice Crimmins of murder. Marty Baron was stunned. Harold Harrison's instinct for combat was aroused. They expected the judge to step in and bring Lombardino within bounds. But Judge Farrell allowed Lombardino latitude. The judge did not even interfere when Lombardino moved onto very shaky legal grounds, suggesting that although no one could connect Alice with her son's death, both deaths were a package.

Baron immediately demanded that a mistrial be declared. Farrell waved him away from the bench and issued a confusing instruction to the jurors. He told them they should consider only the crime of Missy's death, but they were permitted to note that Eddie was dead, too. It was the first sign of the list in favor of the prosecution.

Marty Baron was the wrong man to pit against Tony Lombardino. He did not have Harold Harrison's relish for a gutter fight, and, like James Mosley, he would find himself crowded off the stage by the two brawlers —Lombardino and Harrison. Baron, however, delivered the opening for the defense. He had agonized over it for days, reviewing Harrison's proposed drafts and then deciding to make it brief. "We do not know how this child met her death," he began, "but we will prove that Alice was a loving and a good mother and was emotionally incapable of doing this terrible thing." He was asking the jury to accept an existential mystery that had almost driven dozens of policemen mad. Worse, he was appealing to a level of intellect while Lombardino aimed for the gut. At the prosecution table, Lombardino had trouble keeping his face in an expression of indignant rage. He could tell that his reaction was having an effect on the jury.

Between sessions in the courtroom Alice Crimmins would cross Queens Boulevard to the Part I restaurant, which had become a defense fortress. The movement would be accompained by all the attendant fanfare of backtracking television cameramen, a pause in traffic, and the rushing chorus of bystanders and courtroom spectators, who could never seem to stare at her enough. They would gaze quietly—only outsiders would cry out. They would follow her, the regulars, and stand in the doorway of the restaurant to watch Alice drinking Coca-Cola. It was not just an idle vigil. They waited for the moments when Alice relaxed. If she laughed, it was noted and reported to the others holding a place in line. If she fluffed her hair or nibbled on a hamburger, it was all recorded, and was used to demolish the portrait of grieving parent that Harrison and Baron were trying to paint. Someone would murmur, "Bitch!" and it would undo the courtroom effect so carefully planned by Harold Harrison. Each day Eddie would come over to the defense table, kiss his wife on the cheek, and lead her out of the courtroom. In another part of the courtroom Alice's mother, accompanied by her son, John, would sit clutching her gloved hands into fists of determination. The family would enter and leave together, all performed for the benefit of the jury—the twelve men who would pronounce judgment, but also for the hundreds of others who sat in menacing witness. "I just want to make sure that the bitch gets what she deserves," said a woman towing two reluctant children.

"I didn't think she was a lovely young thing," juror number nine, Lewis Rosenthal, would say later. "Her appearance was interesting. She sat there—she did not impress me as a monster; she didn't impress me as a damsel in distress."

As she sat day after day in the courtroom, stealing glances at the jurors studying her, Alice Crimmins began to have serious doubts that they would understand her complicated innocence.

44

One of the best parts of Peter Farrell's job was the secret of his private theater. Alone in his chambers, he would drop the omniscient forbearance and chuckle over a particular performance. A judge could dine out forever on the things that take place in his courtroom. Trials have been compared to war and chess, but Farrell knew that the tactics of the theater were more apt. Every trial was a unique act of creation—a play that would never be repeated. The production was in the hands of the contending attorneys, who were also the principal actors, but Farrell was the omnipotent director who could sit back benignly or intervene harshly, cutting off one side or the other, leading the plot where he wanted it to go. Farrell had seen fine actors at work. A man like Maurice Edelbaum, virtually unknown to the public, was an expert in matters of timing and pacing and dramatic force. Edelbaum, employed by some of the most notorious Mafiosi, could use a crowd of spectators like stage props to influence the real audience—the jury. Edelbaum, who had a quality much like Spencer Tracy's, was able to refocus attention to himself. A judge watching him work would not be immune to the spell, and among themselves the judges ranked lawyers like connoisseurs. In the Alice Crimmins trial, Farrell knew, he would not hear the splendid eloquence of a Maurice Edelbaum, but he would settle for the tussle of a George Raft and a James Cagney on prosecution and defense.

The opening of the trial was bound to be confusing. There was the obligatory clutter of technical testimony. As nearly as possible, evidence is based on hard proof. A map of the area cannot be introduced without an engineering expert to swear that it fairly represents the neighborhood. It is more than a fussy exercise—it is a habit of taking only the best possible proof.

Detective Frank Frezza said he had taken the photographs of Missy in the lot on 162nd Street on July 14, 1965. He examined his pictures carefully, noted his marks of identification on them, and only then were they accepted as evidence. People's Exhibits One through Eight were passed around for the jurors to examine, their faces puckered as they stared at the corpse of the four-year-old girl. Politely they circulated the pictures among themselves as if they were handling a luncheon menu; yet the jury members were gripped by the impact of staring at a dead child.

Patrolman Bernard Banks, a member of the police engineering section, provided a diagram of the Crimmins apartment, perhaps the only clear reference point throughout the trial. Time and time again, as testimony collided and stories became muddled, some member of the jury could be found staring wistfully at Banks' diagram, a touchstone of reliability.

To establish a moral climate, Lombardino set out to hammer home his point mathematically. It was couched in a flimsy euphemism. How many times, he asked Carl Andrade, the manager of the Steak Pub, had he "seen" Alice Crimmins?

"Quite a few times," answered Andrade.

That wasn't good enough. "Was it more than fifty times?"

"I would say so."

"Was it more than a hundred times?"

"It's very hard to say."

Lombardino had made his point.

The lovers each delivered mileage charts for Lombardino to show how Alice had strayed. Charles Boylan, her supervisor at Hagen Industries, where she worked as a secretary, had slept with her countless times. Even the neighborhood barber, Pasquale Picassio, who had made love to Alice in a car in back of the barbershop in the fall of 1964, was displayed to the jury. And, of course, Joe Rorech.

But somehow the filaments of the testimony could not support the dire charge of murder. The prosecution tried to wrap the wisps of inference into a convincing argument. Detective John Kelly went through contortions describing how eager the police had been to hear Alice's confession, but were only rewarded with defiance. Lombardino tried to make it sound incriminating that Alice Crimmins wouldn't confess. It was like a silent-film melodrama where Lombardino's gestures of horror at such behavior were magnified and telegraphed to the jury. When Piering and Kelly had begged Alice to prove her innocence, she had stalked off and told them to bring her to court.

With a weak case, Lombardino and Mosley were forced to torture the record for anything incriminating. For example, Kelly testified that he had asked Alice to take sodium pentothal to prove her innocence.

"She looked at me and said, 'When you arrest me and take me to court, that's when I will prove I am innocent.'" Kelly paused to allow the natural conclusion to sink in—that she would now have to deliver the proof. It was a strange inversion of presumptive innocence, but in the courtroom it was telling. There was a meaningful exhale among the spectators. When witnesses reported that Alice had spoken about her

245

"guilt feelings," there was a murmur of understanding in the court. Lombardino's weak strands were forming a web.

Evelyn Atkins, the former maid, embellished the major theme by testifying about the infamous boat trip when Alice had deserted her children for the weekend. It left the jury with the feeling that Alice Crimmins had been, at the least, careless about her children. Lombardino would have to produce better evidence to carry it a step further—that she could have actively conspired in their deaths.

Detective Gerard Piering had waited almost three years for his turn to take the stand against Alice. He would provide the prosecution's first piece of hard evidence. On the morning the children disappeared, Piering swore, he had found a film of dust on the dresser and on the sill outside the window. He was unshakable on that point. Sitting almost motionless in the witness stand, Piering testified in a voice that trembled with sincerity. His memory of that morning was sharp and clear, he swore. Alice had told him that she had locked the children in their bedroom. She had fed them manicotti before they were put to bed.

On cross-examination, Piering wouldn't budge; he continued to hurt the defense. Alice was wearing makeup and had her hair "fixed" when he arrived on the scene, he said with obvious malice.

On the third day a man with the distracted manner of a country doctor took the stand. It was Dr. Richard Grimes, who had made the first inspection of Missy's body when it was still covered with flies. "I saw the body of a girl who appeared to be about five years of age; she appeared to be lying on her left side. Her legs were flexed at the knees—flexed at the hips. She was clad in a cotton undershirt, a pair of yellow panties. . . ." Dr. Grimes spoke with dry professional detachment.

A voice broke the recitation. "No!" It was Alice Crimmins.

Harold Harrison put an arm around her, whispered, trying to comfort her. Dr. Grimes squirmed for having caused such a fuss. Judge Farrell pounded his desk and demanded order. Tony Lombardino went through a momentary panic. He felt a backlash of sympathy for Alice in the courtroom. He wanted the jury to hold the memory of Carl Andrade, the natty restaurant manager whose wardrobe fitted like ballet tights. But he misread the reaction.

Dr. Grimes continued: "Around the little girl's face there was a cloth tie. The loose ends of the tie appeared to be the arm of some type of garment. The tie was over the mouth of the child, the knot encircling the neck, and the tie was rather loose. . . ."

Alice Crimmins completely lost control of herself. She made wailing animal noises—sounds that she had never uttered in public and that she had sworn to herself to keep private. In the audience, some few cried out for a recess and some wept aloud. The courtroom was in danger of disintegrating into hysteria, and Judge Farrell gaveled a recess.

Harrison led her away to lunch, across Queens Boulevard, where yellow and orange trucks were grinding up the green malls to build extra traffic lanes. On the sides of the trucks the name of the man who ran the construction company was painted in large green letters—Anthony Grace. The man himself waited in an obscure booth of the Part I restaurant for Alice Crimmins. Harrison planted himself wearily in the booth, ordered a drink, and suggested that when Tony Grace took the witness stand after lunch, he should tear up the courthouse the way his trucks were cracking the streets.

Grace's appearance on the stand worried Peter Farrell. He summoned Lombardino and Harrison into his chambers and warned that he didn't want too much exploration of the purely lurid side of the relationship. Lombardino pledged to keep the sexual emphasis minimal.

"I tried to keep as much of this kind of testimony out as possible," Judge Farrell would recall later. "Of course, she was laying for everybody in creation."

James Mosley handled the questioning of Tony Grace. He would provide the extra ingredient of civility. But without Lombardino's bludgeoning innuendos, it was hard to elicit anything fruitful from Grace. In his own clumsy way, Mosley attempted to trap the witness into admitting that he had taken part in the crime, but Grace curtly denied it, as disdainfully as he would flick off a fly. There were two reasons for keeping Grace on the stand, however. One reason was to display him to the jury. If they were going to accept the prosecution theory, the jurors would have to see the unsavory characters cast in specific roles. Grace's rough grammar and imperious gangsterlike tone and silk suit would form a more lasting impression than any tricks of testimony.

But the more crucial reason for keeping Grace grunting denials all afternoon was a stall. Lombardino was frantically trying to bolster his case. Judge Farrell had let word leak that he was thinking of throwing the case out. Farrell was disgusted with the quality of prosecution evidence. "You have no case," he had told Lombardino. "I have to throw it out as a matter of law." Lombardino had told Farrell that there was more to the case than the grand jury had seen.

Actually, Lombardino was bluffing. There was no more to it, but he thought that, given a little time, he could add a few things. He spent his lunch hour on Monday, May 13, in gloomy despair. If he blew this case, if it never even went to a jury, he would be cast back into the obscure pits of the felony trial part. His popularity, or at least his acceptance, in the District Attorney's office was based solely on his success. He had leapfrogged over too many people, brushed aside too many sensibilities, ignored too much civility to be tolerated on any other terms. He would be like the class bully rendered powerless if he fumbled this case: his enemies, crouching in every shadow, would pounce.

Mosley, who already had a loser's pallor, accepted Farrell's judgment with a shrug. But Lombardino told his partner they were not going to quit. What are you going to do? Mosley asked.

"I'm gonna deliver Joe Rorech," said Lombardino.

In the courtroom James Mosley performed a holding action while his partner gambled on one more ratchet turn for Rorech. Mosley called Dr. Milton Helpern to the stand.

Dr. Helpern's books and articles made an impressive file, and he was listed as a consultant or advisor by the nation's best hospitals and medical universities. There was nothing self-deprecating about his manner: when he took the stand, he wanted it understood that he brought with him the full weight of his standing and experience. Thus introduced, he could adopt a very imposing manner upon being questioned.

"I might say that with regard to the gastrointestinal tract," he began, "the stomach contained a large amount of food that extended from the upper end of the stomach down to the lower opening of the stomach. And this food appeared to be recently ingested. In other words, the contents of the stomach were not empty. The stomach was full. . . ."

Mosley interrupted Dr. Helpern impatiently. He wanted this point driven home to the jury. On this evidence he intended to smash Alice's alibi.

"How soon after this child digested the food was the child dead?" he asked, turning to face the jury.

Dr. Helpern paused for a moment before answering. It was a question upon which dozens of doctors had anguished and disagreed for almost three years. Finally science came down to questions of memory and judgment. "This is a difficult question to answer with any precision," Dr. Helpern replied, and for a flicker James Mosley thought his case was gone. "But the finding of as much food as was found in this case is consistent with a post-ingestion period, that is, a time after the food was ingested, of less than two hours. . . ."

Relieved, Mosley slumped against the jury railing for a moment. Milton Helpern had fulfilled his promise to Tony Lombardino. He had committed the full weight of his reputation to the prosecution's argument that Alice could not have seen the children alive at midnight.

Under relentless cross-examination that took the rest of the afternoon and continued the next morning, Dr. Helpern held his ground. Each time the defense tried to make him hedge or qualify his stout opinion, Dr. Helpern repulsed the effort with a flourish of his own specialty. "In a healthy person, especially a child, the stomach empties rather rapidly," he testified like a patient teacher. He brushed off a defense suggestion that Missy could have died from the venom of a bee sting, and that the marks on her neck might have been the result of the weeds and branches in the lot. Nearly impossible, testified Helpern.

Harold Harrison was at a severe disadvantage. He did not know about the long campaign it had taken to win Dr. Helpern's conclusion that Missy had died within two hours of eating. He was not aware of the conversation that Detective Phil Brady had recorded in which Dr. Helpern said that such a conclusion was "irresponsible and impossible." The defense was ignorant of the undertone of disagreement within the Medical Examiner's office—of the doctors on Helpern's own staff who regarded their chief not as a giant in his field, but as a rather narrow man who was jealous and insecure about his reputation and spiteful about his enemies.

The defense table merely slumped into despair as Dr. Helpern deluged the courtroom with damaging scientific jargon.

"There was one piece of evidence that was indisputable," juror number nine, Lewis Rosenthal, recalled years later. "The medical evidence. The stomach contents. Dr. Helpern could not be disputed. He's a famous man; a reliable doctor. . . . The defense was never able to establish that there was ever any other possibility. Oh, they brought up other doctors, but no one could satisfactorily dispute Dr. Helpern. She claimed she woke the children at midnight and he testified that they had been dead at 9:30 p.m. . . . We seized on that point."

Inside the stomach, the doctor testified, were found a green leafy material, like string beans, a macaroni-type substance, and orange seeds. Little details like the undigested orange seeds left an unbearably plaintive chord haunting the trial.

There had been a final meeting between Joe Rorech and Alice Crimmins on May 13. It had taken place in Harold Harrison's office and was a tearful affair. "I

250

won't be able to see you for a while," Alice had told Joe. "It wouldn't look right during the trial."

"What about after the trial?" Rorech asked.

"I don't know," replied Alice. "Maybe I'll stay with Eddie for a while. Maybe I owe my mother something."

Rorech was inconsolable. As they sat on the couch in the lawyer's office, Rorech caressed Alice's hand, sobbing that he wanted to marry Alice, wanted her to have his baby. Harrison, embarrassed by the scene, stepped outside. Joe frantically tried every appeal. Then he began fondling Alice on the couch, trying to revive her physical dependence.

Harrison, who had re-entered unseen, cleared his throat. He had business to discuss with Rorech, who seemed on the verge of collapse. Harrison wanted to talk about the trial, but all Joe could think about was this further blow, the loss of Alice. Rorech was scheduled to take the stand on Thursday—three days away— and Harrison wanted to know what he planned to say. "Just what I've always said," replied Rorech.

He turned back to Alice and said he had a favor to ask. He held her hand tenderly. The testimony was going to wreck his marriage. Alice nodded sympathetically. "Would you speak to Gloria?" he asked Alice. If Alice would go to his home and explain things to Gloria and tell her how much Joe loved his wife, maybe it could save Joe's marriage.

"Certainly," said Alice, thinking that it was a small price to pay for Joe's loyalty.

But when Joe Rorech walked out of Harrison's office, he was a man almost totally without hope. He had lost his business. Creditors were reclaiming his possessions. He stood a good chance of losing his freedom. His marriage was about to be tested, and he was not certain it would survive. And now he had lost Alice. As he walked to his car and Alice walked with Harrison in another direction, Rorech felt betrayed, isolated . . . and afraid.

At approximately the same hour, Judge Farrell had been explaining to Lombardino that he was duty-bound to dismiss the charges unless the prosecution presented a stronger case. While grand juries may indict for "probable cause," a defendant cannot be convicted unless the presiding judge is persuaded that the prosecution has delivered enough evidence to the jury to form a *prima facie* case of guilt. That is, there must be, by law, evidence of motive and opportunity and guilt.

As Lombardino went over the files, he studied the possibilities. If Alice had confessed, that would have been convincing proof of guilt. Or if the authorities had found an accomplice. There was only one track he had not exhausted and that was to crack Joe Rorech.

The next day, as Mosley took over management of the case in court, Lombardino went across the street to Luigi's restaurant, where he had instructed Rorech to meet him for lunch.

Both men drank through the dinner hour. They were joined during the afternoon by Detectives Kelly and Walter Anderson. Lombardino sensed that Rorech had changed. His puffed ego was deflated. He seemed stripped of pretension and artifice. He drank hard without getting drunk.

The encounter changed the trajectory of the trial, and the lives of many around it. There is only Lombardino's version of the event: " 'You know, Tony,' " he quoted Rorech as saying, " 'you're a good salesman. I'm a salesman too. And one thing I learned is that you can be too good a salesman. You had me sold, but then you oversold yourself.' "

Lombardino was silent for a moment. He knew that he was tantalizingly close to breaking Rorech. All he had to do was find the right combination of promises and threats. Lombardino had to deliver Rorech by Thursday, less than forty-eight hours away. Rorech had sensed Lombardino's weakness, and some of his self-importance began to return.

"Are you afraid of Tony Grace?" asked Lombardino.

"I don't want to end up with icepicks in my eyes," replied Rorech.

The table was littered with half-eaten meals and empty glasses. Suddenly Lombardino wanted to get Rorech out of Luigi's. He knew the man was about to crack and he didn't want it to happen in a restaurant. He turned to Walter Anderson and told him to get a car and reserve a suite at a nearby motel.

At a motel flanking La Guardia airport, Rorech settled into a chair and continued drinking Scotch. Lombardino had warned his men not to try to keep up with Rorech, but sociably hold onto a drink while they tried to pry information out of him. Joe Rorech never went home that night. Nor did Walter Anderson or Tony Lombardino. On Wednesday Lombardino made a token appearance in court, but quickly left to return to the motel room.

Harrison, who had been trying to reach Rorech, was becoming alarmed. Rorech's wife said mysteriously that she didn't know where Joe was, but that he had called to say he was all right. Harrison dismissed it from his mind. He noted and was alarmed by the disappearance of Lombardino, but he didn't connect the "coincidence."

Throughout Wednesday, Lombardino fed liquor to Rorech. One of his men picked up a change of wardrobe and they bought some toilet articles to prepare for the appearance in court on Thursday. Sometime on Wednesday—Lombardino cannot pinpoint the moment —Joe Rorech came over to his side. It was accomplished without promises. Somehow it came to be understood by everyone in the room that when Rorech took the stand, he would hang Alice Crimmins.

Lombardino had committed himself, too. Rorech testified against Alice Crimmins under a grant of immunity, knowing the slate would be wiped clean and there would be no criminal prosecutions. "The charges weren't that serious against him," Lombardino would say years later, defending the grant of immunity.

After the luncheon recess on Thursday, May 16, Joseph Rorech was called to take the witness stand. It was almost fifty yards down the center aisle of the courtroom, and the eyes of the spectators followed his every step. Rorech did not look to either side as he took his place on the stand. His hair was combed straight back and there was no expression on his face. His expensive suit was not paid for. Alice tried to smile at him, but he never looked in her direction.

He took the oath and bent forward in the witness stand, his hands clasped together and his voice muted. It was not normally a quiet voice. When he had peppered Alice with five calls a day for five years, he had made a booming, cheerful sound, alive with possibilities. He would take Alice's slipping moods and carry her back to giddiness. "Things are never that bad," he would say.

But as he sat in the witness stand, appearing like a condemned man, he spoke as if he were looking down the barrel of a gun. He had to be reminded to keep his voice up. Harold Harrison, sensing something ominous, asked for a sidebar conference, a conference which takes place out of range of the jury. He made a motion for an offer of proof—which is a motion out of the range of the jury asking the District Attorney to indicate the general area of the forthcoming testimony and its relevance to the trial. Farrell was brusque with Harrison: "No."

Then to Rorech: "Nice and loud now. I can hardly hear you."

Rorech: "I'm sorry."

Harrison kept throwing up objections, trying to prevent Rorech from what seemed to be building into a terrible blow against the defense. "What's wrong?" whispered Alice to Harrison. He didn't answer her. She would see soon enough.

Tony Lombardino led Rorech carefully. The story came out slowly at first. The testimony concerned a meeting between Alice and Joe in a cocktail lounge in Nassau County a month before the custody hearing, when the children were both alive. Harrison objected; he couldn't see the relevance, but the judge denied every motion. Each objection was like a plea to Rorech —Harrison was saying, "Don't do it, Joe." But the story continued; there was no turning back for Rorech.

RORECH: Well, we kept discussing the fact that Eddie wanted the children. She did not want Eddie to have the children. She did not want her mother to have the children. Regardless of what happened, she wasn't going to let them have the children. . . . The day that she was going to court [he had to be reminded again about his voice] she was not going to bring the children to court with her. And she was going to drop them off at her girlfriend's house. And when she went to court that day, if she had to produce the children, she would go back to her friend's house, pick up the children, and take off.

Harrison began to have hope. Perhaps this was the extent of Rorech's damaging evidence. But it was hard to believe that Lombardino would lay such suspenseful groundwork unless he had something explosive.

"Did she say anything else, Mr. Rorech?" asked Lombardino.

Rorech: "She did not want Eddie to have the children. She would rather see the children dead than Eddie have them."

The impact was lost since hardly anyone could hear it. "Wait a minute," said Farrell, straining to hear. "You see," he said, pointing to the stenographic reporter, "they couldn't even get that. Repeat it, Mr. Reporter."

It was a surprise, but Harrison could live with that kind of testimony. There wasn't much that was terribly incriminating; just more of the same attack on morality. Alice's first impulse was generous. They must have put Joe through a lot to squeeze this out of him, she thought. But Rorech wasn't through. There had been a night in 1966 when Joe and Alice were talking, Rorech testified. She had been filled with remorse. If only Joe had come over on the night the children disappeared, this wouldn't have happened, she had told Rorech. The implication of this testimony was that Alice knew what had happened that night and that Joe's presence could have prevented it. It was vague, but Lombardino threw it in.

Harrison was worried about something besides Joe's testimony. He was afraid of being involved in a terrible conflict, since Joe Rorech was also his client. As he listened in fascination with everyone else, Harrison decided he would have to drop Rorech as a client and possibly remove himself from the case. He had not done anything unethical, but he feared he might have compromised his client's defense.

Rorech's testimony continued: On another occasion Alice had told him emphatically that the children went out the front door, not the window. On the night the children disappeared, he told the jury, he called Alice twice, and the second call she never answered although he let it ring five times. He still remembered the number: Boulevard 3–7851.

And then Lombardino brought Rorech to the night of September 9, 1966. He had jumped all over the calendar with Rorech, putting him at ease in the witness chair, establishing his identity as a prosecution witness. But the point of it all was September 9, 1966. Rorech asked for a glass of water. What happened on September 9, 1966? asked Lombardino.

With his head low, Rorech said that he and Alice had gone to a motel—the Kings Grant Inn in Nassau County. Alice had started crying.

"This went on for a period of time, and she said there was no reason for them to be killed. It was senseless. The reason had been eliminated. I said to her, 'You mean Evelyn?' "

One of the jurors had difficulty hearing, and Rorech spoke a little louder: "And she kept crying. She started to say again that they will understand, they know it was for the best. And I said to her, 'Missy and Eddie are dead. No one can speak for them. Only you and I can help them.' And she repeated over and over again, 'They will understand, they know it was for the best.' And this repeated on and on quite a few times. And then she said to me, 'Joseph, please forgive me, I killed her.' "

The courtroom exploded. Alice leaped out of her chair, her fists banging on the defense table, her eyes on fire with anger. People all around the room were screaming or shouting. But it was as if the two were alone in the room—just Alice and Joe; two former lovers.

"Joseph!" she cried, her voice breaking. "How could you do this? This is not true! Joseph . . . you, of all people! Oh, my God!"

There was one person who could have challenged Rorech's testimony. On the night when Rorech swore that Alice made her confession, Detective Phil Brady had spoken to Rorech for two hours. After he had come back from the Kings Grant Inn, Rorech had called Brady. The detective had asked Rorech over and over if Alice had said anything incriminating, but Rorech had said all the conversation was innocent. Brady remembered the conversation clearly, and he remembered that Rorech had been emphatic in denying that anything important had been said.

But Phil Brady had been pulled off the case and he didn't follow it in the newspapers. By the time his conscience bothered him, it was too late. No one wanted to listen.

On May 16, 1968, no one knew about Detective Phil Brady. There was only the undisputed testimony of Joseph Rorech. Lombardino smiled as decorum broke down. He had enough now to take the case to the jury.

45

Peter Farrell hadn't yet put on his robes and Harold Harrison sat nervously on the edge of his chair in the judge's chambers before the start of court on Friday, May 17.

"I think I should withdraw," said Harrison.

He had outlined his reasons to Farrell: he represented both Alice Crimmins and Joe Rorech, and now that one had turned against the other, he couldn't represent the interests of both. He had dropped Rorech as a client after his appearance on the stand, but he was worried that he might have compromised Alice's defense.

Farrell shook his head. If Harrison pulled out of the case, it would mean long delays. A new attorney would have to be hired and brought up to date. They would have to go through all the pretrial motions and the trial again. It might be assigned to another judge. Furthermore, Harrison believed that Farrell was sprinting through the case so that he would be able to attend his son's college graduation—as he did the day after the trial ended on May 30.

Alice waited for Harrison in his office. She had thought she was immune to further shock and pain, but when Rorech turned against her, it hurt. She sat on the couch—the same couch where he had begged her to marry him a few days earlier—mumbling over and over: "Joseph, you were my best friend!" When Harrison returned from Farrell's chambers, he sat with her, holding her hand, while she spoke to Rorech's ghost: "Joseph, how could you? You were my friend!"

"It's going to be a busy weekend for me," said Harrison. "I want you to get as much rest as possible."

She looked at him without expression. "It's been a bad week," she said.

On Monday the prosecution was scheduled to call its mystery witness. On Thursday, Harold Harrison had found out her name. When Lombardino handed Harrison a copy of the grand-jury minutes of Joe Rorech's appearance, he had carelessly left an unfamiliar name on the cover. Harrison immediately guessed that "Sophie Earomirski" was the "woman in the window" and sent investigators to interview her. Mrs. Earomirski wouldn't unchain the door when Harrison's men rang her bell. She slammed the door in their faces and called Tony Lombardino to tell him they'd been there.

On Friday afternoon Mosley complained to Judge Farrell that Harrison's people were "hounding" his witness. Mosley summoned Mrs. Earomirski to court and swore her in—out of turn—thus invoking immunity from defense questioning. Then Farrell summoned Harrison to his chambers again.

"Have you been bothering the People's witness?" Farrell asked Harrison.

"I tried to talk to her, yes, Your Honor," replied Harrison. "It's my job."

"This witness has now been sworn, and if you bother her again, I'll ram it up your ass."

Learning the identity of the mystery witness had become almost a contest among newspaper reporters. Friends and sources within the District Attorney's office were tapped, but the security held. One day *Newsday*'s Manny Topol approached a stout woman sitting in the rear of the courtroom to ask if she were the mystery witness.

"No," she said pointing at the blushing prosecutor, "I'm Tony's mother. I'm taking him home for lunch."

"Aw, ma," whined Lombardino.

Harrison's office became a combat headquarters over the weekend as he dispatched investigators to research Sophie Earomirski. It was a frustrating job, since most offices were closed, and it would continue even while Mrs. Earomirski was on the stand.

If Joe Rorech had slunk into the courtroom, Sophie Earomirski entered like a champion on Monday morning. She smiled inadvertently at her own celebrity. Urged on by the gentle questioning of James Mosley, Sophie told her tale.

It was hot, she remembered, on the night of July 13. "Very, very hot," she said. She had gone to bed at 11:00 p.m. Trying to be vivid in her testimony, she helpfully offered the opinion that the bricks in her building retained the heat during July. Her husband had been asleep, but she was unable to sleep, so she crept out of bed and wandered into the kitchen. She poured herself a glass of iced tea, and when she glanced at the clock, it was 2:00 a.m. These little details seemed to lend a note of authenticity to Sophie's testimony. The clock on the shelf where she stored her plastic glasses was a touch her listeners could almost visualize.

Restless, she drifted into the living room and started to work on a crossword puzzle. A breeze came in through the living-room window and it distracted her. She shut off the light and leaned out the window, letting the draft wash away the heat. She stubbed out her cigarette on the sill and watched the sparks disappear like fireflies. And then something off to the left caught her attention. She noticed a group of people approaching, what seemed to be a family. The man was walking ahead and the woman was trailing, carrying a bundle in one hand and walking with a child in the other. The bundle was under the woman's left arm. The child let go of the woman's hand and walked faster toward the man. There was also a dog sniffing around on the mall, looking, it appeared, for a place to relieve itself. The woman waited for the dog, and the man became impatient.

EAROMIRSKI: He [the man] was looking left and right, up and down the street, and he called over to her to hurry up, will you, and she said that she was waiting for the dog. She said, "The dog is pregnant." And he said to her, "Did you have to bring it?" She made a remark which I didn't get. He went over to her and he took the bundle and he swung the bundle under his arm . . . and he walked very quickly to the car that was parked going the wrong way opposite my window. He opened the back door of the car and he took this bundle and he threw it in the back seat of the car.

MOSLEY: Go on.

EAROMIRSKI: She ran over to him and she said, "My God, don't do that to her." And then he looked at her and said, "Now you're sorry?" and something else and then she looked up at him and she said, "Please don't say that, don't say that." The little boy . . . got into the back seat of the car. He had climbed over and I saw him in the front seat. He looked like he was trying to get the window open there. At that point I became very upset. I became very numb. . . .

Judge Farrell interrupted to remind her that her feelings were not relevant; they were in court to hear sworn statements of fact, not personal emotions.

MOSLEY: What, if anything, did you do?

EAROMIRSKI: I tried to close the window. I picked up the crank and I turned the handle and it squeaked. She said to him, "Somebody's seen us," and they turned and they looked in back of them at the building for a while. Then they turned and they looked into my apartment, the apartment downstairs, the one on the first floor, and

260

they kept looking up at my apartment and I had ducked behind my drape.

MOSLEY: What happened then?

EAROMIRSKI: I waited there for a while and I looked and I seen this other fellow was crossing from Kissena Boulevard over, and they were looking at him and they had this conversation and the man turned away from her and he was like facing me, and when this other man passed by them she acknowledged, like a hello, a greeting, and he walked down the area towards the mall; and again I stood back. I sat down. I lit a cigarette.

The testimony was breathtaking. Every eye was on the heavy woman, but drifted now and then to see the effect on Alice, who was as struck as anyone else.

EAROMIRSKI: Well, then I got up and I looked out the window and I saw the car turn around and go towards the area by Kissena Boulevard.

There was a pause. Mosley waited until he had the courtroom's attention. "Now, the woman you say you saw carrying this bundle and the woman you heard say 'Don't do that to her,' and the woman you heard say 'Somebody seen us,' do you see that woman in this courtroom?"

Sophie snapped her head and looked at the defense table. Her right arm went up straight as an arrow and a finger pointed at Alice Crimmins. "That's the woman!" she said.

There was a rumble from the spectators and Alice Crimmins screamed at Sophie Earomirski: "You liar! You liar!"

"I heard you!" Mrs. Earomirski shouted back.

"You liar! You liar!"

Judge Farrell was trying to rap down the exchange with his gavel, but Alice kept shouting: "You liar! You liar!"

"This will stop from this point on," ordered Judge Farrell vainly. "You are instructed to disregard this outburst," he told the jury.

During the weekend and on Monday the defense staff had worked on Sophie's background. However, the defense had temporarily been sapped of its greatest energy source—Harold Harrison. His father, Louis Harrison, died that Monday and Harold was called out of the courtroom. He would not return for a week, and so Marty Baron would have to lead the attack on Sophie Earomirski.

The witness sat with her defensive armor bristling as Baron circled for a moment, reading the file his detectives had brought in. Softly, almost innocently, Baron began probing for soft spots. Did you recognize the man? he asked. No, replied Sophie, but he had a big nose. Baron picked up a copy of Sophie's grand-jury testimony. He noted what seemed to him like a discrepancy. In court she displayed an impressive memory for detail. The woman's legs were bare and she wore a triangle scarf; her hair was dark and fell below the shoulders. But the only thing that Sophie had told the grand jury was that the woman had on a pair of shorts and a blouse.

To the spectators it seemed that Baron was nit-picking. To many, this moment in the trial had turned into a contest between a hapless woman and a tricky lawyer. Each time she scored a point, there was a cheer. When she left the stand for a recess, she held her hands up in a boxer's salute and the audience laughed appreciatively.

When she returned to the stand, Baron was ready with some tough questions. He asked her about the concussion she had received when working at the World's Fair, and Sophie dismissed the injury as trivial. What did the hospital at the Fair do for you? Baron asked. When she replied, "Nothing," the spectators roared.

During her two days on the witness stand, Sophie's testimony grew stronger with the encouragement of the audience. She denied having seen a psychiatrist. She denied having made suicide attempts, although her stomach had once had to be pumped after an overdose of pills. Another time her husband had found her unconscious with her head in the oven, but she claimed she had fallen asleep when checking on something she was cooking. There was never any risk of a perjury charge against Sophie, since she was the prosecution's star witness and her explanations had been accepted.

Baron confronted another handicap. Judge Farrell was limiting the range of questioning. Before he left the trial, Harrison had ordered a psychiatrist profile of Sophie Earomirski from Dr. Louis Berg, a specialist in neurology and psychiatry.

That Wednesday—May 22—Dr. Berg examined the Workmen's Compensation file of Sophie Earomirski. He explored her case with other doctors and reported his findings to Harrison in a written report. On August 25, 1967, he noted in his report, Mrs. Earomirski had been treated at Booth Memorial Hospital after taking an overdose of librium—presumably a suicide attempt. Her stomach had had to be pumped.

It is my considered opinion after reading and evaluating these hospital reports and the compensation file that Mrs. Earomirski suffered first a head injury [at the World's Fair] which resulted in permanent brain damage. This is evidenced by the fact that her compensation case was terminated by the carrier on the basis of a permanent partial disability of the brain. Secondly, Mrs. Earomirski made at least one suicide attempt [which] is further evidence of her emotional instability. Finally, it is an established clinical fact that a hysterectomy, which brings a woman's menstruation function [to an end], is accompanied by emotional and sometimes even mental symptoms.

The clinical picture presented by the hospital records . . . shows a heavily unstable individual. . . .

(signed) LOUIS BERG, M.D., M.A.P.A.

Dr. Berg's affidavit was sworn to on May 22, 1968, but Judge Peter Farrell, within his discretionary powers, ruled that it was inadmissible to the case.

There were sharp inconsistencies in Sophie Earomirski's testimony. She claimed she had never had trouble sleeping except on this one night. And yet when she was seeking damages for her injury, she had sworn before many medical boards that she was an insomniac.

In the letter she wrote to the District Attorney, she

said that what she saw that night "may be connected and may not be" connected to the case. In the letter she described just "a woman," and yet she had known Alice Crimmins from the neighborhood and was later able to pick her out from police photographs. On the witness stand the first soft assertion hardened into cement.

Finally, there was the testimony about the dog. Mrs. Earomirski swore that she had heard the woman on the mall say that the dog was "pregnant." But several other witnesses swore that no one knew Brandy was pregnant that night. When the dog gave birth to a single pup the week after the killings, it was a complete surprise to Alice, her family, and the neighbors. She had even been negotiating with one of the neighbors to buy another dog—she wanted one for each child.

With Sophie, it was hard to know where reality left off and the power of suggestion began. When she was questioned about her eyesight and brainwave tests, she announced proudly that they were all "perfect," and the spectators applauded her spunk.

It was finally too much for Judge Farrell. "What do you think this is," he said sternly, addressing the audience, "the Hippodrome? I will not allow any more of this."

It was hard not to hold Sophie up to ridicule. When she said it was not a suicide attempt when she was found unconscious with her head in the oven, that she was just checking on dinner, there was a good-natured wave of applause. The spectators admired the bravery of someone who would expose herself to that kind of laughter. Sophie didn't distinguish between those who laughed with her and those who laughed at her. She basked in the limelight.

But there was more to it than a fearless performance. When Sophie left the stand, she was pleased with herself. She asked Lombardino how she had done, and he said, "fine, fine," as if he were grading her on an oral exercise. More compelling, though, was the effect Sophie's testimony had on the jury. If Sophie was uncertain about her story, if she had lapses of memory, she did provide the jury with a story that linked Alice

Crimmins with the District Attorney's version of the children's death. The jury had been shown the complete circle—the deaths, a possible motive, and opportunity.

The prosecution case was completed. Its effect on the jury was impossible to measure. But what it had done to the woman sitting in volcanic fury at the defense table, no more the demure little housewife in a white collar, was evident. This was what Tony Lombardino wanted the jury to see—Alice seething with rage, capable of violence.

Harold Harrison, in mourning for his father, was consulted by Marty Baron. Both men agreed that the defense had been injured badly by Joe Rorech's defection. They had a string of character witnesses who would testify to Alice's good nature and assert that she had been a good mother. The testimony of her husband, who had blurted out his belief in his wife's innocence on the witness stand, was not enough. Only one person could save Alice, they agreed—Alice Crimmins herself.

46

The first-strike advantage belongs to the prosecution. The defense must remain calm and stitch the wounds, one by one, with surgical patience. But the efforts of Harold Harrison and Marty Baron seemed feeble and doomed.

Choosing Theresa Costello as the first defense witness was a mistake. At seventeen, she was too young, and Alice's former baby-sitter left an aftertaste of youthful defiance with the jury. The testimony itself was too complicated. By now a high-school junior,

Theresa swore that she had heard the children reciting their prayers at 8:30 p.m. the night they disappeared. This was intended to challenge the medical testimony.

She told the jury she had seen the porter's stroller that night and noticed the screen inside the window of the children's room. The next morning the stroller had been moved under the window and the screen was down on the mall. The suggestion was that someone had used the stroller to take the children out through the window where the screen had been removed. But the testimony was too abstract to gain attention.

Mrs. Mary Buttner testified that Alice Crimmins' hair was worn an inch below her ears before the disappearance; Sophie Earomirski said that the woman on the mall had hair falling below the shoulders. Robert Levins, a neighbor, was among a group who said that the lighting on the mall was poor—too poor for someone to notice false eyelashes, as Sophie had sworn she had done. Others swore that Alice Crimmins had been a good mother and that it would have been out of character for her to strike a child, much less murder her own.

But the effect was less telling than the prosecution's brutal suggestions. The jurors were plainly dissatisfied with what they regarded as diversionary attacks on Sophie Earomirski.

Alice never really had time to prepare herself. There was a quick drink at lunch, accompanied by Marty Baron's hard warnings, but Alice was still stung by Sophie's testimony when she took the witness stand on Wednesday afternoon.

Judge Farrell, in the indirect and impersonal manner of the courtroom, had cautioned Alice through her attorney that by taking the stand she was waiving her right to stand mute.

"Does your client understand, Counselor?"

"Yes, Your Honor," replied Marty Baron.

But Baron was not certain that Alice really understood. Once she took the oath, she would be left open to the harshest assaults of the prosecution. Anthony Lombardino was waiting for just such an opportunity.

The rules of the courtroom are precise. A defendant may guard him/herself against character attacks by remaining silent and the court is obliged to respect that privacy unless the evidence directly bears upon the case. But once a defendant takes the witness stand, the prosecution, under a broad cloak of authority to impeach his/her word, is allowed to explore every aspect of character.

There would be no more prim hesitation about the propriety of examining her sex life. Nothing would be private on the witness stand. Lombardino was sure to use this license to bait and taunt her, trying to provoke her temper to give the jury a glimpse behind the shadows of Alice Crimmins' defenses.

But Alice had a very important motive for going to the witness chair. She wanted her own voice. From the start of the trial she had sat back helplessly, hearing herself depicted as a homicidal slut, and she was determined to correct that image. She was under the misapprehension, as she swore an oath to tell the truth, that she would at last be given a voice. What she did not understand was that the law was such a fine instrument that a cunning surgeon could cut her throat with a scalpel of objections and questions.

At first the voice was inaudible. "Alice, I'm going to ask you to speak up," said Marty Baron, but she had such a thin voice that it could never rise to the occasion. Farrell finally installed a microphone-and-loudspeaker system so that she could be heard.

Alice retraced her background . . . childhood in the Bronx . . . meeting Eddie at fifteen . . . the marriage in St. Frances de Chantal Church on November 8, 1958 . . . the disintegration of the marriage as Eddie worked from midnight to 8:00 a.m. as a mechanic for Trans World Airlines. The story was flat. She was unable to flesh it out with subtle details, important nuances. She couldn't make the people in the courtroom understand the overwhelming loneliness she had felt in her marriage, or the gradual numbing of feeling, the loss of respect. She could recite the fact that her husband was an airline mechanic, but "Did you know he couldn't even fix his own car?" she wanted to shout. That was irrelevant or immaterial to the court, but it had been a powerful influence on her feelings. Testimony, she was beginning to discover, was not always the whole truth.

It was late in the afternoon, almost 3:00 p.m., when Alice took the stand. Baron had wanted to counteract Sophie's impact on the jury. When Alice reached the point where she was talking about her children, she began to tremble. She turned to her right and whispered something to Judge Farrell.

"She says she can't go on," Judge Farrell told Baron, but his voice was skeptical. When Alice began to sob softly, Farrell declared a recess. Marty Baron put his arm around his client and helped her into a small room off the courtroom, where she slumped into a chair and stared hopelessly at the tile floor. Eddie bent over his wife, making consoling gestures. John Burke hovered near his sister. But Alice couldn't regain her composure. The trial would have to be postponed until the next day.

As she entered the courtroom on Thursday, a curtain had once again come down over her face, like the white gloves that her mother wore to conceal her hands. Alice was wearing the black crepe dress with the white fluted collar. She carried a handkerchief.

Carefully, almost gracefully, Baron led her through her past and up to the present. She was now working as an executive secretary for the North American Phillips Company, a fact that the defense hoped would mitigate the cocktail-waitress image. It was a futile hope.

Shrewd attorneys bring out the worst about their clients, assuming it will take out the sting and disarm the prosecution. If something bad is sprung by the prosecution, it has the double disadvantage of seeming furtive and shameful. Better to have a sympathetic questioner bring out the worst in the best light. And so Baron asked Alice about her boat trip with Tony Grace.

BARON: Did you bring a suitcase with you when you went on that boat?
CRIMMINS: No.

268

"I was working that day," explained Alice, "and Tony had told me that he was going to have a *bon voyage* party. . . . I had gone down there with a friend of mine, Margie Fischer, and we're on the boat, and I guess we were fooling around. . . . I couldn't get off."

The explanation seemed unsatisfactory and she wanted to make the jury understand. She hadn't taken a suitcase because it was totally unplanned, she insisted, her sense of frustration leading her on. There had been no deliberate neglect of the children. Evelyn, the maid, had known that there was always between $80 and $100 in cash in the house for emergencies. She looked desperately at the jury, as if to say, "Don't you see?"

Baron moved the questioning to the night of the disappearance. Alice twisted the handkerchief tighter and her voice softened. She couldn't remember whether or not the front door had been locked; she couldn't recall if she had clapped the hook in the eye. When the subject of Joe Rorech came up, her voice flared with emotion. He was a liar, she said. His testimony was based on the fact that she had recently spurned him, and she denied the "confession." Rorech's story was an amazing reversal, she told the jury. Just two weeks ago, she recalled, they had been at the Red Coach Grill in Westbury having drinks and Joe had kept saying that he thought Eddie had killed the children. Sam [Spade] Gianopoulos had been with her that night and would back her up. It was all very sad, she said; Joe Rorech had brought his children to meet her—and this was after the alleged confession—and left them alone with her. Would he have risked that with a confessed murderess? she asked. Joe had always sworn she was innocent—until last week in court. And she shook her head tragically.

"Did you ever say, 'I'm sorry, Joe, I killed her'?" Baron asked.

"Never," she said in a powerful voice.

Lombardino, meanwhile, could hardly contain his impatience. He was going to cross-examine Alice Crimmins and it would be brutal. He had boasted about it in private, entertaining friends by saying, "Let me at her." He had thought about his attitude, and from the start he treated her without pity, his voice betraying more than professional anger and magnified in the cloistered courtroom. At first Mosley had thought *he* might handle the questioning of Alice, but Lombardino had said no. Although Mosley was the titular head of the team, it was apparent that Lombardino had snatched the leadership from his hands. When the trial began, newspaper reporters had sought information from Mosley; now they instinctively turned to Lombardino. Without protest, Mosley had slipped into the background.

As Alice and Tony faced off in the courtroom, the cold antipathy between them was manifest.

LOMBARDINO: Mrs. Crimmins, would you mind getting a little closer to the microphone so everybody in this jury panel can hear you?
CRIMMINS: They can hear me, sir.
LOMBARDINO: Madame, will you please do that!

There was to be no velvet on the fist. These two people, virtual strangers who knew each other mostly by reputation, were going into combat without the pretense of chivalry. The first exchange was meant to demonstrate who was in control. Instinctively, Alice understood and resisted. She was helpless as Lombardino lunged directly into her sex life.

LOMBARDINO: When you were working at the Heritage House, did you know a Mr. John Walters?
CRIMMINS: Yes, I did.
LOMBARDINO: Was he a married man?
CRIMMINS: I knew him as separated.
LOMBARDINO: Did you go out with him?
CRIMMINS: Yes, I did.

Everyone in the courtroom understood the code. For "going out," they read "sex." Lombardino reestablished her identity as a cocktail waitress at the Heritage House. John Walters had also worked at the Heritage House. Had she stayed overnight with Walters? Lombardino asked. Yes, she said, she had.

270

"You know," she would say years later, "going back over the transcripts—I mean, reading them—I know I sounded like a bitch. But that man started on me as soon as he got up. And I got angry. I just wanted to tell my side of the story, and all he was interested in was my sex life. I wanted to say I was innocent, but he never let me. He just kept hammering at that one point—my sex life."

Lombardino was promiscuous with names—he would ruin a marriage or a relationship or poison a reputation with the flick of his tongue. How about Carl Andrade? he asked, as Marty Baron rose wearily from the shambles of the defense table, by now the camp of a beaten army.

"I know in what direction the District Attorney is going," said Baron. "It's something that is going to defame this witness and lead her up to ridicule."

Lombardino was prepared for the objection. He recited the law: "The rules of evidence are such that the People have an absolute right to inquire into every act involving moral turpitude of any defendant who takes the stand, in order to attack and impeach her credibility and/or her character."

Farrell nodded and told Lombardino to proceed. The Assistant District Attorney, pacing thoughtfully, asked Alice if she remembered the time when Eddie surprised her in bed with Carl Andrade.

She did.

LOMBARDINO: How was Carl Andrade dressed?
CRIMMINS: He was in a state of undress.
LOMBARDINO: Will you tell the men of this jury panel what you mean by a state of undress?

Alice Crimmins looked at Lombardino for a moment, wondering how deliberately explicit he would force her to be. She felt as if he were making *her* undress in public. "Just what I said, sir," she replied coldly. "A state of undress."

The enmity had grown overwhelming, as she pointedly called him "sir" and he struck her with "madame." Lombardino wanted all the details about Andrade's sudden flight through the window after a quick scuffle with Eddie. Speaking calmly, Alice said she had got dressed and taken Andrade's clothing out to where he waited in his car.

If there was triumph at the prosecution table, it was because they had done their homework. Lombardino had a file on Alice Crimmins that was like a link to every secret. As she sat exposed on the witness stand, Lombardino reminded her of a job she had held briefly at the World's Fair in 1964. She knew what was coming. She had had an afternoon tryst with a buyer named Stanley Bauman. The names tumbled out and Alice acknowledged each one. There were some names that Tony Lombardino did not dare bring out. When he brought up another boat trip, he carefully omitted naming the important guests aboard the boat. She had shared a cabin with Tony Grace in 1964 when she sailed to the Democratic National Convention in Atlantic City, New Jersey. The trip was aboard Sal Lo-Curto's boat, and it was on that trip that she had met Robert Wagner and Paul Screvane.

"Oh, I knew about those people," Lombardino said later, "but why drag them into it?"

"The audience is directed to stop comments," ordered Judge Farrell. "Again, I warn you that you must keep quiet. It's important to the fairness of the situation."

Lombardino waited until the judge had finished. He was at the prosecution table, his back to the court, reading from a legal pad full of hasty scrawls.

LOMBARDINO: Do you know the name of Pasquale Picassio?
CRIMMINS: I know Pat Picassio.
LOMBARDINO: What is his occupation?
CRIMMINS: He's a barber.
LOMBARDINO: And did you ever take anyone to his barbershop?
CRIMMINS: I took my children to the barbershop.
LOMBARDINO: And did Pasquale cut your children's hair?
CRIMMINS: Yes.
LOMBARDINO: How many times?
CRIMMINS: I'd say ten times.

LOMBARDINO: Did you ever have a relationship with Pasquale Picassio in the back of his automobile?

CRIMMINS: No, I don't believe I did.

LOMBARDINO: Would it refresh your recollection if I told you that you had a sexual relationship with him in the back of that car behind the barbershop [in the fall of 1964]?

CRIMMINS: I don't remember it.

She had finally found a defense against Lombardino's relentless remonstration—lapse of memory. There was no end to Lombardino's scolding pursuit and she realized she was losing badly. Lombardino was doing what the police had done ever since the children were killed—trying to connect her sex life to their deaths. She could never comprehend what one had to do with the other.

In public Lombardino demanded that Alice be judged by her sexual conduct. Who was out looking for the killer while the police were tapping her telephone and listening to her passion? she wanted to know. Lombardino spent all of his energy proving that she slept with a lot of men while Alice believed he should have been looking for murder clues. In any event, the tone of the trial never recovered from the encounter about the barber.

Lombardino returned to the subject of Joe Rorech, trying to squeeze the last bit of scandal out of that relationship. Alice admitted she had been to Rorech's home when his wife was away.

LOMBARDINO: Does he have a swimming pool there, Mrs. Crimmins?

CRIMMINS: Yes, he does.

LOMBARDINO: Did you ever go swimming in that pool?

CRIMMINS: Yes, I did.

LOMBARDINO: What were you wearing when you went swimming in that pool, Mrs. Crimmins?

CRIMMINS: One time a bathing suit; one time, no bathing suit.

LOMBARDINO: Where were your children when you were swimming without a bathing suit in Joe Rorech's swimming pool?

CRIMMINS: They were dead.

At the Part I restaurant, where the defense regrouped for lunch, Morty Allerand, the owner, made certain that everyone was comfortable. Allerand was a fussy, generous man who provided everything for his guests. If he didn't have a certain dish in his restaurant, he would send someone to fetch it from another restaurant. A natural host, Allerand provided food, liquor, and an appreciative audience. He was always laughing at his friend Jimmy Breslin, even when Breslin wasn't saying anything particularly funny. Allerand listened more to tone than substance, and he thought Breslin sounded funny.

Whatever people said about Alice Crimmins, Morty Allerand liked her. He listened to her tone and his instinct told him she was a good person. He didn't pay much attention to details of the trial—after all, some of his best customers were members of the District Attorney's staff and it wouldn't do his business any good to antagonize them. They accepted Morty's geniality toward Alice for what it was—the manners of a natural host. Gradually, though, Allerand found that he was no longer neutral about the trial. He was rooting for Alice Crimmins. She was a generous, largehearted woman, he believed, and as a thoughtful host, he wanted to make some gesture of appreciation. He bought a case of domestic champagne for the party he was going to throw when she was acquitted. There was no doubt that she would be acquitted. He heard it personally from Harold Harrison every day at lunch. Among the people he invited were a number of reporters, who injected this premature cockiness into color stories surrounding the trial. The word got back to the people waiting in the lines every day, and it was mangled in the retelling. The version that swept the corridors was that Alice herself had ordered a case of champagne for her victory celebration.

Every night, when Lewis Rosenthal came home from the hectic day in court, he read all the newspapers and watched the television news programs about the trial. The judge had toyed with the idea of sequestering the jury, but

274

decided against the expense and trouble of putting the jury under guard in a hotel. He believed that the jury would not be influenced by the outside world. Lewis Rosenthal, however, could never escape the trial. One day he went to his doctor for a checkup. The receptionist found out that he was a member of the jury and rose out of her seat, shaking a fist at him: *"You have to find her guilty! You can't let her go free!"*

After Thursday's luncheon recess Lombardino wanted to explore Alice's job at Hagen Industries, where she had worked for Charles Boylan, then thirty-eight, married, with a family in Virginia and an apartment in New York.

LOMBARDINO: How long did you live with Charles Boylan, your supervisor?

CRIMMINS: Until you people gave him such a hard time that we couldn't see each other any more.

LOMBARDINO: Did his wife give you a hard time, Mrs. Crimmins?

CRIMMINS: Through you, yes.

LOMBARDINO: Did you ever have your clothing up at this apartment, Mrs. Crimmins?

CRIMMINS: I told you, I moved in there.

LOMBARDINO: Did you ever get your clothing out of the apartment?

CRIMMINS: No.

LOMBARDINO: What happened to your clothing?

CRIMMINS: His wife threw them out.

LOMBARDINO: Did she do anything else to your clothing that you know of?

CRIMMINS: I was told she tore them up.

Lombardino raised the name of an executive at Norelco, but apparently the relationship was only friendly. "Nothing ever happened, if that's what you want to know," she snapped. Lombardino put on the record the fact that both Rorech and Grace had helped support Alice Crimmins. Knowing that the omission of something can often be more significant than allowing a denial to go into the record, Lombardino let the jury draw the conclusion that all Alice's lovers were

275

helping support her. Another technique for suggesting things to a jury is to ask a question in such a way that even a denial doesn't erase suspicion.

LOMBARDINO: Did you ever cry when you were talking to the police about [your children]?
CRIMMINS: Yes, I did.
LOMBARDINO: When was that?
CRIMMINS: I don't know. You broke me down so many times it's ridiculous. I was there eight or ten hours at a clip with you people—voluntarily, too.

Judge Farrell was becoming impatient. He got up and began to wander around his chair. He paced as Lombardino hammered at Alice's crumbling defenses. Lombardino missed the signal and kept up the attack. End it, Farrell finally said.

Alice Crimmins walked away from the witness stand stunned by her ordeal. She knew it had been a failure. Her protests had sounded feeble, almost like technical denials. She had wanted to be open, but it came out guarded. She had wanted to explain, but it all seemed to serve the prosecution's cause. It had turned out like her relationship with the police—the first hope of cooperation had turned to defiance. And the defiance had spoiled her appearance.

"A tramp like that is capable of anything." Lewis Rosenthal heard his fellow juror Sam Ehrlich make that remark, and he found it a fair reflection of the jury sentiment. Ironically, Sam Ehrlich would eventually come to Alice's rescue.

47

There were a few loose ends to tie up on Friday, May 24, but for all practical purposes the trial ended with Alice's appearance on the stand. The legal maneuvers and technicalities would flesh out and harden decisions that had already formed in the minds of the jurors.

Despite the myth that dramatic shifts of opinion occur during summation, it is usually too late by then. What a summation does, in reality, is to muster the arguments each side will take into the jury room to try to influence the other jurors.

The defense sums up first. Harrison's wife, Muriel, was among the spectators. It was the first time she had come to court during the trial. She knew how much this case meant to her husband. He had not slept the night before. His clothes were carefully chosen—a dark, sober suit and plain shirt and tie. Harrison had been working on the summation since the first day of the trial, keeping notes on a dozen legal pads scattered around the defense table. At breakfast that morning he had been unable to eat. The enormity of the trial had now struck him. Not only Alice Crimmins' destiny hung on how he handled himself. If he made a fool of himself today, it would be in the full glare of the public. He had brooded about it all weekend. Instead of being fresh and rested that Monday, May 27, Harrison was still grieving for his father and afraid that he was unprepared.

"Innuendoes, dirt, filth, that's what you were subjected to in this case," began Harrison, trying to match indignation to the words.

Harrison had to create a reasonable doubt about the testimony of the prosecution witnesses. One by one, he ran down the list, trying to make them all sound unsavory. When he reached the name of Rorech, he paused.

"He talks about pangs of conscience? He doesn't know what that means with his seven children and his running around. . . . He's a pawn in this case. Somebody tightened the screw on Joe Rorech and made him say what he said, because he never said it before until he said it to you."

Sophie Earomirski? "Just too incredible," pronounced Harrison. "Sophie is a spurious letter-writer and I was always warned against people like that . . . who won't sign their names." Harrison attacked specific points, such as the fact that Alice couldn't have known the dog was pregnant on the night of the disappearance, and alluded to the medical doubts about Sophie's stability.

There are turning points during any trial when a lawyer knows he has won. A juror will give off such powerful signals that the message is unmistakable. Harold Harrison had waited for such a moment, but it never arrived. The two rows of faces in the jury box were grim and unsympathetic. A jury may pick up a fragment of speech, lock on to it, and ignore everything else. Harrison had attacked Sophie in a manner that was unforgivable to some jurors. Sophie was a pathetic woman, they could agree, but it was better left unsaid.

"We can't bring back this innocent child, but, as God Almighty knows, Alice didn't do it!"

That statement irritated a few of the men on the jury. Harold was defending Alice against the accusation of killing one child, but they were all aware of two dead children and it seemed wrong to them that she didn't grieve equally. Harrison's statement was correct, but it jarred and seemed a mere technical statement of innocence.

The summation took a little more than an hour,

but Harrison had paid too much attention to accuracy and style to be effective.

Tony Lombardino began by defending himself. "There were times, gentlemen, that by necessity this case went into the cesspool, but that wasn't by the District Attorney of Queens' doing. We don't select the evidence."

Lombardino was sorry if he had raised his voice, but excused himself because he had become so engrossed in the case. The prosecution had presented twenty-three witnesses, and Lombardino was prepared to defend them all. No one could challenge Dr. Helpern, he declared flatly.

"Joe Rorech doesn't merit a Legion of Honor," he said disarmingly. "Joseph Rorech is Joseph Rorech, a man who finally got caught up in his life and in his escapades, but he didn't deny them. . . . He got up on that stand and not only did he tell you gentlemen and everybody in this courtroom, but he told the world and he told his wife and he told his family what had transpired. I'd like to know how many men, honestly and sincerely, could have taken that course of conduct."

Tony Lombardino found heroic qualities in Sophie Earomirski. "A decent, simple, honest woman, not psychotic, not a liar, not someone who wants to gain attention. . . . I don't think it would be a bad world if we had more Sophies around."

If Tony Lombardino could find virtue in every prosecution witness, he found nothing redeeming in Alice Crimmins. He saved her for last, for he wanted to leave an image with the jury.

"When Alice Crimmins testified on that stand, I couldn't help but think about . . . the one object in this world that has the most beautiful shape and symmetrical design—the egg. Just beautiful on the outside in shape and form. But when you break the egg open, if it should be rotten inside, it's probably the worst stench you can find anyplace in this world." If there was an analogy that stuck with the people in the courtroom, it was the one about the beautifully rotten egg.

The trial had not taken as long as had been expected. It lasted a total of thirteen courtroom days—there were forty-two witnesses and the transcript ran to 1514 pages.

Judge Farrell outlined five possible verdicts—guilty of murder, first or second degree; guilty of manslaughter, first or second degree; or innocent. And then he turned it over to the jury, after reading them the law. The case had been made out of circumstantial evidence, Farrell said. However, circumstantial evidence was enough to convict if it was convincing. "We are not trying Mrs. Crimmins' morals," he said finally. "We are trying a homicide."

But that offhand disavowal didn't seem strong enough to neutralize the long concentration on Alice Crimmins' sex life. More than one juror resolved the confusing instruction by ignoring it. Why had all that testimony been allowed if they couldn't consider it?

The spectators did not disperse while the jury deliberated; they did not go home and wait near the television set for the verdict. They stayed in the corridors, or outside on the ramps, or in the fast-food restaurants across the street, never straying far, dropping their guard only when the jury went to dinner. They sat along the long plate-glass window of the courthouse corridor, waiting in blank patience, or insisting on their own interpretation of the facts. The law students lounged under the best light, reading their textbooks, maintaining a kind of sanitized distance from the more passionate spectators.

Alice Crimmins left the courtroom and went to a friend's place on the eighth floor of an apartment house across Queens Boulevard. She stared down at the patient crowd milling in front of the courthouse. She carried a copy of *Airport,* but it was only a prop. She didn't have the stamina to read. Finally she couldn't stand the isolation and went downstairs to the Part I restaurant, where everyone assured her that the signs were good. There was a relay system into the Part I, where rumors and gossip raised and lowered moods.

"It's nine to three for conviction," someone said out of Alice's hearing, but she could tell by the grave expressions that not everyone was optimistic. Harrison and Baron made repeated attempts to brighten things, finding cause for hope in delay. When they heard that it was nine to three against, they reversed it and said the jury was three to one in her favor.

"The majority of us were quite careful about the verdict," recalled Lewis Rosenthal. "We leaned over backwards to give her the benefit of the doubt." In the beginning Rosenthal was one of a handful who voted for acquittal. His instinct told him that she was probably guilty, but he had doubts about the proof. And even if the proof was adequate, he could not see any profit in finding her guilty. "She would be no danger to society," he told fellow jurors. "She is not likely to commit another crime like this." The others on the panel sensed something weak in Rosenthal's position, as if he were asking to be convinced. He was vulnerable. An appeal could be made to Rosenthal on the very grounds on which he defended Alice Crimmins—her danger to society. On tables and mantels and surfaces around the Rosenthal home are the links in a complex chain. In stiff formal poses are the great-grandparents. European ancestors march in an unbroken procession of yellowing photographs. There are modern color photographs of Rosenthal and his wife and his daughter, who he hopes will one day inherit all the traditions and become the picture caretaker. Something about contemporary society nags Lewis Rosenthal: the disappearance of marriage, the rupture of family life. It bothers him that his daughter may grow to adulthood and never marry, thus breaking the family chain.

As Monday, May 27, passed into Tuesday, there were different interpretations of the long deliberation. Some felt it was a good sign for the defendant because the jury was absorbed in doubt. Others said those holding out for acquittal were being whittled down, since jurors bent on conviction were usually more tenacious and less easy to convert. Still another view was that the jurors wanted as many free meals as they could get out of the state.

At 1:45 a.m., after the jury had asked a few questions and requested a few instructions on the law, a call came to Louis Warren's apartment, where Alice Crimmins waited: "There's a verdict." Warren, a friendly bail bondsman, wished Alice luck as she straightened her hair.

Alice Crimmins was wearing a red dress and her face was chalk as she hurried through the strangely crowded street, in which people stood in the middle of the traffic lanes as they do in Times Square on New Year's Eve.

"The first thing I'm going to do when I get home is take a hot bath," she said bravely as she waited with Muriel Harrison in the filling courtroom.

Judge Farrell entered suddenly, seeming preoccupied, as if he had been taken away from something truly important. "Now, as this verdict is announced," Farrell warned the spectators, "anybody that makes a sound or stands up will be liable to contempt. Now watch yourselves. This is going to be in order. That's what's required by law."

Court attendants took up positions around the large room. The jurors came in looking haggard and miserable, trying to conceal the verdict by staring at their hands or feet. And suddenly Alice Crimmins knew that she was lost. A matron moved in behind her.

"Have you agreed upon a verdict?"

Alice was standing as Carl Boyer, the foreman, replied: "Yes, sir." She sagged slightly and Harold Harrison held her by the elbow.

"Your Honor, we, the jury, find the defendant guilty of manslaughter in the first degree."

Alice went limp in Harrison's arms, moaning, "Oh, my God."

In the first row Eddie Crimmins buried his head in his hands and wept.

Most of the spectators were too stunned to react. It was a verdict that most agreed with and had hoped for, and yet the impact was powerful, as if for the first time they realized the consequence of the wish.

"Your Honor," appealed Harrison, "may she see her husband before she's taken out?"

"She's remanded," said Farrell remorselessly. "No."

The matron moved Harrison out of the way and took charge of Alice's rubbery body. She led her into another room, where for a few moments Alice was able to say goodbye to her family.

Lombardino shook hands with Jim Mosley wordlessly. Mosley gathered up his papers while Lombardino left the courthouse with John Kelly and Jerry Piering. Strangely, only Lombardino seemed elated. He laughed and congratulated the two detectives and then clicked his heels in the air in celebration. "Cut it out, you jerk!" said Jerry Piering. It had been too long, too hard, and their feelings were too complicated for that kind of demonstration.

As Alice was being taken to the detention pen, she collapsed again. Dr. Lester Samuels, a city Health Department physician, was summoned. "We'll have to put her in the hospital," said Samuels.

Now semiretired, Samuels will no longer talk about the case, but in the next few days members of the prosecution staff began calling newspapermen they considered reliable to pass along something Samuels reportedly told them. It was contended that a sedative Dr. Samuels administered to Alice had acted as a truth serum, and that under it she had confessed killing her children. Samuels was horrified by the reports. He denied the stories, claiming that Alice had ranted incoherently under the sedative but had said nothing that could be regarded as a confession. The poisonous effect of the stories, however, reached into the community, and nothing that Samuels said afterward worked as an antidote to the first reports. In the years ahead it would be faithfully related by those familiar with the case that Alice had confessed under truth serum.

48

On the cover of Alice Crimmins' probation report Jerry Piering had written: "There is no doubt that Alice Crimmins killed her two children!"

The report took three months to compile. After the

verdict Alice remained under heavy sedation for two weeks. Gradually she came to accept her new status. Harold Harrison visited her regularly in the prison hospital and told her cheerfully that he was working on an appeal and that there appeared to be considerable grounds for a reversal. John Burke, her brother, urged her to hire a new set of attorneys. He had nothing personal against Harold Harrison or Marty Baron, but Burke argued that they were clumsy and she needed more talent.

And almost daily Eddie Crimmins went to Elmhurst General Hospital to see his wife, but he was not allowed in. He would stand outside staring at the windows of the prison ward, trying to pick out her face.

In June, Alice was transferred to the Women's House of Detention in Manhattan's Greenwich Village to await sentencing on July 12. The matrons there reported that after a first burst of hysteria she settled into prison routine. She worked in the office, filing and typing, and was found to be efficient.

The police, meanwhile, made a halfhearted effort at finding the "mystery man" who had purportedly helped Alice dispose of the children—which was the essence of their case. But it seemed more a public-relations justification of the verdict than a real manhunt.

Harold Harrison, although believing he would soon be leaving the case, discovered that three jurors had improperly visited the scene of the crime during the proceedings, and filed a writ for a new trial. Harrison obtained an affidavit from one of the jurors, who swore he had driven to the area during the trial. Sam Ehrlich, juror number three, was the first to admit it. And then Harry Tunis and Irving Furst said they had visited Kew Gardens Hills to learn whether Sophie Earomirski could have seen what she claimed from her window. Judge Farrell had blundered by failing to remind the jury regularly to stay away from the area. Instead of sentencing Alice on July 12, Farrell heard defense motions that the verdict should be turned aside because of the unauthorized visits. He postponed sentencing until August 9 after deciding that the visits were not a grave violation.

When Alice appeared for sentencing, Judge Farrell

asked her if she had anything to say before he pronounced sentence.

"I am not guilty of this charge," she said. "This horrible charge. I did not do it, and Mosley, Lombardino, and Mackell, all down the line, are rotten through and through. . . ."

The judge interrupted to say that he was not interested in her "personal" attacks.

"You don't care who killed my children," she shot back angrily. "You want to close your books. You don't give a damn who killed my kids!"

Harold Harrison had nothing further to say.

"It is the sentence of the court . . . that she be confined in the New York State prison for women at Westfield State Farms, Bedford Hills, New York, for a term of not less than five years, nor more than twenty years."

"Until this I always had a very deep respect for the law, you know?" Alice Crimmins would say years later. "I thought that people get justice in the courtroom. I don't know what I believe in any more."

Standing in the courtroom when Alice was sentenced were two men who were to become her new attorneys. William Erlbaum, in his thirties, was a large rawboned man with waves of dark hair that kept flopping in his face as he took frantic notes. Erlbaum was the detail man—a painstaking fanatic for fact, with wild, blazing eyes.

The senior man was two decades older. Herbert Lyon, who had a deliberately somnolent look, was considered by many the most skilled forensic attorney in Queens. He had a thriving practice—taking large fees for successfully defending alleged mobsters—and was warned that the Crimmins case would only bring him grief. "It's a no-win case," his colleagues along Queens Boulevard told him. But Lyon was outraged at the verdict and the sloppy handling Alice had received. As she was led away to prison, he saw her for a moment and promised that she would not remain in prison long. With Harrison's help, he got her out in less than a month. On September 4, Harrison, still the attorney of record, obtained a certificate of reasonable doubt and she was free on $25,000 bail.

For more than a year Erlbaum buried himself in the paperwork of the appeal, taking direction and broad approaches from Lyon. Sixteen months after stepping into the case, Lyon and Erlbaum argued Alice's appeal before the Appellate Division. One week later they were rewarded for the great care they had invested in preparation. By a four-to-one decision, the court ruled that the improper visits to the crime scene were enough grounds to grant Mrs. Crimmins a new trial.

District Attorney Thomas Mackell announced immediately that he would bring Mrs. Crimmins to trial again.

After her conviction and before she engaged her new lawyers, Harold Harrison persuaded Alice to sign a paper giving him exclusive book and movie rights to the story of her life. He did it because she had run out of money and he said he could not work for free. In addition, there had been inquiries from writers and movie producers. None of them came to anything and the document would be renounced by Harrison, but according to Anthony Lombardino, one of the factors that influenced the District Attorney's office to take Alice to court again was to prevent her from exploiting her story in a book or a movie.

Indignation about Alice Crimmins was still high in Queens County and there was never any doubt that she would be retried, but Tom Mackell decided he would bring in a new team to match Lyon and Erlbaum. Lombardino was too heavy-handed and Mosley too ineffectual to succeed against the talented new combination. Mackell had learned through experience to respect Lyon, who had beaten Mosley when the latter came out to Queens and tested his feet in the water.

Lyon was particularly effective in a courtroom. Juries found him full of wisdom and understanding, capable of resolving knotty complications with benevolent even-handedness. To Herb Lyon, prosecutors were never mean or cruel, they were merely mistaken and lacking a forgiving perspective. There were broader, more informed dimensions to Lyon than to most Queens lawyers. He had a taste for literature and had, in his youth, written a modest novel. He appreciated music and good food, and the partnership between him and the younger Erlbaum was nourished by mutual respect. Their conversations were not girded by the boundaries of local politics and lunch-hour vendettas. This catholicity set Lyon and Erlbaum somewhat apart from their colleagues, but there were common interests. Herb Lyon and Bill Erlbaum would put in hours drinking at Luigi's bar with the personnel who inhabited the courtrooms across the street, showing not a trace of performing a grudging duty.

Harold Harrison accepted Alice's decision to switch attorneys with good grace, but Marty Baron felt somewhat betrayed. He believed he had devoted more time and effort to the case than was repaid—financially or in consideration. While Harrison had wanted to remove himself from the case the moment that Rorech turned against Alice, and regretted the book-and-movie document because it made him look greedy, Baron felt he had done nothing wrong. The result was hurt feelings. And when it came time to turn files over to Lyon and Erlbaum, the old firm was slow.

Even before Mackell announced his decision to retry Alice, Lyon and Erlbaum went to work with energy to prepare a defense. They hired a talented private detective, Irwin Blye, to re-examine the evidence. Unlike the stereotyped private detectives, Blye was a quiet family man who made his way by being polite and thorough. He retraced all the previous steps and found himself stumbling over the carefully guarded police theory of the case, which turned on the man they believed had helped Alice kill her children.

His name was Vincent Colabella and his police record was that of a viper. He was now being held on robbery charges in the Tombs. One of Colabella's fellow inmates reported that he had boasted of driving the car the night the children disappeared.

John Kelly and Jerry Piering immediately went to see Colabella. "All right, hump," began Kelly, "I'm giving you a choice—you can either be a witness or a defendant in the Crimmins case."

Colabella was surprised; he had spoken carelessly to a fellow prisoner in the morning and by afternoon two detectives were waiting for him. A man in prison might drop coy hints about cooperation and being able to solve this or that crime, and it could take months before some harassed Assistant District Attorney would show up to drive a hard bargain. But the Crimmins case was different.

"What can you guys do for me, huh?" said Colabella, his face a smirking slate. At the age of thirty-three, Colabella was toughened to life in prison. He had spent a third of his life in some kind of confinement and the threat of doing time did not hold terror for him. "What can you guys do for me?" He was not asking; it was a statement. Kelly slammed his fist on a table and demanded that Colabella tell them his role in the case.

"I was kidding," said Colabella. "I don't know anything about it."

Kelly, a great believer in the polygraph, asked Colabella if he would take a lie-detector test. Colabella replied that he didn't mind, but that he would like to talk to his lawyer first. After speaking to the lawyer, Colabella refused to take the test.

Colabella's withdrawal was a disappointment to the District Attorney. There were some in Queens who felt that Alice Crimmins was being persecuted by Mackell's office. The conviction had merely strengthened that opinion, and the appearance of Colabella stirred hope among police and staff in the District Attorney's office that their case would be vindicated. There was a powerful desire to produce one solid, incontrovertible piece of evidence in court instead of the chain of inferences.

Strategists in Mackell's office did not want to get involved in another sordid name-calling contest. The prosecutor began to re-examine the case, as Irwin Blye was doing, trying to develop additional evidence. Privately, the police were convinced that they had solved the case and that Vincent Colabella had helped Alice dispose of the children. But he was a hardened criminal, unlikely to violate his own code of silence. So the only tactic available was to try and bolster the existing case.

John Kelly had been saving something, he told Piering and, later, Tom Mackell. A week after he testified against Alice, Joe Rorech had been drinking with Kelly at a bar at La Guardia Airport. Rorech had been tormenting himself for having turned on his lover. "I hated to blow the whistle on Alice," Rorech reportedly had told Kelly. "I hated to do that to her, but I didn't have any choice. They were beautiful kids. I can't see why she wanted to take their lives."

Kelly said that when he heard this, he had blanched. "What the hell are you talking about?" he said he had asked. "I thought that you testified that she only admitted she killed the girl."

"I told Lombardino and Anderson before I testified about the boy, too, but they didn't want me to mention it on the stand," Rorech had said, according to Kelly. "They said it would be prejudicial and that the judge would call a mistrial."

"What did you tell Tony and Walter?" Kelly said he has asked Rorech.

"Only that Alice told me that she had help in killing her son," Rorech reportedly had replied.

Kelly brought this conversation to the attention of the District Attorney's staff and the seeds of a variation on the first prosecution began to grow. The new prosecution tactic would be to bring Alice to trial for the murder of both children. A conviction for the murder of the boy was not likely since no one could testify about a cause of death. But if Alice was indicted for both murders, the jury might be persuaded that it was doing her a favor by convicting her of only one. This was a ploy, but in the absence of substantial new evidence, the District Attorney and his staff felt compelled to expand the first theme.

If the first trial of Alice Crimmins was like an enormous frontier brawl, the second seemed almost subdued. It was an argument that engaged the intellect and did not threaten, like the first trial, to burst its boundaries and spill out of the courtroom. There was also something weary about the supporting cast; and some athletic second effort seemed necessary to get through it.

The trial began on a cloudy Monday, March 15,

1971; it was almost six years since the deaths of Missy and Eddie. Time had wrung out much of the outrage. The trial was held in a smaller courtroom than the "Hippodrome," and was presided over by a huge man with an austere manner named George Balbach. There had been public criticism of the conduct of the first trial and Balbach was determined not to repeat Farrell's mistakes. He laced the corridors and courtroom with court attendants. Again there were crowds waiting for every vacant seat but they were quiet.

The scope of the trial was larger than its predecessor, since the charges were enlarged. On July 13, 1970, a Queens grand jury had reindicted Alice Crimmins, this time charging her with the murder of her son as well as manslaughter in Missy's death. She had gone through another ritual of arrest and collapse, falling this time into the arms of John Kelly when she was being booked at the Fresh Meadows Precinct. By now only the most optimistic policemen held out any hope that she would confess. Jerry Piering, however, was at the booking to monitor her reaction, comparing it to the day he had met her; he was like a patient research chemist working toward a correct formula.

Alice still insisted upon her innocence, but that didn't affect the detectives' basic faith in her guilt. It was apparent, as she was again freed on $25,000 bail, that she had changed. She had a haggard, hounded look and no longer displayed the jaunty overconfidence that had characterized her attitude during the first trial. In unguarded moments she was hesitant and aware of a vulnerability she had only guessed at before. Her drinking didn't make her giddy or high, but was driving her into despair.

Tony Lombardino had joined the United States Attorney's office in the Southern District in Brooklyn. James Mosley had been reduced to bureaucratic chores. Tom Mackell had decided to orchestrate the second trial of Alice Crimmins with more dignity and attention to legal points. To handle the case, he chose forty-five-year-old Thomas Demakos, chief of the office's trial bureau, a solid, sober man, who though lacking flourishes of eloquence, was refreshingly direct. What recommended him even more, perhaps, was the fact that he had beaten Herbert Lyon in a murder case—one of the few prosecuting attorneys who could make that boast. Demakos was handsome in a mature way, with gray hair and wrinkles to give texture and depth to his expression. He never displayed temperament or vanity, relying instead on what passed for an urban kind of homespun self-deprecation.

For his assistant, Demakos selected Vincent Nicolosi, who had the virtue of fresh indignation. Nicolosi had his own identification with the case. He had taken his bar examinations on July 14, 1965—the day Alice's children disappeared. He would be prepared to perform whatever unpleasant hatchet work was demanded in the second prosecution of Alice Crimmins. Under his bright blond hair he had an engagingly elfin face that seemed incongruous with his nastier chores. The new team was both better matched and more harmonious than Lombardino and Mosley, who had seemed to struggle for control. Nicolosi never challenged Demakos' position.

Lyon was surprised by the indictment of his client for the death of her son, but guessed correctly that the extra charge had been thrown in to make the manslaughter accusation seem trivial. He prepared his case as if defending Alice for the death of her daughter, believing that the murder charge would fall under the weight of law. Private detective Irwin Blye compiled dossiers on the major characters, but they were frustratingly similar to the information Harold Harrison had unearthed. He wondered if Alice's familiarity with politicians and show-business people could have had anything to do with the killings, but it was a blind alley. The police contacts Blye knew dismissed his questions, saying that nothing would be served going into that area. Lyon was totally uninterested in pursuing it, so Blye tracked other areas. He found himself hacking at a great jungle of facts, getting almost nowhere. He thought he could dispose of the murder charge involving little Eddie, however. In the first few days after the disappearance, he found, police had carefully searched the undergrowth where Eddie's body was found, leading him to deduce that the body had been deposited there later. Since Alice had been under constant police surveillance, it must have been done by someone other than her. Of course, this was not necessarily inconsistent with the police theory that Alice had had help.

Lyon and Erlbaum neglected other clients to concentrate on the Crimmins case. In the fall of 1970, Eddie and Alice had finally been divorced. They had attempted several reconciliations, but Eddie could no longer ignore her affairs and she had grown weary of the pretense that kept them together. For the sake of the trial, Lyon decided, they needed Eddie. Alice's reputation was bruised enough and they were desperate to win sympathy for her.

Eddie would again stand by his ex-wife. He would offer to put up bail; he would swear in court that she was innocent, and he would admit that, despite everything, he still loved her.

Irwin Blye, moving a few paces behind the police, managed to locate most of the people involved in the case. It was not easy—their lives were scattered like autumn leaves. Theresa Costello, the former babysitter, was a married woman. She and her husband, an Air Force sergeant, lived in Arizona. Some witnesses had died. Others had moved. Joe Rorech was separated from his wife and was working as a carpenter—his first trade—in Connecticut. Several marriages had collapsed because of Tony Lombardino's cross-examination of Alice Crimmins. Tony Grace's wife, brokenhearted, had been hospitalized after the first trial. She had begun divorce action, but had died soon afterward. Policemen and doctors had retired. Most didn't want to be reminded of Alice Crimmins.

By 1971 the outrage at Alice's past behavior had cooled. The nation had changed and women's emancipation was not so frightening or unusual. Queens had not yet accepted it, but Alice Crimmins was not the contaminating symbol she had seemed to some in 1968.

In the foreplay of the trial Thomas Demakos consented to bail, but insisted that Alice Crimmins should not be permitted to speak to the press. He was determined to control the atmosphere during the trial.

And before the start of jury selection, inside Judge Balbach's chambers Demakos won his first victory. Balbach warned Herbert Lyon that he would remand his client if she violated this accord. He would put her in prison if she granted one interview. This was a terrible threat. Alice had recurrent nightmares about her brief time in prison and shuddered at the thought of going back.

The decision annoyed Lyon. It gave Demakos almost exclusive access to the press. If Lyon wanted to get out his version, he would have to do it indirectly, without attribution. Lyon had always enjoyed a fine working relationship with courthouse reporters. He understood the ground rules and knew which reporters to trust and who would report back to the District Attorney.

By the second trial a small corps of reporters had begun to ask tougher questions about the District Attorney's case. Perhaps it was because there were more women covering the second trial or perhaps the cause of Alice Crimmins was no longer so lonely, but there was sympathy for Alice among a minority of the press. Demakos was aware of the trend and was pleased by the judge's ruling isolating Alice.

Herbert Lyon's office was a converted three-bedroom apartment diagonally across the boulevard from the courthouse. The walls were covered with signs of the occupant's vanity. There were sketches and photographs of Herbert Lyon, documents and diplomas he had acquired. In his inner office he was particularly fond of a pencil rendition of himself pacing before an expectant jury. In his sanctuary Lyon kept a bar inside a large globe. There was also a naugahyde couch upon which Lyon and Erlbaum plotted strategy or recovered from the daily contest.

The small conference room outside was formal, and Lyon preferred the comforts of his own office, with its telephone console, its soft swivel chair, and an iron rendition of the lonely and heroic Don Quixote. Like most good lawyers and actors, Lyon had a large ego. In his case, it was qualified by his ability and a sense of humor.

William Erlbaum, a brilliant dialectician, was a more tentative personality. It was almost as if he didn't trust his own intellect; he tended to make people nervous with incessant probing questions as he sought reassurance on any given decision.

In the opening stage of the trial, a small group met in Lyon's office to outline Alice's conduct during the trial. She would no longer lunch in the Part I restaurant, entertaining reporters and bystanders. Lyon's office receptionist would bring in sandwiches and coffee, and Alice would eat in her lawyer's office. Lyon spoke to Alice in severe, fatherly fashion. He wanted her to understand that this was serious. He believed that she hadn't gone through the first trial with the proper spirit.

"What about Alice's testifying?" asked Erlbaum.

Lyon shrugged; he didn't know yet. He was convinced that she had impaled herself on the witness stand in the last trial. But he knew how important it was for a defendant to proclaim innocence. Every lawyer is instructed that juries punish defendants who stand mute—an emotional reaction having nothing to do with evidence or law. Lyon would play it by ear.

"Now, Alice," he began in his deep, half-sleepy voice, and she would bolt to attention, "I want you to pay attention to this!" Lyon would pick her wardrobe and her moods. He would orchestrate the trial so that she would appear the wronged party. The main line of attack against Alice during the last trial had been that she was a "cold bitch." Lyon would show a woman who suffered. Many people were convinced that she had been punished enough, and Lyon would expand from that base. It was a small price if she had to sit out the lunch hour in Lyon's office.

When Harold Harrison or Marty Baron had told Alice to do something, she would sometimes ignore them. But that had been before she felt the nameless, faceless, impersonal brutality of prison. Alice's letters to Harrison, full of gratitude for his visits, had reflected the cold shock she felt in jail. If that was the result of ignoring legal advice, she would not make the same mistake twice.

There were important differences between her relationships with Lyon and Harrison. During a pretrial conference Harrison was called into Judge Balbach's office. Harrison knew his livelihood came from his relationships with the men in Balbach's chambers—Demakos, Mackell, Balbach. He understood that they were hostile to Alice and regarded her as someone unworthy of any display of human emotion. But when Harrison walked into the room and saw Alice, he smiled and kissed her on the cheek. A small gesture, but it took courage. Lyon, who witnessed it, was impressed. Alice might not have listened to Harrison as she would to Lyon, but she liked him better.

In the past Alice had suffered at the hands of the press. Even the reporters who genuinely liked her had mauled her in print. As a consequence, there were large gaps in her story. She had never sat down with a reporter and explained her version of the events. Most of the reporting had been from the District Attorney's vantage point, partly because of Harold Harrison's initial blunder of deceiving reporters into believing Alice was pregnant. In addition, the public was captivated by her sexual exploits. The District Attorney's staff, on the other hand, was accessible and provided fresh material. During the first trial James Mosley had been the subject of a flattering biography, *The Prosecutor*. He had allowed the author, James Mills, unparalleled access to the secret workings of his office. He had even tried to infiltrate Mills into the actual investigation by introducing him to Joe Rorech as just another "investigator." Mosley was rewarded by heroic depiction in print.

Ironically, Alice always felt some affection for reporters—men that she romantically believed led lives of high adventure—but she never trusted them with revealing insights into her personality. Her reticence was so profound that even Harold Harrison never dared ask certain questions and retained doubts about his client.

One afternoon before the start of jury selection for the second trial, Alice sat in the oak-paneled artificial night of a Long Island steak house having lunch with a stranger. Lyon and Erlbaum were close by, a backup of protection. The newcomer was a reporter for *Newsday* who was researching a magazine article on Alice Crimmins. Lyon had decided that it was time for Alice to display her wounds. It was painful, and a little mechanical, because such public intimacy did not come naturally. Yet there were glimpses behind the cosmetic barriers.

"It's not easy for me," she said staring into the bottom of a whiskey glass. Her face, even in the dark, seemed a decade older than it had three years ago. "It's very hard," said Alice. "They want me to break down for them." She never said who "they" were. "That's what they've always wanted. They wanted me to cry and break down. I'd never give them the satisfaction." The anger seemed more comfortable for her.

The reporters had been handpicked by Lyon. He asked Alice why she didn't grieve for her children.

"Grief?" she flared. "That's mine! They took my chil—" She couldn't finish the word. She took another swallow of whiskey and went on quietly. "Afterward, everybody was talking about Alice. 'What about Alice?' they said. Everybody was thinking about Alice. Who was thinking of the children?

"Oh, God," she said hopelessly. "I can't explain it. They were mine. *Mine!* The children were mine. The grief, it was mine. I wasn't going to give them my grief. When this is over, I'll grieve. Or maybe this is my grief."

296

So Alice Crimmins had postponed her grief and devoted herself to defiance or whiskey and kept the pictures of the children in her wallet, and when no one was around to see, she would take them out to weep over. After the trials were finished, she would grieve.

"The people who felt sorry for Alice, didn't they realize that I was suffering for my children? Didn't they know I wanted them to think of my children? There was not one day, not one minute when they are not on my mind."

Alice Crimmins' grief was complicated—it was connected with resistance to the District Attorney's office, and with self-punishment. She would not give "them" the satisfaction of showing pain. But at the end of the interview, when the talk had turned elsewhere, something that had been in the back of her mind troubled her and she touched the stranger's arm.

"Missy would have been ten and little Eddie would have been eleven, you know. I keep seeing children that age on the street or somewhere and wondering what they would have looked like."

The two aspects of the case—the one taking place in the courtroom and the drama surrounding it—were related. One couldn't help affecting the other. But Herbert Lyon was handicapped in the one outside. In the courtroom, his tactic was to understate things and hope the jury would develop trust in him. It was a brilliant plan and depended for effect on a slowly growing faith. Flashes of temper or indignation would merely create doubt about the defense.

The jury seemed to take a liking to Lyon. During the voir dire when the jury was chosen, Lyon went out of his way to affirm that he would not require a special jury to acquit Alice Crimmins. Middle-level male Queens workers, of the sort that inevitably were picked, would see the justice of voting not guilty. Since he had very little chance of getting anyone but such people on the jury, it flattered those who were selected. As in the first trial, women excused themselves from the prospective panel, admitting to opinions about Alice Crimmins' guilt. Demakos and Nicolosi, on the other hand, appeared tense and contentious in comparison with Lyon's nerveless good humor. In his opening statement Lyon's skill was deceptively masked behind what seemed a rambling, pointless essay on life's random possibilities. The case was a mystery, he told the jury. There are such things in life, and people must learn to accept that, even when doubts are troublesome. The children were dead; of that there was no doubt. They could have been abducted by a sex pervert, fed a last meal, molested, and then murdered. Or they could have got out of their room by themselves and been picked up by someone. There were a hundred possibilities, and only one involved Alice Crimmins. That possibility, Lyon told the jury, was the least likely. They would find the prosecutor's evidence unconvincing, he said.

It was a beginning. Lyon didn't expect much—it was hard for the jurors to keep their eyes off Alice Crimmins, now thirty-two years old. As the trial began, a subtle change took place in the copy flowing out of the courtroom. Instead of referring to Alice as a swinging cocktail waitress, the description had a slightly different tone, calling her "a 32-year-old former barmaid."

Alice was too fidgety to remain idle during the trial. During breaks and on the lunch hour she worked in Lyon's office, typing briefs, filing, or clipping newspaper stories. On most days Anthony Grace waited there for her; he would sit almost motionless in Lyon's inner office, saying nothing. There were rumors that he contributed toward her legal defense, but it is a point upon which neither he nor Lyon will comment. Grace would pay for her apartment and her new car and give her walking-around money; and he would remain loyally behind her. One of his major concerns was to keep out of the case the famous men Alice had known. None of the former city officials—still influential in political and business affairs—could afford to be linked to the case, even after six years. Tony Grace was still doing business with the city and he had given his word to protect the former officials. Demakos always read sinister implications into the relationship between Tony and Alice, claiming that it proved they were in on the crimes together.

Lyon and Erlbaum had learned to take Alice's

counsel. She had become adept at reading character and more than once warned against a particular prospective juror. They trusted her intuition.

Eddie Crimmins, looking forlorn, seldom missed a court session. He would sit alone on a window ledge staring out at the monotonous rows of cars in the parking lot, his brow pinched into a scowl. Occasionally, one of the familiar detectives would pass by and nod, but Eddie remained an enigma. "It never seems to end," he said almost to himself one day as a reporter stood next to him at the window. "I thought I'd be over it by now, but I'm not. It just goes on and on."

Eddie would listen to the conversations of the spectators in brooding detachment. They always thought Alice was guilty. "I know Alice didn't do it," he told the reporter. "The police kept trying to make me say she did it; they kept trying to show me she did it. But I know her better than anyone. She couldn't do it. She *couldn't*. I guess it's never going to end. I mean, I know it's over between me and Alice, but this"— and his head swiveled to take in the whole courthouse —"this is never going to end until they find her innocent. Then it'll be over. Maybe then the pain of the kids being killed like that'll go away. Maybe I'll be able to stop thinking about it. When this is all over."

A few yards away a line of spectators waited for a participant to leave the courtroom. A young construction worker remembered the headlines of the case and wanted to know more details. A housewife who had attended every session of the first trial felt obliged to see it through, as though a lingering ache couldn't be ignored.

"She's presumed to be innocent, but she is not innocent," Demakos told the jury.

"I am *too* innocent," cried Alice. "You know I'm innocent!"

Flustered by the outburst, Demakos had trouble relocating himself in the opening questioning of members of the jury. He was a legal technician, but an interruption of courtroom decorum jarred him. Jury selection consumed four days, and the trial began on March 15.

The formal prosecution opening was delivered by Nicolosi, whose voice became high and irritating when he was excited. "We are going to prove to you that the body [Eddie] was so decomposed that the Medical Examiner could not arrive at a cause of death," said Nicolosi. "And you will hear that maggots—"

Lyon rose with objections, claiming that the prosecutor, lacking real proof, was appealing to emotion and trying to provoke an outburst from Mrs. Crimmins.

Judge Balbach told Nicolosi to continue

"They found the body in the blanket covered with maggots—"

Again Lyon appealed to Balbach to stop Nicolosi, but the judge rapped down each objection.

"You are going to hear that decomposition resulted not only from maggots, but from weather; five days exposed to the elements. And we are going to prove to you gentlemen that in the latter part of 1966 Alice Crimmins confessed. She stated, 'I killed my daughter and I agreed to the murder of my son.'"

Lyon wondered what Nicolosi could mean. If he was referring to Rorech's testimony, Rorech had sworn that Alice had mentioned only the girl. In 1966, according to Rorech, Alice had delivered a partial confession about the murder of her daughter. What Lyon didn't know was that Kelly had provided a way out of the dilemma. Now Rorech would allege that Alice had said: "I killed Missy . . . and I agreed to the murder of my son." It allowed the District Attorney to take the alleged confession piecemeal, using one segment when it suited the first trial and two parts for the second trial. It was a very tricky business, for if in 1966 Alice had simply told Rorech straightforwardly that she had killed her "children," the statement would have been inadmissible in the first trial. But in the more complicated construction of the second trial the District Attorney could bring back an embellished Rorech.

The charges against Alice Crimmins in the second trial were strung together like afterthoughts. The indictment and the proof were cut to fit each other by legal tailors. In the first trial Alice had been tried for the murder of her daughter, but had been convicted of manslaughter. Thus, she could not now be charged with first-degree murder in Missy's death. The manslaughter conviction was, in effect, an acquittal of the more serious charge of murder, and the rules of double jeopardy forbade retrial on the murder charge.

Alice had never been accused of anything concerning Eddie's death, so the District Attorney decided to use the harshest possible charge.

Curiously, the evidence in Eddie's death—the more serious charge—was even weaker and more circumstantial than in Missy's case. Indeed, there was only one way to prove that Eddie had been murdered: first prove that Missy had been murdered, then somehow link the two deaths. The chain was very flimsy and had to be strung together backward. Unless the jury accepted the premise of Missy's murder and that it was related to Eddie's, there was no way to conclude any criminal liability in Eddie's death.

Technically, Rorech's testimony could be construed as an admission from Alice, although, at best, a dubious one. However, the jury could not even consider the prosecution's thesis unless it was provided with some basis in testimony. But Dr. Milton Helpern testified that Eddie's murder could scientifically be "inferred" because of the circumstances of Missy's death. He further swore that the deaths were related, since both children were found in vacant lots and both had disappeared at the same time.

Lyon was astounded. Dr. Helpern could, perhaps, give competent medical testimony concerning the results of an autopsy, the results of laboratory tests. But what he was testifying to in the second Crimmins trial was pure police hypothesis. There was, however, no way for Lyon to make a frontal assault on Helpern's testimony, and so he got him off the stand as soon as possible.

Working for the prosecutor was the natural confusion of the jurors. Once they became convinced that the evidence supported guilt on one charge, it was natural that the proof should blur, covering the entire case.

There is a precious aspect to the District Attorney's argument. Alice was accused of having killed Missy, yet the charge was manslaughter; she was accused of merely "consenting" to the murder of Eddie, but was charged with murder. It was a hard reversal for the jury to follow.

Many of the witnesses of the first trial reappeared in the second. Alice lost control more frequently. She would bite back tears when the children were mentioned. When Eddie Crimmins was on the stand and the prosecution attorney was questioning him on the routine facts of his life—where he lived, where he worked—he was asked if he had children. Eddie faltered, his voice breaking when he answered. When the prosecutor persisted and asked their birthdays, he lost his voice for a moment. He sat on the witness stand, clenching his fists, fighting for control. Alice couldn't bear to watch and sobbed into her hands. Even the stoic court officers were affected at such moments.

The trial was also marked by the eloquence of Herbert Lyon. "We expect that when [this trial] is over," he told the jury, "you will feel that this is a woman who suffered the greatest tragedy in the world in that she lost her two children and now she is falsely accused of having killed them. . . . And we expect that . . . plain simple, human, decent justice requires that after six years of this torture, that this woman be vindicated and sent home free."

The prosecution tactic once more was to depict Alice's morals as an issue. It was done by suggestion, by a kind of raised-eyebrow innuendo. Michael Clifford, then a patrolman, now a detective, was asked by Vincent Nicolosi how Mrs. Crimmins had looked when he first appeared on the scene. Clifford swore she was wearing makeup and had her hair "all teased up" when he answered the first alarm—leaving the jury with the impression that she was more concerned with her beauty than with her children.

Lyon cross-examined, trying to undo the subliminal damage.

LYON: You noticed her that day pretty well, didn't you?
CLIFFORD: Yes, I did.
LYON: You noticed the color of her blouse?
CLIFFORD: Yes.
LYON: The color of the pants she was wearing?
CLIFFORD: Yes.
LYON: Did you know what color your wife's blouse was that morning?

Demakos objected and Balbach sustained him, but later, in the third-floor corridor, Clifford told Demakos that he had made a mistake, he should have let him answer. Why? asked Demakos. "Because I'm not married," replied Clifford.

Jerry Piering's memory in 1971 was just as crisp as it had been in 1968. He could still see the manicotti in the garbage. He remembered that Alice had told him the children had been unruly and that at one point, in the car, "she swung and hit the girl."

Anthony Grace, a little older, with a little more dignity to lose, spent longer on the witness stand than he did during the first trial. The prosecution case, which had to be presented to the jury with oblique precision, was to suggest that Alice and Tony were partners in the murders. Demakos attacked the contractor as if Grace were on trial. He wanted to know about their relationship, emphasizing their contacts since the murders. In 1969 and 1970 Grace had taken Alice on cruises, and underlying the questioning was the resentful accusation of lives continuing.

"Does the defendant reside with you?" Demakos asked.

Grace replied that she sometimes "stays" with him. "Comes and goes just like that," said Grace inelegantly.

The second trial lasted six weeks, and gradually the prosecution became worried about the strength of their case. Again and again Lyon was approached by Demakos offering Alice "a deal"; she spurned them, but Demakos regarded her hesitation as evidence of guilt.

Detective John Kelly was on the verge of retirement when he testified that he had offered Alice a deal. She had said she had to discuss it with her attorney when Kelly told her she could get "full im-

303

munity" from prosecution. In his summation Demakos would point to that offer and argue that Alice's reaction was not that of an innocent person. An innocent person would have dismissed the offer immediately.

The prosecution hinged a large part of its case on such negative points. Kelly said he had listened to hundreds of hours of tapes from Alice's telephone taps and she had never discussed the children. Lyon would make it clear that Alice knew about the telephone taps and would never pick up the receiver without the greeting: "Hello, boys, drop dead," before beginning her normal conversations.

Joe Rorech's suit was paid for this time, but it was a cheaper cut than the one he had worn at the first trial. Now a laborer, Rorech seemed drained of fight. He recited mechanically, swearing that Alice had told him she had killed Missy "and consented" to the murder of her son. Alice's outcry was tinged with sympathy. She could see that he was a broken man. Lyon dredged up Rorech's drinking, his sloppy business habits, and made the jury aware that he had escaped criminal prosecution through his testimony.

By the time he was finished with his cross-examination, Lyon thought he had demolished Rorech's testimony. But he understood that the jury could still take the word of a thoroughly discredited witness when it wanted.

If the years had punished Rorech, Sophie Earomirski seemed to have flowered since her last public appearance. She was slimmer and her hair had been coiffed. Her story, with all its inconsistencies, conflicts, and self-serving explanations, was still popular.

Alice screamed from the defense table: "You liar . . . Do you even know what the truth is?" But Lyon understood that in some fashion Sophie had managed to cast herself in the role of underdog. He gently brought out her medical history, allowing her to make her denials, attempting to damage her testimony without destroying Sophie.

On April 7 the prosecution rested, mildly depressed. Demakos glumly told friends at lunch that he thought he had blown the case. Rorech had not been particularly effective and Sophie's story was hard to swallow.

304

Nicolosi, however, was unfailingly optimistic. Wait until Alice gets on the stand, he told Demakos.

But Lyon had decided against putting Alice on the stand. At the first trial she had been unconvincing. Lyon decided to risk his case by continuing the tactic of understatement. He played tapes of long conversations—between Rorech and Alice Crimmins, recorded before the first trial. Boring, meandering, they were punctuated by ardent declarations of Joe's affection. Lyon wanted the jury to try to reconcile the man on the tapes with the witness who swore that Alice was a killer. A proper reading would show him as a spurned lover.

On April 12, in the midst of the defense testimony, Demakos asked Judge Balbach to allow him to reopen the prosecution case—he had a new witness. Mrs. Tina DeVita was a small, nervous woman who had lived in the Kew Gardens Hills development at the time of the disappearance. On the night of July 13/14, 1965, she was coming home from visiting relatives. Her husband was driving, and as she sat on the passenger side of the car she looked out the driver's window, past her husband, and saw something on the mall where Alice Crimmins lived. What she saw, she said, was "people . . . walking . . . a man carrying a bundle, a woman, a dog and a boy." She had kept the story to herself for almost six years, she said, because she was afraid. Lately, with the story in the newspapers, she had told her husband, and he had urged her to come forward.

Herbert Lyon seemed to lose his temper for the first time. Why should anyone believe you after all these years? he asked angrily. He could see that the effect on the jury was powerful. This testimony tended to corroborate the prosecution's shakiest and most important witness—Sophie Earomirski. It added another coating of paint on Demakos' cracked portrait. Mrs. DeVita couldn't identify anyone in the grouping. Her husband had noticed nothing because he had been driving. Another slim reinforcement of a crumbling line, it heartened Demakos and unsettled Lyon.

The defense would have to improvise. The next morning, accompanied by Irwin Blye, Alice Crimmins marched into the courthouse pressroom and made a public appeal for someone to come forward to help her. She pleaded for anyone who had been on the mall that morning to contact her. Lyon remained in his office while Alice made the appeal.

Judge Balbach was furious. He brought Lyon into his chambers and threatened to clap Mrs. Crimmins into prison. Lyon said it was all an innocent mistake and it wouldn't happen again. The attorney had decided that the risk was worth it. If Mrs. De-Vita's testimony remained unchallenged, his case was wrecked.

That afternoon a chubby young salesman named Marvin Weinstein called Lyon's office and said he had something interesting to tell him. Weinstein lived in Massapequa, and Irwin Blye, the private detective, drove out to interview him. A day later Weinstein was on the stand. He too, he said, had been on the mall that morning, walking under Sophie's window.

LYON: Who was with you?
WEINSTEIN: My wife, my son and my daughter . . . and my dog.
LYON: How tall is your wife?
WEINSTEIN: Approximately five feet two-and-a-half.
LYON: And how old was your son?
WEINSTEIN: Three and a half.
LYON: How old was your daughter?
WEINSTEIN: Two.

Weinstein said his dog might have appeared pregnant, and that he had carried his daughter under his arm "like a sack" when he walked to his car under Sophie's window. When Mrs. Weinstein appeared in the courtroom, she looked very much like Alice Crimmins. On the stand, she too swore that they had been on the mall that evening.

Anthony King, the man the Weinsteins said they had visited on the night of the disappearance, thought that the visit had taken place on another night. Herb Lyon countered by bringing out that Weinstein and King had been business partners and were now enemies. The business had folded, leaving both men embittered. It was not clear what point had been established, beyond an obvious clouding of the case. The jury was forced to choose between identical sets of witnesses. They could believe Mrs. DeVita, who seemed almost impacted with anger. Or they could accept the Weinsteins, a young couple who seemed to live and dress beyond their means. The prosecutors campaigned against the Weinsteins, hinting that he owed money to gambling casinos in Las Vegas and had worked his way clear by testifying for Alice Crimmins. The Weinsteins would claim later that they had opened themselves to years of "official harassment" by coming forward.

Lyon had one more tactic. The prosecution's case was full of rumor, innuendo, and sly secrets. In one way or another, it had been suggested to the jury that the actual killer of little Eddie was known, that he was a man serving a fifteen-year term in Atlanta Penitentiary on a drug charge. Lyon wanted to stop the whispers and so he called Vincent Colabella as a witness. It was another moment from another era. Colabella, the smirking gangster escorted into the courtroom in handcuffs between federal marshals, seemed utterly out of place in this domestic melodrama. Colabella, predictably, denied any part in the killing, chuckling on the witness stand, swearing that he had never seen Alice Crimmins before.

Demakos was furious. He felt as if his nose were being tweaked and he stalked the corridor afterward, muttering. Why hadn't he offered Colabella a deal to testify, as he had Alice Crimmins? a reporter asked.

"I wouldn't offer a killer a deal," he replied sharply.

In his summation, Lyon dismissed Joe Rorech as the "man with the lisping mouth and evil heart." Sophie Earomirski was an "irresponsible neurotic." He spoke sadly about the need for the limelight and how the truth was often not a trick of selective testimony. Rorech wanted revenge and a way out of his financial and legal traps, while Sophie needed a way to reclaim her credibility.

Jerry Piering had his motives, too, he said. Piering he called inept. "Piering never made a note about dust.

The Police Department needs more space every day for the volumes of reports it must make, and Detective Piering doesn't make a note. He goes before the grand jury and he never mentions the dust."

Lyon paused and shook his head in disbelief.

"The question is, is she guilty or not? Six years have passed by. Mrs. Earomirski said she heard the children crying from the grave . . . if they are crying from their grave, they are saying: 'Let my mother go; you have had her long enough!' "

It was a summation that affected several jurors.

Demakos' summation was more direct, less literary, angrier: "She doesn't have the courage to stand up here and tell the world she killed her daughter—"

"Because I didn't!" cried Alice.

"And the shame and pity of it is that this little boy had to die, too. . . ."

The day that the case went to the jury Alice was preparing to go across the street to Lyon's office when Balbach told her to wait. When the jury had disappeared, he ordered her to remain within the courthouse. After the deliberations were adjourned for the night, Balbach held everyone in the courtroom until the last juror had gone, then ordered Mrs. Crimmins remanded to a detention pen.

"No," she pleaded. "Please, no."

Lyon was shocked. She had not expected to be remanded and was psychologically unprepared for it. Balbach was firm that she would not be permitted to remain free. "Not during jury deliberations," said Balbach.

Lyon pleaded that he would be responsible for Alice, that she could sleep on the couch in his office. Alice was crumpled in tears as if a verdict of guilty had already been pronounced.

"She will be remanded tonight," said Balbach.

Alice gripped her chair. "No. Please, you can't do this to me!"

Erlbaum said that Mrs. Crimmins had a rheumatic heart. Four court officers were prying her fingers from the chair.

From the back of the courtroom, where she had silently sat from the beginning, a sob broke from Alice's mother: "Your Honor, let my daughter go!"

The deliberations began after lunch on Thursday, April 23, and resumed Friday morning, after Alice had spent a sleepless night in a prison cell. At 5:45 p.m. on Friday there was an urgent summons from the third-floor courtroom. It was a verdict.

When the jury foreman began to read the verdict, Bill Erlbaum held his client's elbow. Behind her like a cloud was the frowning matron.

"Guilty of murder in the first degree . . ."

Almost everyone sobbed. Alice fell on the defense table and wailed, "Dear God, no! Please, dear God!"

The verdict of guilty in the manslaughter charge was almost lost in aftermath. John Burke stood shaking his fist and weeping. Mrs. Burke slumped back in the bench, crying, "Sweet Jesus, no! Not again!"

"She didn't kill her children," her brother cried. "She didn't kill them."

Eddie Crimmins wept into his large, clumsy hands.

Demakos and Nicolosi seemed stunned; they hadn't really expected victory. And Herbert Lyon looked bewildered. "I guess I convinced everyone but the jury," he said.

EPILOGUE

Alice Crimmins would have to postpone her grief again. On Thursday, May 13, 1971, still protesting her innocence, she was sent back to Bedford Hills prison. Supreme Court Justice George Balbach imposed a life sentence for the murder of her son, and no less than five nor more than twenty years in prison for the death of her daughter. The sentences were to run concurrently, so that she would be eligible for parole at the age of fifty-eight. On the day after the jury verdict Erlbaum began drafting her appeal.

Alice became a model prisoner at Bedford Hills. Every Sunday, Tony Grace drove up the Saw Mill River Parkway, brought her cigarettes, and told her that work on her appeal was progressing.

In the summer of 1973, after she had spent more than two years in prison, Alice was freed. The Appellate Division of the Supreme Court, Second Department, in Brooklyn, reversed the conviction in the case of little Eddie—ruling that there was no evidence of murder—and ordering a new trial in the manslaughter conviction of Missy. Demakos had erred in his summation when he said that Alice didn't have "the courage to stand up here and tell the world she killed her daughter." The statement went beyond the limits of fair summation and suggested that a defendant who didn't take the stand was admitting guilt.

The District Attorney's office began working on an

appeal of the court's ruling, but permitted Alice to be free in $25,000 bail. Technically, she was still under indictment for the death of Missy. Meanwhile, she tried to work and went through the motions of a normal life. She attended baseball games and went out drinking at night with Tony Grace. But she never opened her door without the fear that someone would be waiting in ambush to take her back to prison.

In February 1975, in an unusual decision, the Court of Appeals, the highest court in New York State, unanimously upheld the dismissal of Alice's conviction of murdering her son; however, by a 5–2 vote the judges ordered the count involving manslaughter of her daughter sent back to the Appellate Division of the Supreme Court for reconsideration. In May the Appellate court upheld the manslaughter conviction, and while her attorneys prepared another round of appeals Alice Crimmins was returned to prison to complete her sentence.

In the decade since Alice Crimmins, an obscure Queens housewife, became a public figure, the nature of family relationships has changed. Divorce has become easier, even in Queens. Casual relationships are no longer exceptional, even in Queens. The borough is still a collection of small towns, and some of the men who pursued Alice Crimmins so relentlessly spend occasional nights in dark bars trying to seduce the women who serve them drinks.

Lives were touched and altered by the Crimmins case. Vincent Nicolosi was elected to the State Assembly, in some measure because of the fame he achieved in the trial. Nat Hentel is a judge. Thomas Mackell resigned in disgrace and was convicted for shielding a cheap swindle in his office.*

Sophie Earomirski disappeared into another section of the borough, refusing to discuss her night at the window. John Kelly works as a private investigator. Jerry Piering has made second-grade detective. Phil Brady, retired from the Police Department, has spent

---

* In April 1975, Mackell's conviction was overturned by a higher court.

a few sleepless nights because of what happened to Alice Crimmins. George Martin, also retired, has more time to fly his private airplane. Dr. Milton Helpern retired with many honors and died in 1977. Harold Harrison tried practicing law in Manhattan, but moved back to Queens.

The graves of Missy and Eddie are still unmarked and, according to the caretaker of the Bronx cemetery, unvisited. Their pictures are buried in the folds of a secret compartment of Alice Crimmins' wallet, where she keeps them forever four- and five-year-old angels in heaven. Eddie Crimmins still works as a mechanic and uses his airline credentials to make long, distracting trips.

And the name of Alice Crimmins still ruptures some blister of guilt, but no one is ever certain of whose.

> Still she haunts me, phantomwise,
> Alice moving under skies
> Never seen by waking eyes.
>
> Children yet, the tale to hear,
> Eager eye and willing ear,
> Lovingly shall nestle near.
>
> In a Wonderland they lie,
> Dreaming as the days go by,
> Dreaming as the summers die.
>
> —*Through the Looking-Glass*

INDEX

321